TKO STUDIOS

SALVATORE SIMEONE - CEO & PUBLISHER

TZE CHUN - PRESIDENT & PUBLISHER

JATIN THAKKER - CHIEF OPERATIONS OFFICER

SEBASTIAN GIRNER - EDITOR-IN-CHIEF

EVE OF EXTINCTION #1-6.

Copyright © 2019

TKO Studios, LLC. All rights reserved.

Published by TKO Studios, LLC.

Office of Publication: 450 7th Ave., Suite 2107. New York, NY 10123.

All names, characters, and events in this publication
are entirely fictional. Any resemblance to actual persons
(living or dead), events, or places, without satiric intent,
is unintended and purely coincidental. Printed in the USA.

ISBN: 978-1-7327485-7-6

TKO PRESENTS A WORLD BY:

SALVATORE A. SIMEONE & STEVE SIMEONE
WRITERS

NIK VIRELLA
FULL COLOR ART #1, LINE ART #2-4

ISAAC GOODHART
LINE ART #5-6

RUTH REDMOND
COLOR ART #2-6

ARIANA MAHER
LETTERER

SEBASTIAN GIRNER
EDITOR

MARIA NGUYEN
COVER ART

JARED K FLETCHER
TITLE & COVER DESIGN

JEFF POWELL
BOOK DESIGN

EVE of EXTINCTION

CHAPTER 1

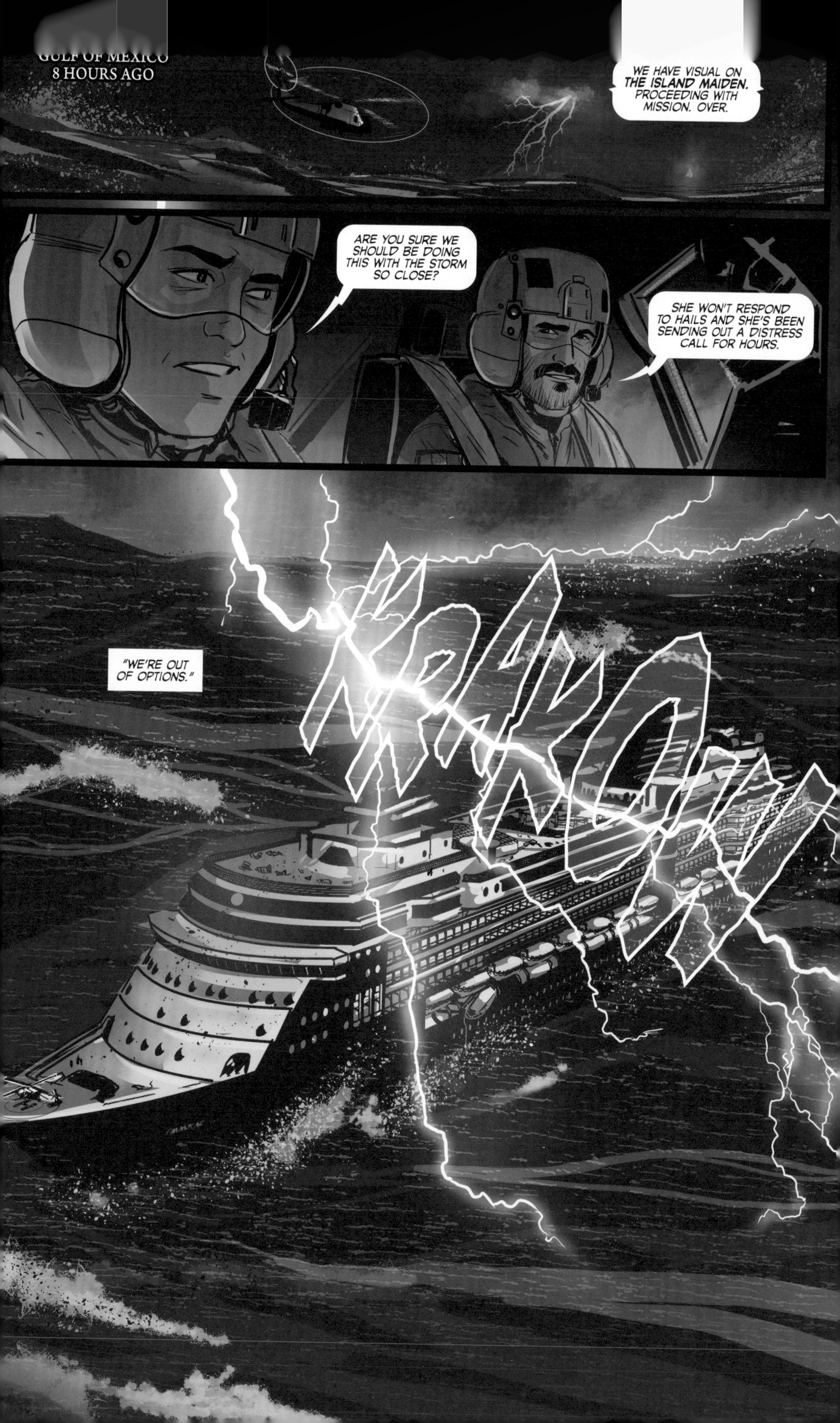
GULF OF MEXICO
8 HOURS AGO
WE HAVE VISUAL ON THE ISLAND MAIDEN. PROCEEDING WITH MISSION. OVER.
ARE YOU SURE WE SHOULD BE DOING THIS WITH THE STORM SO CLOSE?
SHE WON'T RESPOND TO HAILS AND SHE'S BEEN SENDING OUT A DISTRESS CALL FOR HOURS.
"WE'RE OUT OF OPTIONS."
KRAKOOM

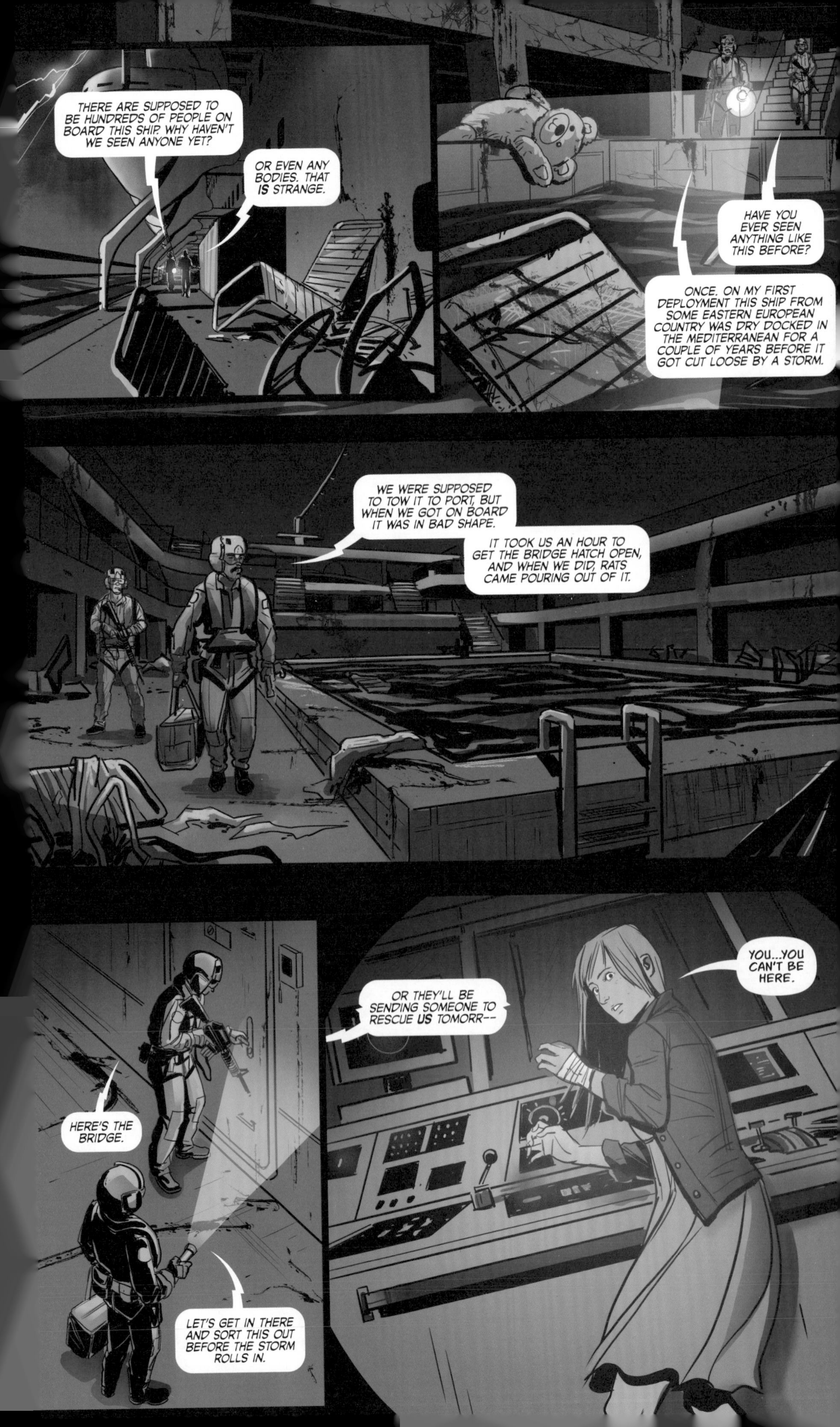
THERE ARE SUPPOSED TO BE HUNDREDS OF PEOPLE ON BOARD THIS SHIP. WHY HAVEN'T WE SEEN ANYONE YET?
OR EVEN ANY BODIES. THAT **IS** STRANGE.
HAVE YOU EVER SEEN ANYTHING LIKE THIS BEFORE?
ONCE. ON MY FIRST DEPLOYMENT THIS SHIP FROM SOME EASTERN EUROPEAN COUNTRY WAS DRY DOCKED IN THE MEDITERRANEAN FOR A COUPLE OF YEARS BEFORE IT GOT CUT LOOSE BY A STORM.
WE WERE SUPPOSED TO TOW IT TO PORT, BUT WHEN WE GOT ON BOARD IT WAS IN BAD SHAPE.
IT TOOK US AN HOUR TO GET THE BRIDGE HATCH OPEN, AND WHEN WE DID, RATS CAME POURING OUT OF IT.
HERE'S THE BRIDGE.
LET'S GET IN THERE AND SORT THIS OUT BEFORE THE STORM ROLLS IN.
OR THEY'LL BE SENDING SOMEONE TO RESCUE **US** TOMORR--
YOU...YOU CAN'T BE HERE.

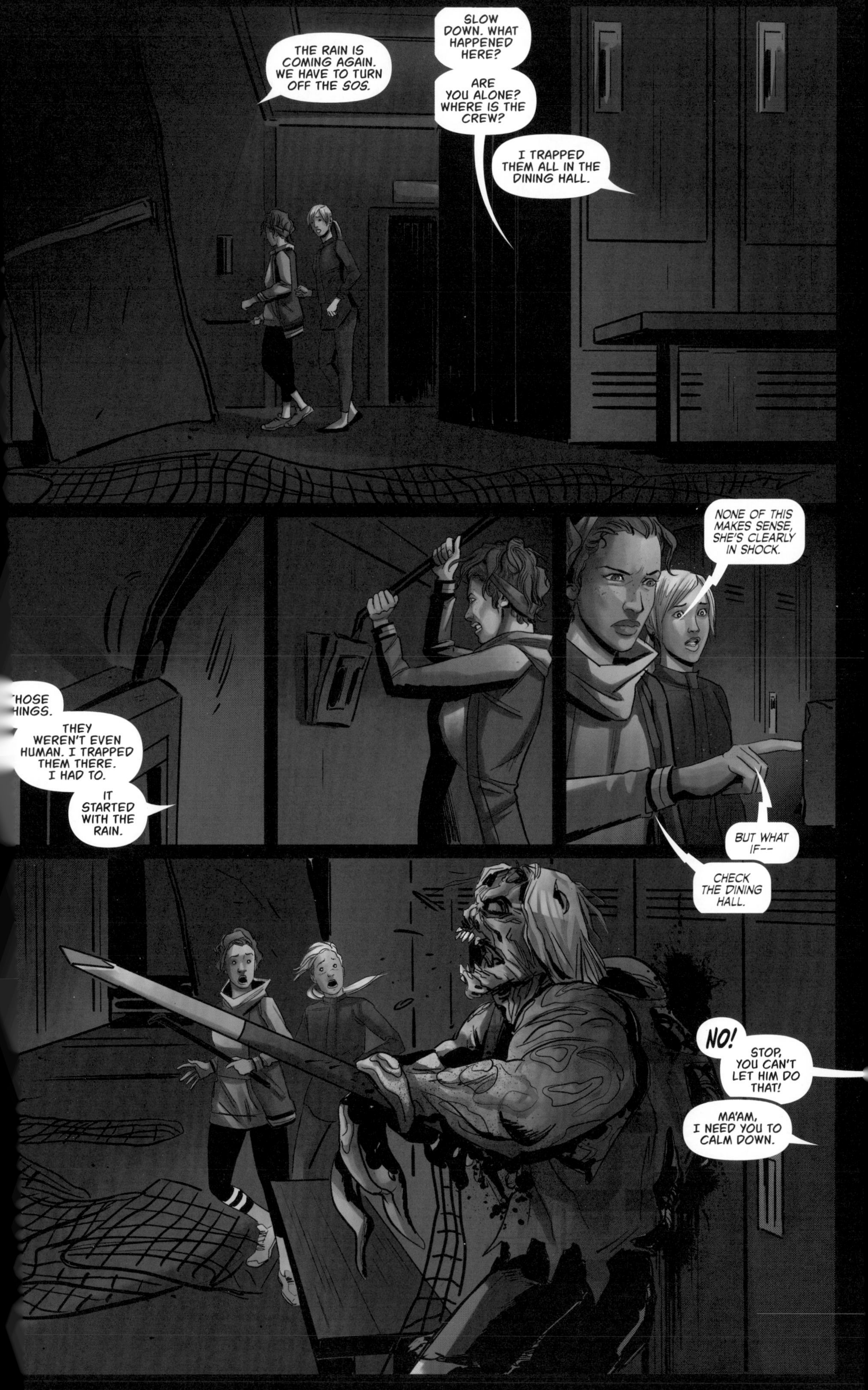
THE RAIN IS COMING AGAIN. WE HAVE TO TURN OFF THE SOS.
SLOW DOWN. WHAT HAPPENED HERE?
ARE YOU ALONE? WHERE IS THE CREW?
I TRAPPED THEM ALL IN THE DINING HALL.
HOSE HINGS.
THEY WEREN'T EVEN HUMAN. I TRAPPED THEM THERE. I HAD TO.
IT STARTED WITH THE RAIN.
NONE OF THIS MAKES SENSE, SHE'S CLEARLY IN SHOCK.
BUT WHAT IF--
CHECK THE DINING HALL.
NO!
STOP, YOU CAN'T LET HIM DO THAT!
MA'AM, I NEED YOU TO CALM DOWN.

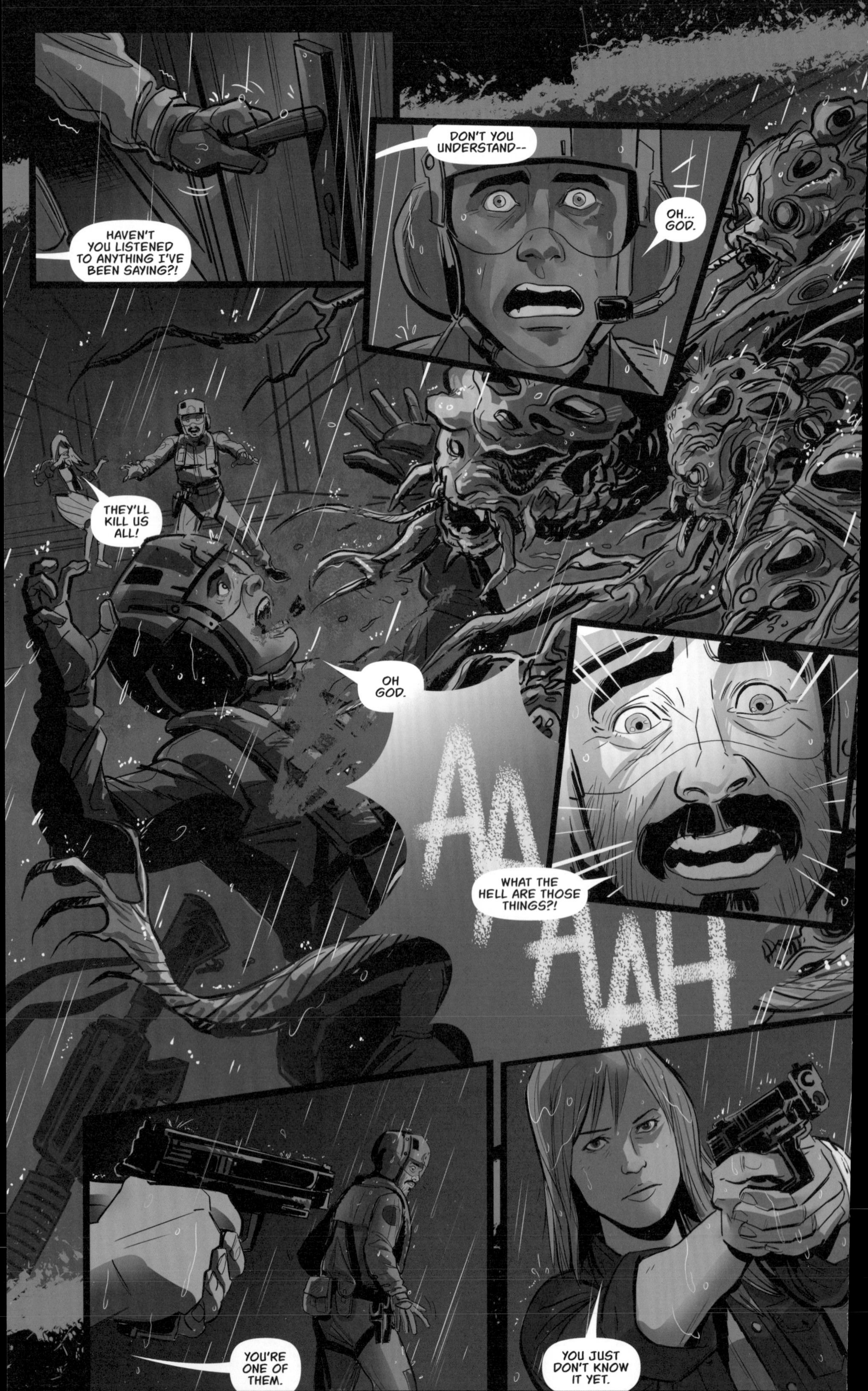
HAVEN'T YOU LISTENED TO ANYTHING I'VE BEEN SAYING?!
DON'T YOU UNDERSTAND--
OH... GOD.
THEY'LL KILL US ALL!
OH GOD.
AAAAH
WHAT THE HELL ARE THOSE THINGS?!
YOU'RE ONE OF THEM.
YOU JUST DON'T KNOW IT YET.

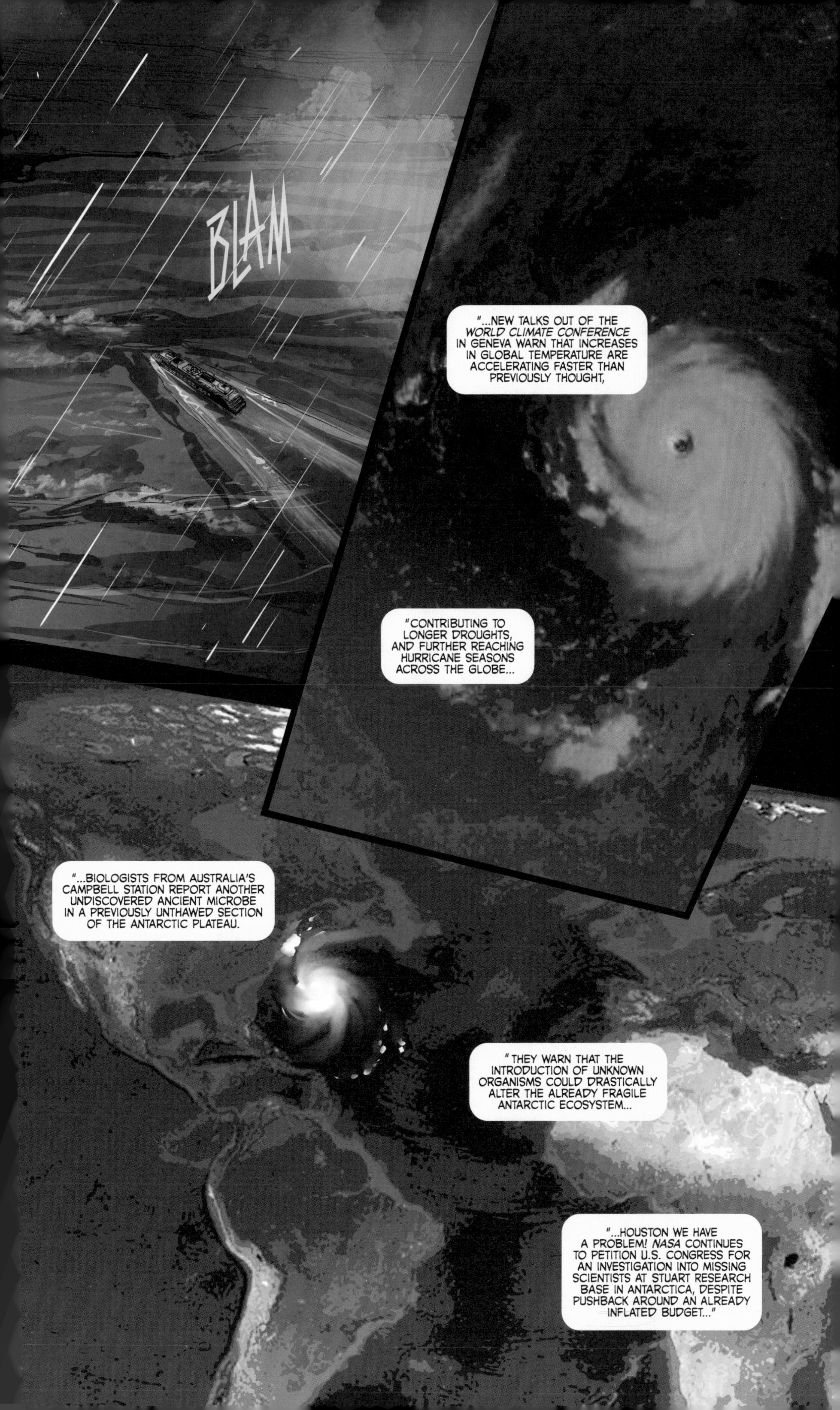
BLAM
"...NEW TALKS OUT OF THE *WORLD CLIMATE CONFERENCE* IN GENEVA WARN THAT INCREASES IN GLOBAL TEMPERATURE ARE ACCELERATING FASTER THAN PREVIOUSLY THOUGHT,
"CONTRIBUTING TO LONGER DROUGHTS, AND FURTHER REACHING HURRICANE SEASONS ACROSS THE GLOBE...
"...BIOLOGISTS FROM AUSTRALIA'S CAMPBELL STATION REPORT ANOTHER UNDISCOVERED ANCIENT MICROBE IN A PREVIOUSLY UNTHAWED SECTION OF THE ANTARCTIC PLATEAU.
"THEY WARN THAT THE INTRODUCTION OF UNKNOWN ORGANISMS COULD DRASTICALLY ALTER THE ALREADY FRAGILE ANTARCTIC ECOSYSTEM...
"...HOUSTON WE HAVE A PROBLEM! *NASA* CONTINUES TO PETITION U.S. CONGRESS FOR AN INVESTIGATION INTO MISSING SCIENTISTS AT STUART RESEARCH BASE IN ANTARCTICA, DESPITE PUSHBACK AROUND AN ALREADY INFLATED BUDGET..."

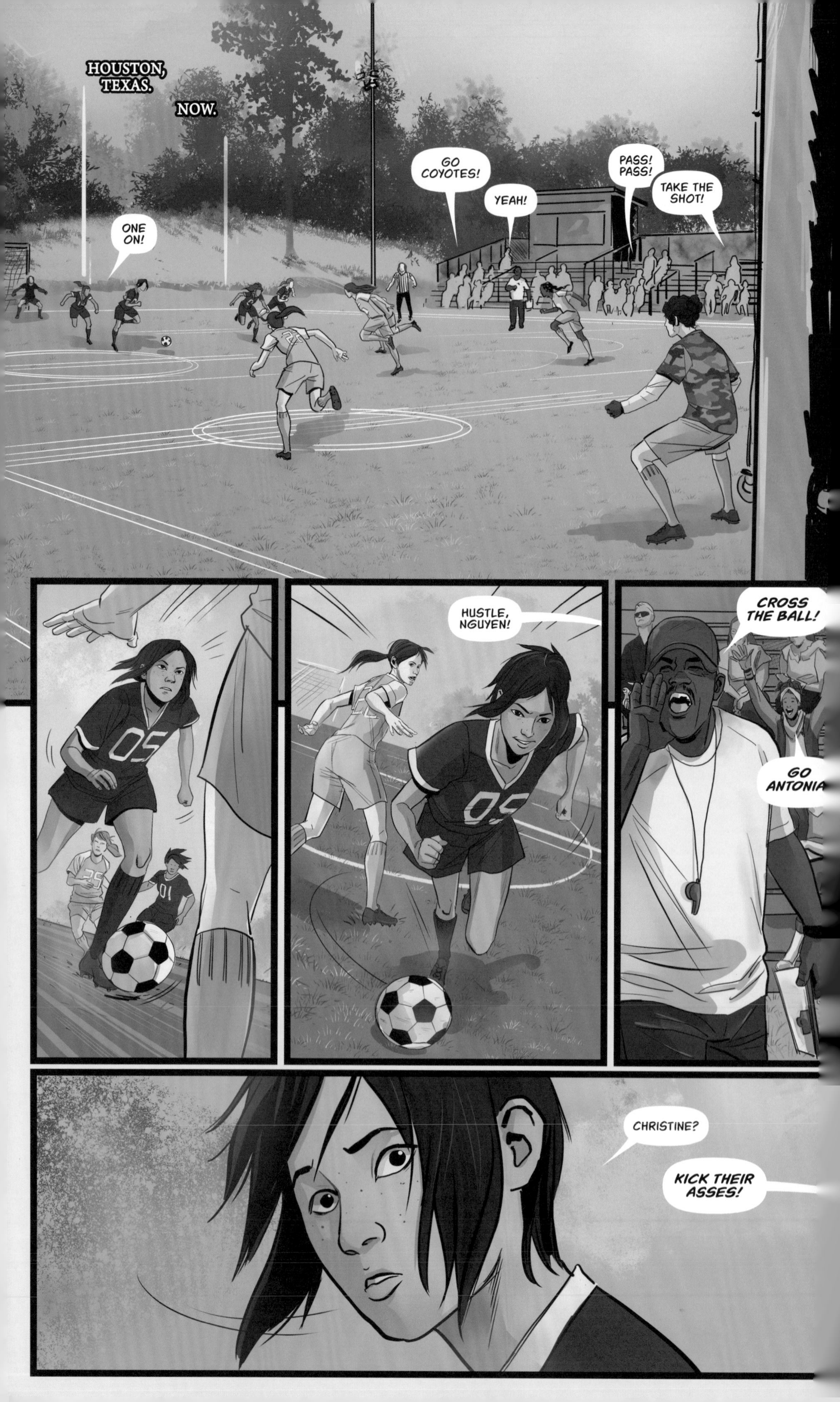
HOUSTON, TEXAS.
NOW.
ONE ON!
GO COYOTES!
YEAH!
PASS! PASS!
TAKE THE SHOT!
HUSTLE, NGUYEN!
CROSS THE BALL!
GO ANTONIA
CHRISTINE?
KICK THEIR ASSES!

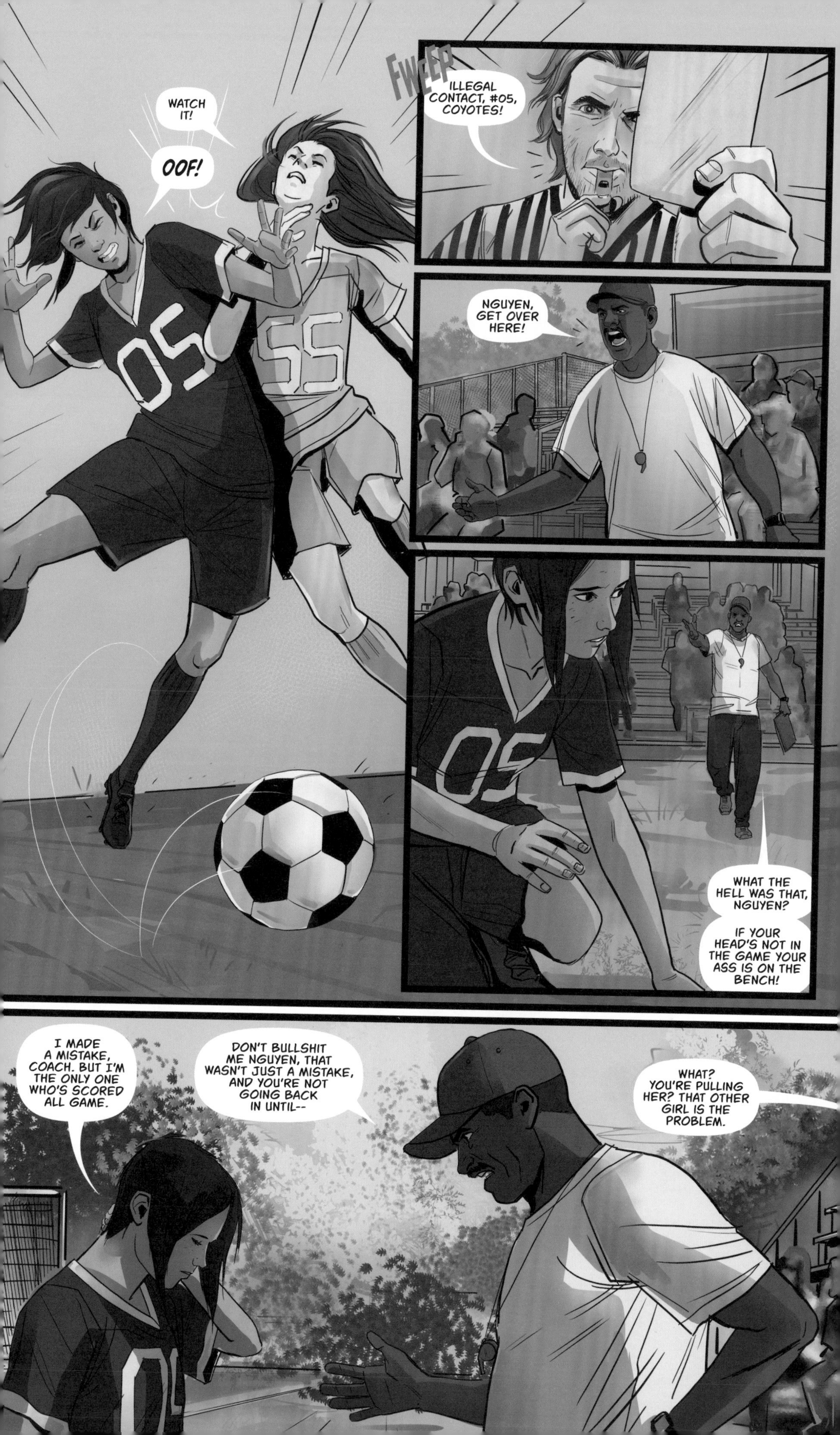
WATCH IT!
OOF!
FWEEP
ILLEGAL CONTACT, #05, COYOTES!
NGUYEN, GET OVER HERE!
WHAT THE HELL WAS THAT, NGUYEN?
IF YOUR HEAD'S NOT IN THE GAME YOUR ASS IS ON THE BENCH!
I MADE A MISTAKE, COACH. BUT I'M THE ONLY ONE WHO'S SCORED ALL GAME.
DON'T BULLSHIT ME NGUYEN, THAT WASN'T JUST A MISTAKE, AND YOU'RE NOT GOING BACK IN UNTIL--
WHAT? YOU'RE PULLING HER? THAT OTHER GIRL IS THE PROBLEM.

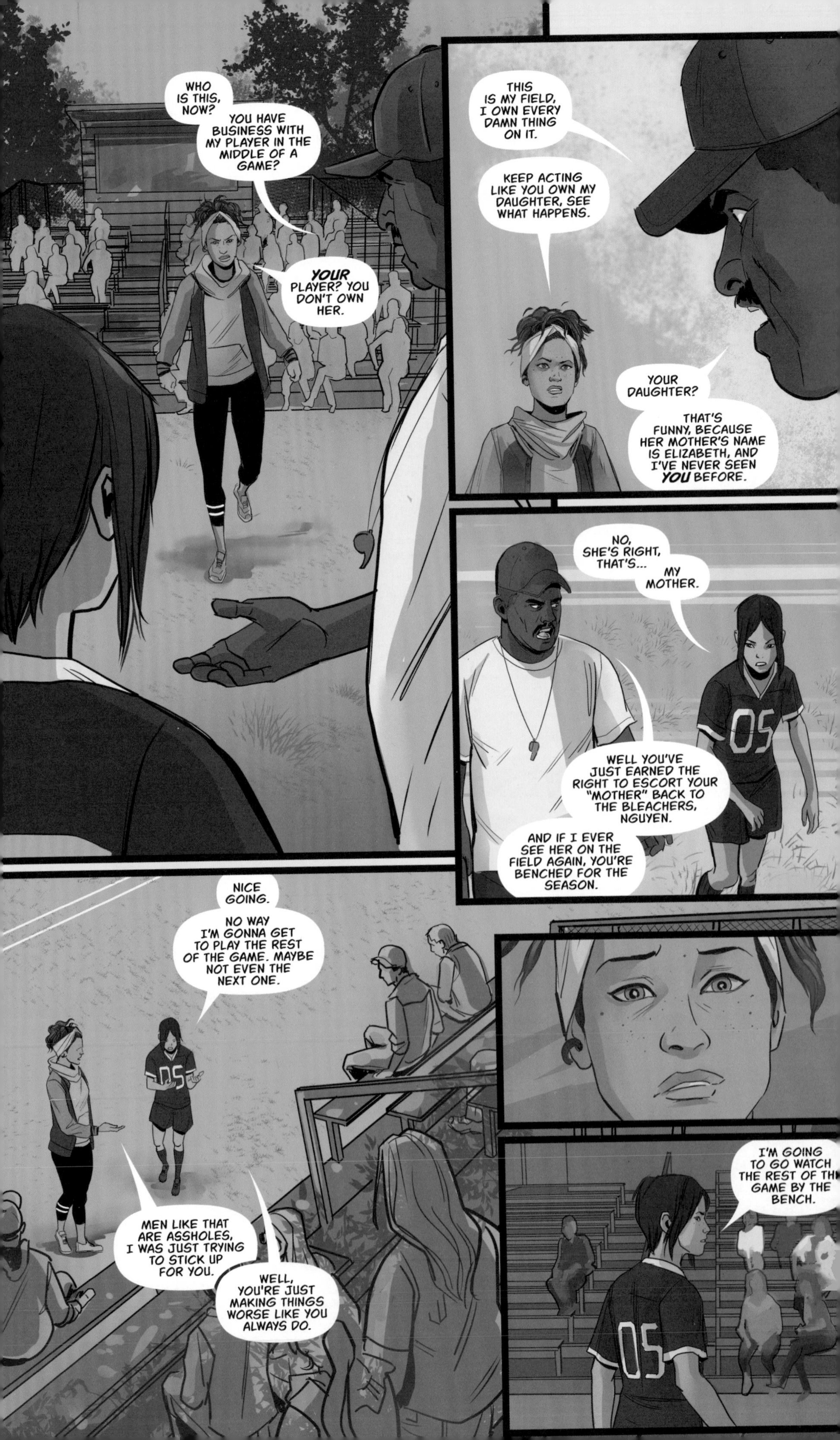
WHO IS THIS, NOW?
YOU HAVE BUSINESS WITH MY PLAYER IN THE MIDDLE OF A GAME?
YOUR PLAYER? YOU DON'T OWN HER.
THIS IS MY FIELD, I OWN EVERY DAMN THING ON IT.
KEEP ACTING LIKE YOU OWN MY DAUGHTER, SEE WHAT HAPPENS.
YOUR DAUGHTER?
THAT'S FUNNY, BECAUSE HER MOTHER'S NAME IS ELIZABETH, AND I'VE NEVER SEEN YOU BEFORE.
NO, SHE'S RIGHT, THAT'S... MY MOTHER.
WELL YOU'VE JUST EARNED THE RIGHT TO ESCORT YOUR "MOTHER" BACK TO THE BLEACHERS, NGUYEN.
AND IF I EVER SEE HER ON THE FIELD AGAIN, YOU'RE BENCHED FOR THE SEASON.
NICE GOING.
NO WAY I'M GONNA GET TO PLAY THE REST OF THE GAME. MAYBE NOT EVEN THE NEXT ONE.
MEN LIKE THAT ARE ASSHOLES, I WAS JUST TRYING TO STICK UP FOR YOU.
WELL, YOU'RE JUST MAKING THINGS WORSE LIKE YOU ALWAYS DO.
I'M GOING TO GO WATCH THE REST OF TH GAME BY THE BENCH.

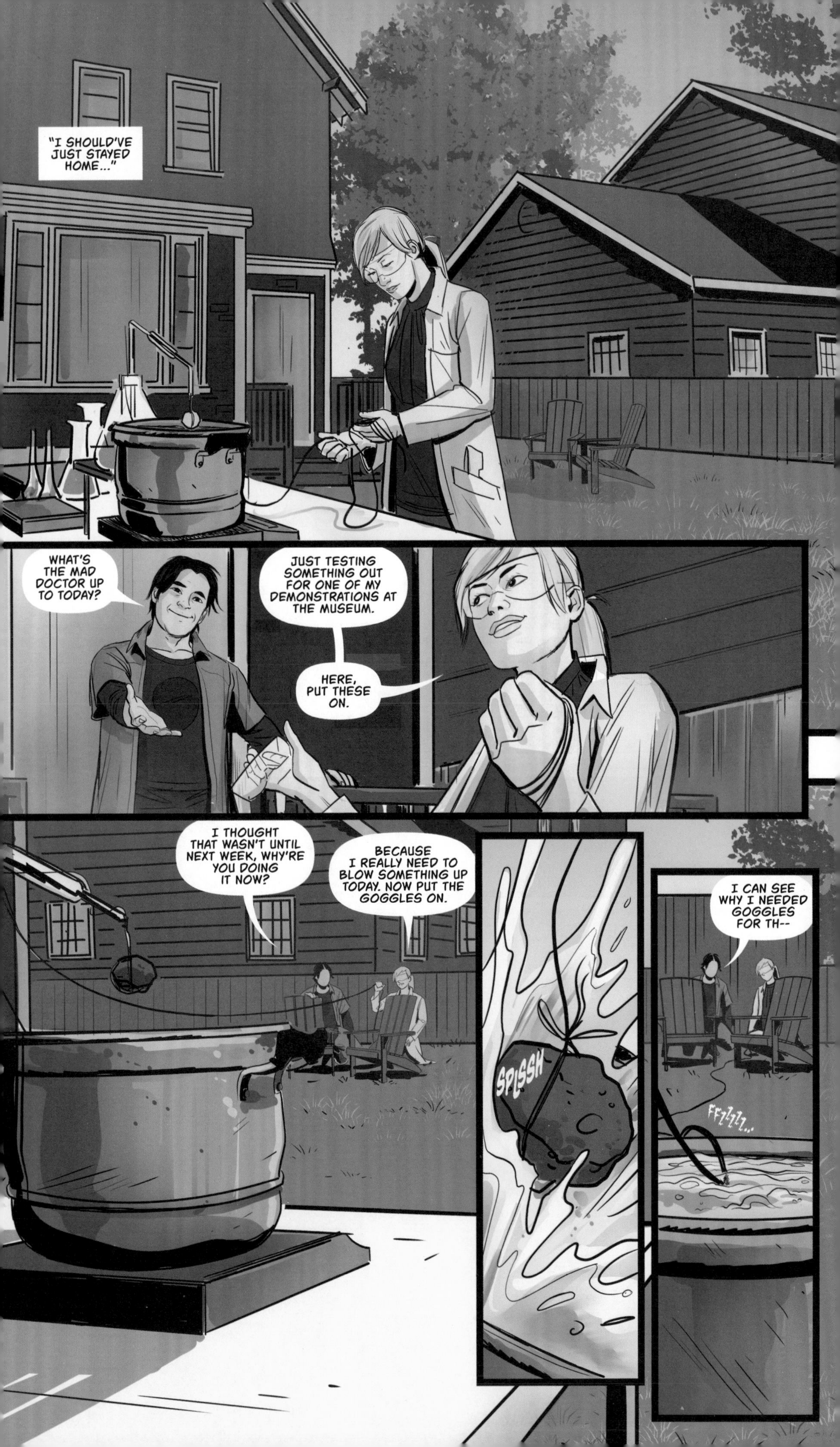
"I SHOULD'VE JUST STAYED HOME..."
WHAT'S THE MAD DOCTOR UP TO TODAY?
JUST TESTING SOMETHING OUT FOR ONE OF MY DEMONSTRATIONS AT THE MUSEUM.
HERE, PUT THESE ON.
I THOUGHT THAT WASN'T UNTIL NEXT WEEK, WHY'RE YOU DOING IT NOW?
BECAUSE I REALLY NEED TO BLOW SOMETHING UP TODAY. NOW PUT THE GOGGLES ON.
SPLSSH
I CAN SEE WHY I NEEDED GOGGLES FOR TH--
FFZZZZZ...

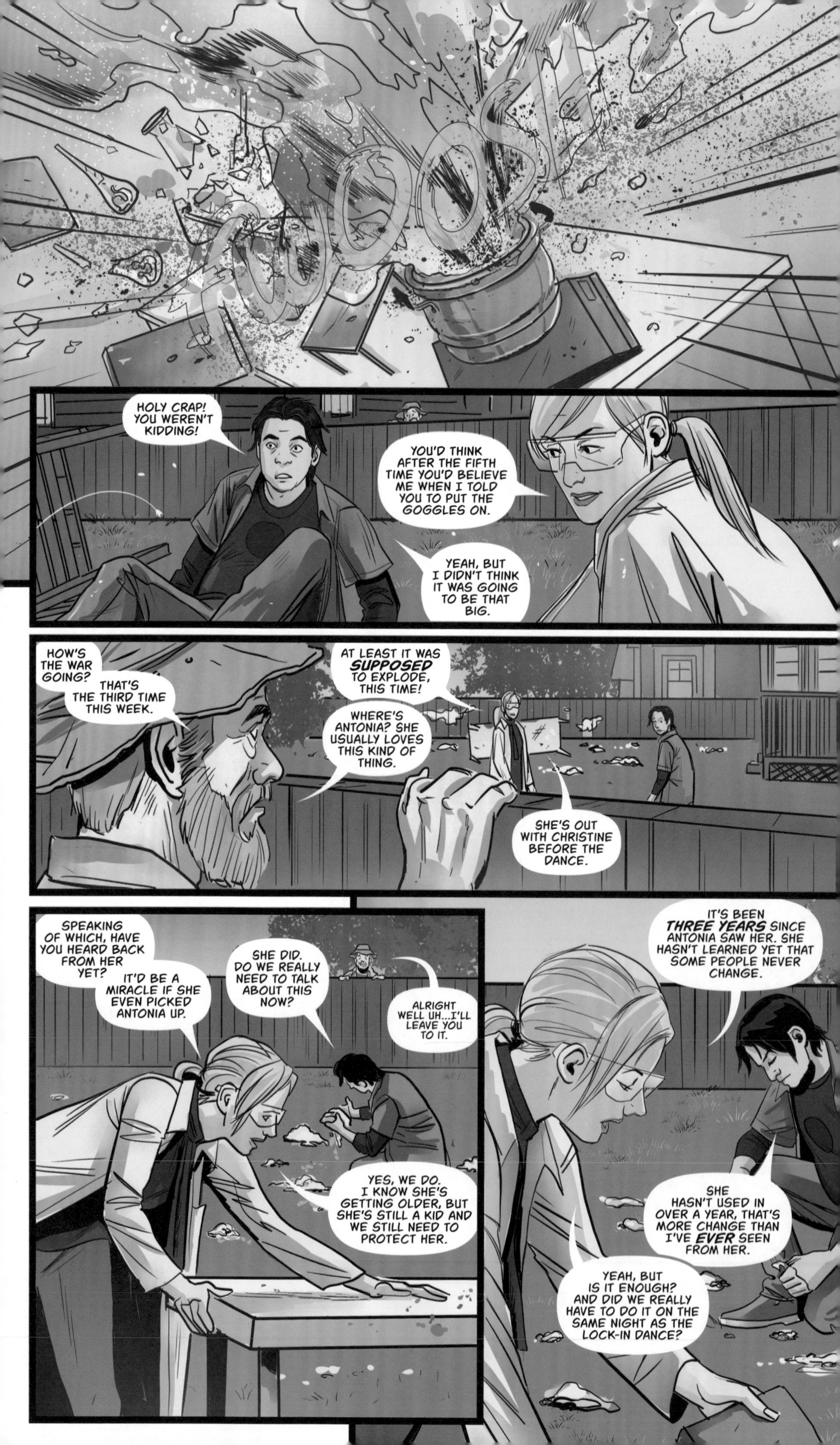
HOLY CRAP! YOU WEREN'T KIDDING!
YOU'D THINK AFTER THE FIFTH TIME YOU'D BELIEVE ME WHEN I TOLD YOU TO PUT THE GOGGLES ON.
YEAH, BUT I DIDN'T THINK IT WAS GOING TO BE THAT BIG.
HOW'S THE WAR GOING?
THAT'S THE THIRD TIME THIS WEEK.
AT LEAST IT WAS SUPPOSED TO EXPLODE, THIS TIME!
WHERE'S ANTONIA? SHE USUALLY LOVES THIS KIND OF THING.
SHE'S OUT WITH CHRISTINE BEFORE THE DANCE.
SPEAKING OF WHICH, HAVE YOU HEARD BACK FROM HER YET?
IT'D BE A MIRACLE IF SHE EVEN PICKED ANTONIA UP.
SHE DID. DO WE REALLY NEED TO TALK ABOUT THIS NOW?
ALRIGHT WELL UH...I'LL LEAVE YOU TO IT.
YES, WE DO. I KNOW SHE'S GETTING OLDER, BUT SHE'S STILL A KID AND WE STILL NEED TO PROTECT HER.
IT'S BEEN THREE YEARS SINCE ANTONIA SAW HER. SHE HASN'T LEARNED YET THAT SOME PEOPLE NEVER CHANGE.
SHE HASN'T USED IN OVER A YEAR, THAT'S MORE CHANGE THAN I'VE EVER SEEN FROM HER.
YEAH, BUT IS IT ENOUGH? AND DID WE REALLY HAVE TO DO IT ON THE SAME NIGHT AS THE LOCK-IN DANCE?

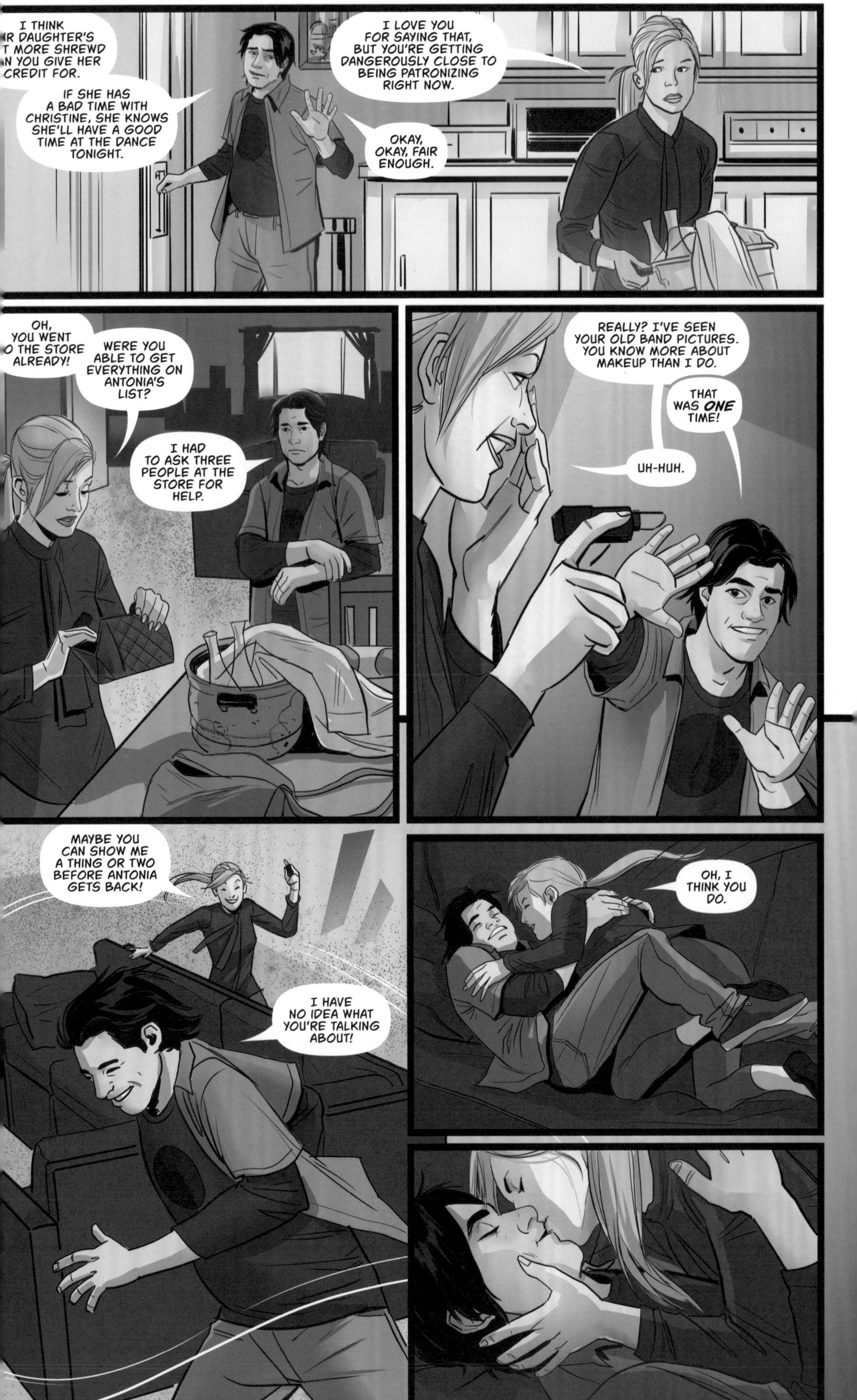
I THINK
R DAUGHTER'S
T MORE SHREWD
N YOU GIVE HER
CREDIT FOR.
IF SHE HAS A BAD TIME WITH CHRISTINE, SHE KNOWS SHE'LL HAVE A GOOD TIME AT THE DANCE TONIGHT.
I LOVE YOU FOR SAYING THAT, BUT YOU'RE GETTING DANGEROUSLY CLOSE TO BEING PATRONIZING RIGHT NOW.
OKAY, OKAY, FAIR ENOUGH.
OH, YOU WENT
O THE STORE
ALREADY!
WERE YOU ABLE TO GET EVERYTHING ON ANTONIA'S LIST?
I HAD TO ASK THREE PEOPLE AT THE STORE FOR HELP.
REALLY? I'VE SEEN YOUR OLD BAND PICTURES. YOU KNOW MORE ABOUT MAKEUP THAN I DO.
THAT WAS ONE TIME!
UH-HUH.
MAYBE YOU CAN SHOW ME A THING OR TWO BEFORE ANTONIA GETS BACK!
I HAVE NO IDEA WHAT YOU'RE TALKING ABOUT!
OH, I THINK YOU DO.

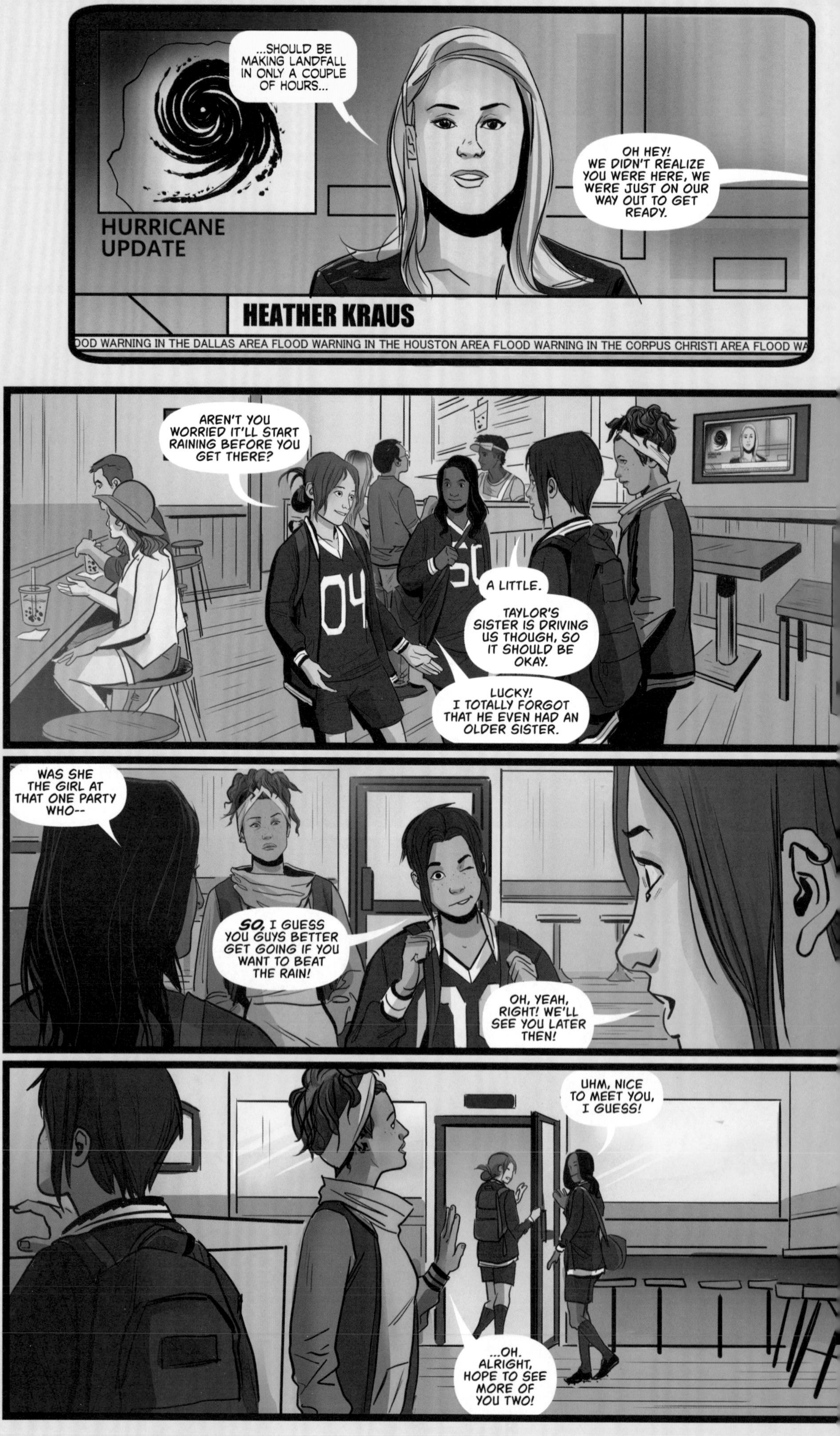

...SHOULD BE MAKING LANDFALL IN ONLY A COUPLE OF HOURS...
HURRICANE UPDATE
HEATHER KRAUS
OOD WARNING IN THE DALLAS AREA FLOOD WARNING IN THE HOUSTON AREA FLOOD WARNING IN THE CORPUS CHRISTI AREA FLOOD WA
OH HEY! WE DIDN'T REALIZE YOU WERE HERE, WE WERE JUST ON OUR WAY OUT TO GET READY.
AREN'T YOU WORRIED IT'LL START RAINING BEFORE YOU GET THERE?
A LITTLE.
TAYLOR'S SISTER IS DRIVING US THOUGH, SO IT SHOULD BE OKAY.
LUCKY! I TOTALLY FORGOT THAT HE EVEN HAD AN OLDER SISTER.
WAS SHE THE GIRL AT THAT ONE PARTY WHO--
SO, I GUESS YOU GUYS BETTER GET GOING IF YOU WANT TO BEAT THE RAIN!
OH, YEAH, RIGHT! WE'LL SEE YOU LATER THEN!
UHM, NICE TO MEET YOU, I GUESS!
...OH. ALRIGHT, HOPE TO SEE MORE OF YOU TWO!

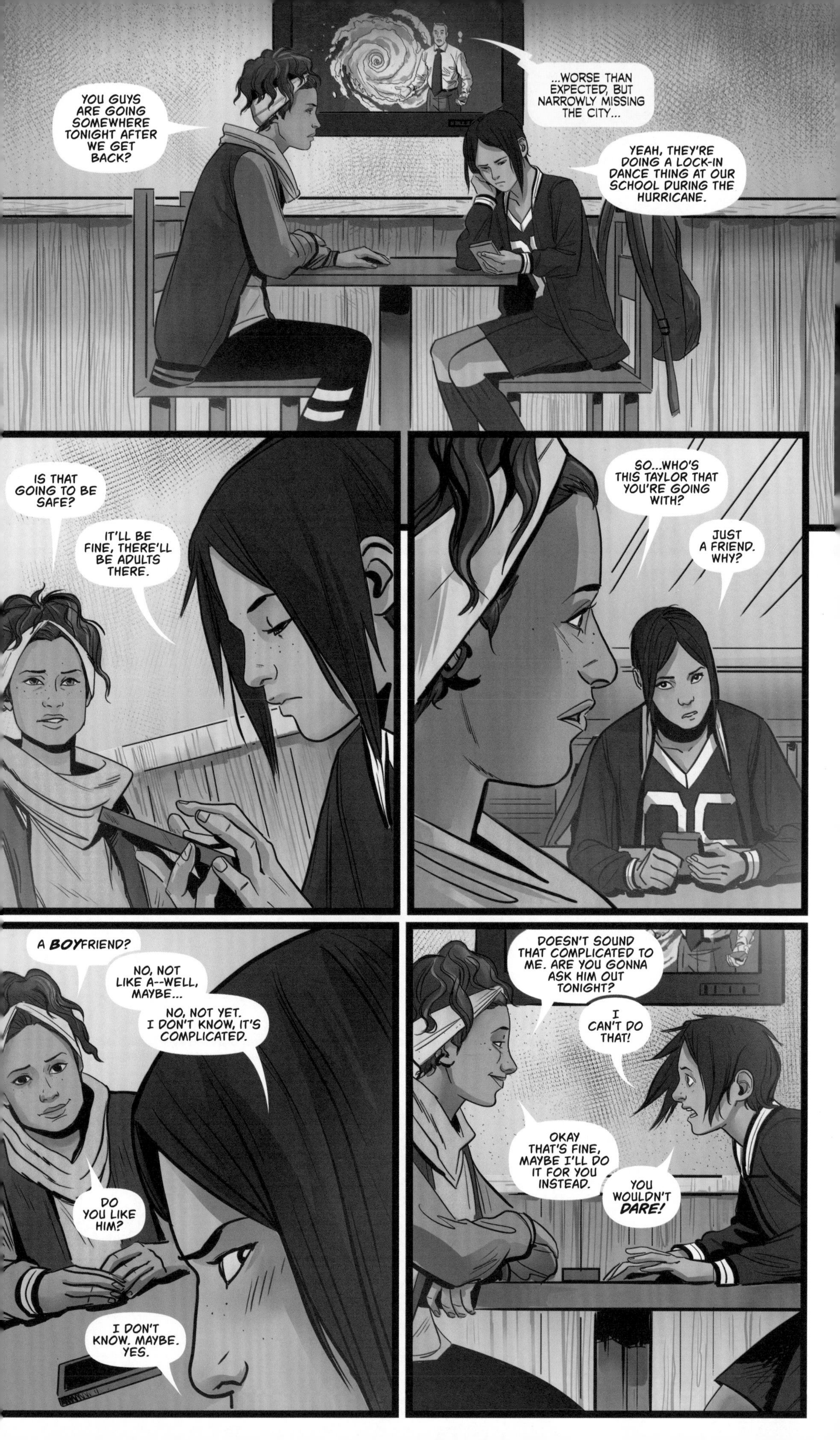

YOU GUYS ARE GOING SOMEWHERE TONIGHT AFTER WE GET BACK?
...WORSE THAN EXPECTED, BUT NARROWLY MISSING THE CITY...
YEAH, THEY'RE DOING A LOCK-IN DANCE THING AT OUR SCHOOL DURING THE HURRICANE.
IS THAT GOING TO BE SAFE?
IT'LL BE FINE, THERE'LL BE ADULTS THERE.
SO...WHO'S THIS TAYLOR THAT YOU'RE GOING WITH?
JUST A FRIEND. WHY?
A **BOY**FRIEND?
NO, NOT LIKE A--WELL, MAYBE...
NO, NOT YET. I DON'T KNOW, IT'S COMPLICATED.
DO YOU LIKE HIM?
I DON'T KNOW. MAYBE. YES.
DOESN'T SOUND THAT COMPLICATED TO ME. ARE YOU GONNA ASK HIM OUT TONIGHT?
I CAN'T DO THAT!
OKAY THAT'S FINE, MAYBE I'LL DO IT FOR YOU INSTEAD.
YOU WOULDN'T ***DARE!***

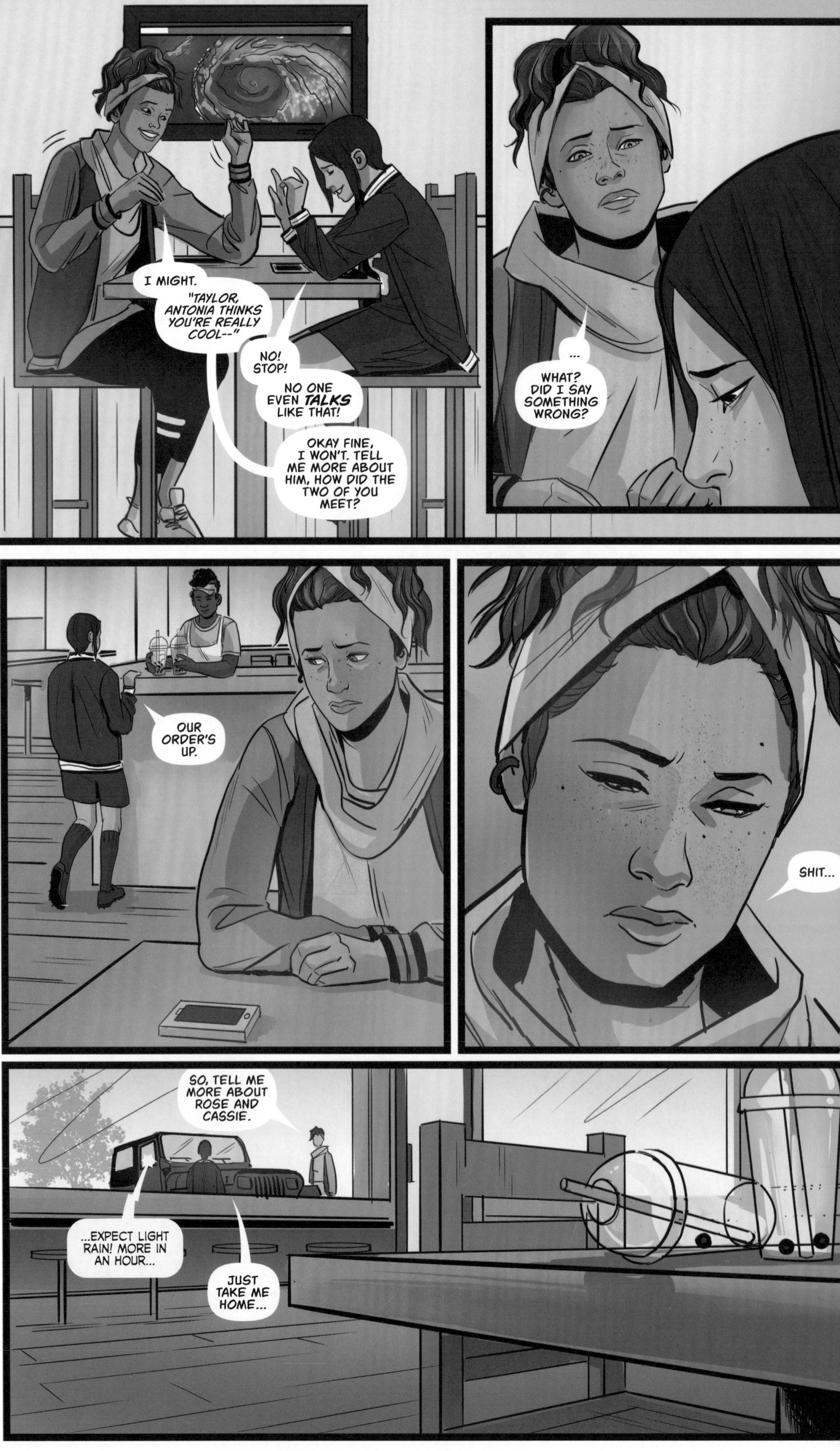
I MIGHT.
"TAYLOR, ANTONIA THINKS YOU'RE REALLY COOL--"
NO! STOP!
NO ONE EVEN TALKS LIKE THAT!
OKAY FINE, I WON'T. TELL ME MORE ABOUT HIM, HOW DID THE TWO OF YOU MEET?
...
WHAT? DID I SAY SOMETHING WRONG?
OUR ORDER'S UP.
SHIT...
SO, TELL ME MORE ABOUT ROSE AND CASSIE.
...EXPECT LIGHT RAIN! MORE IN AN HOUR...
JUST TAKE ME HOME...

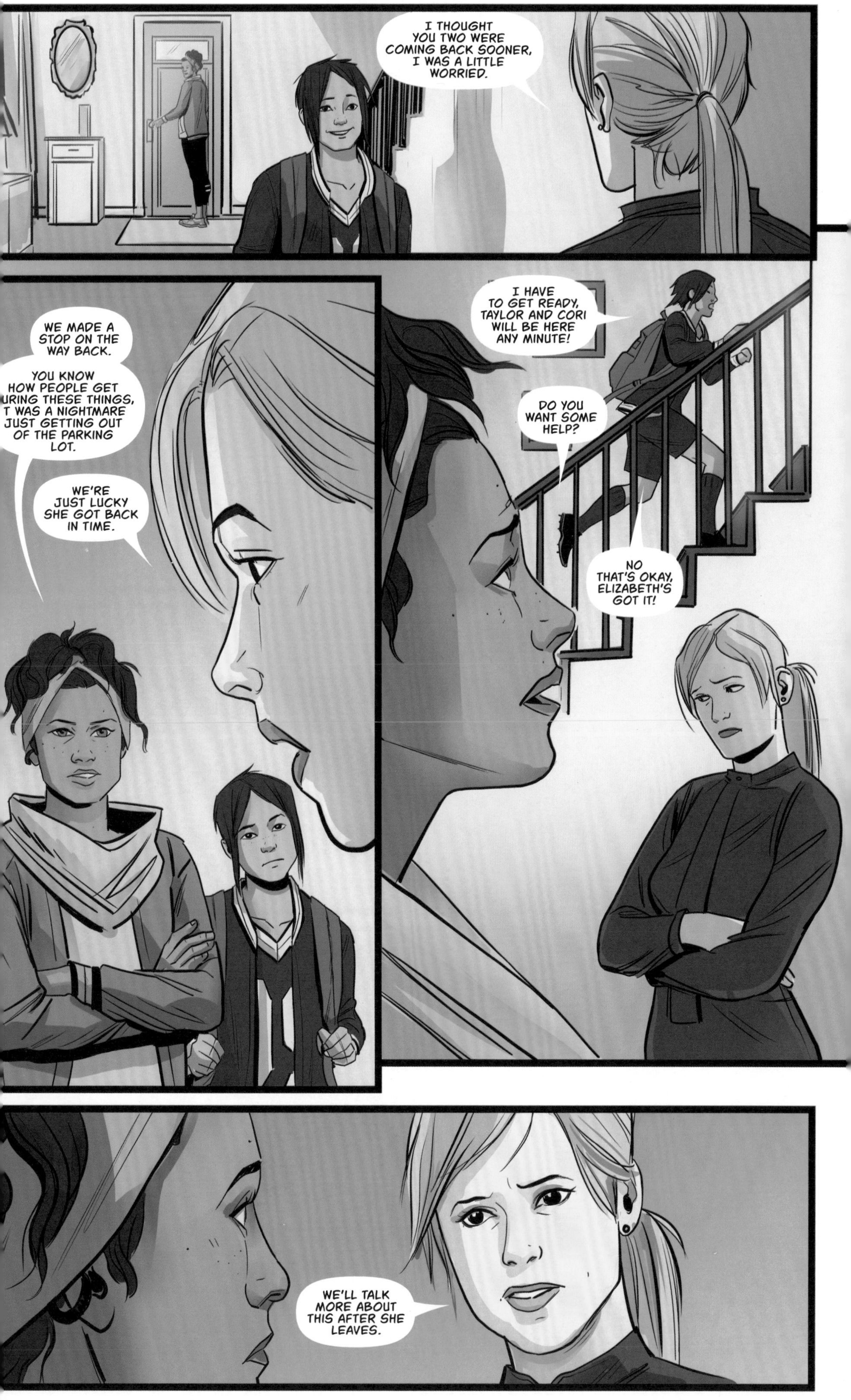
I THOUGHT YOU TWO WERE COMING BACK SOONER, I WAS A LITTLE WORRIED.
WE MADE A STOP ON THE WAY BACK.
YOU KNOW HOW PEOPLE GET URING THESE THINGS, T WAS A NIGHTMARE JUST GETTING OUT OF THE PARKING LOT.
WE'RE JUST LUCKY SHE GOT BACK IN TIME.
I HAVE TO GET READY, TAYLOR AND CORI WILL BE HERE ANY MINUTE!
DO YOU WANT SOME HELP?
NO THAT'S OKAY, ELIZABETH'S GOT IT!
WE'LL TALK MORE ABOUT THIS AFTER SHE LEAVES.

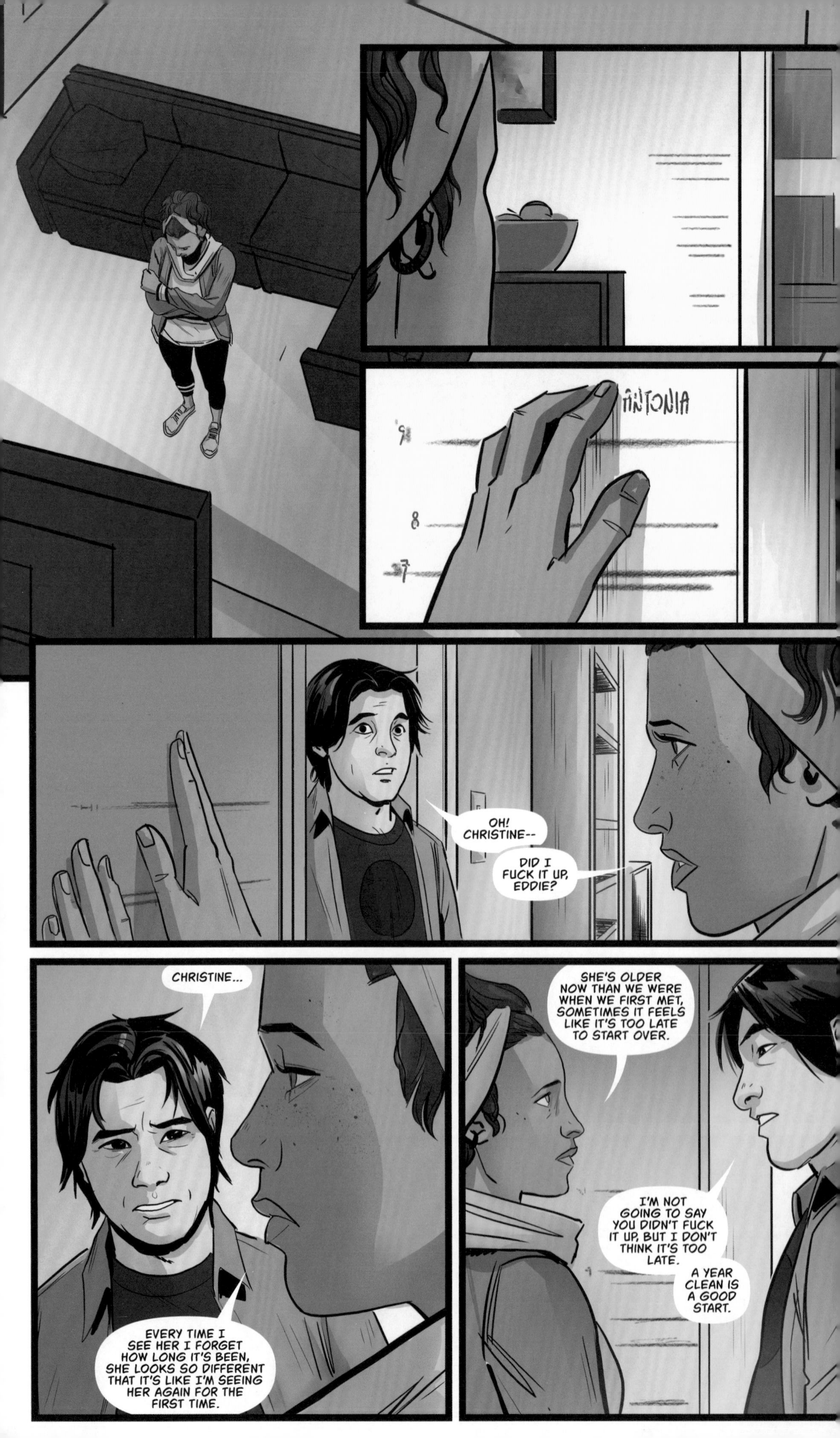
ANTONIA
OH! CHRISTINE--
DID I FUCK IT UP, EDDIE?
CHRISTINE...
EVERY TIME I SEE HER I FORGET HOW LONG IT'S BEEN, SHE LOOKS SO DIFFERENT THAT IT'S LIKE I'M SEEING HER AGAIN FOR THE FIRST TIME.
SHE'S OLDER NOW THAN WE WERE WHEN WE FIRST MET, SOMETIMES IT FEELS LIKE IT'S TOO LATE TO START OVER.
I'M NOT GOING TO SAY YOU DIDN'T FUCK IT UP, BUT I DON'T THINK IT'S TOO LATE.
A YEAR CLEAN IS A GOOD START.

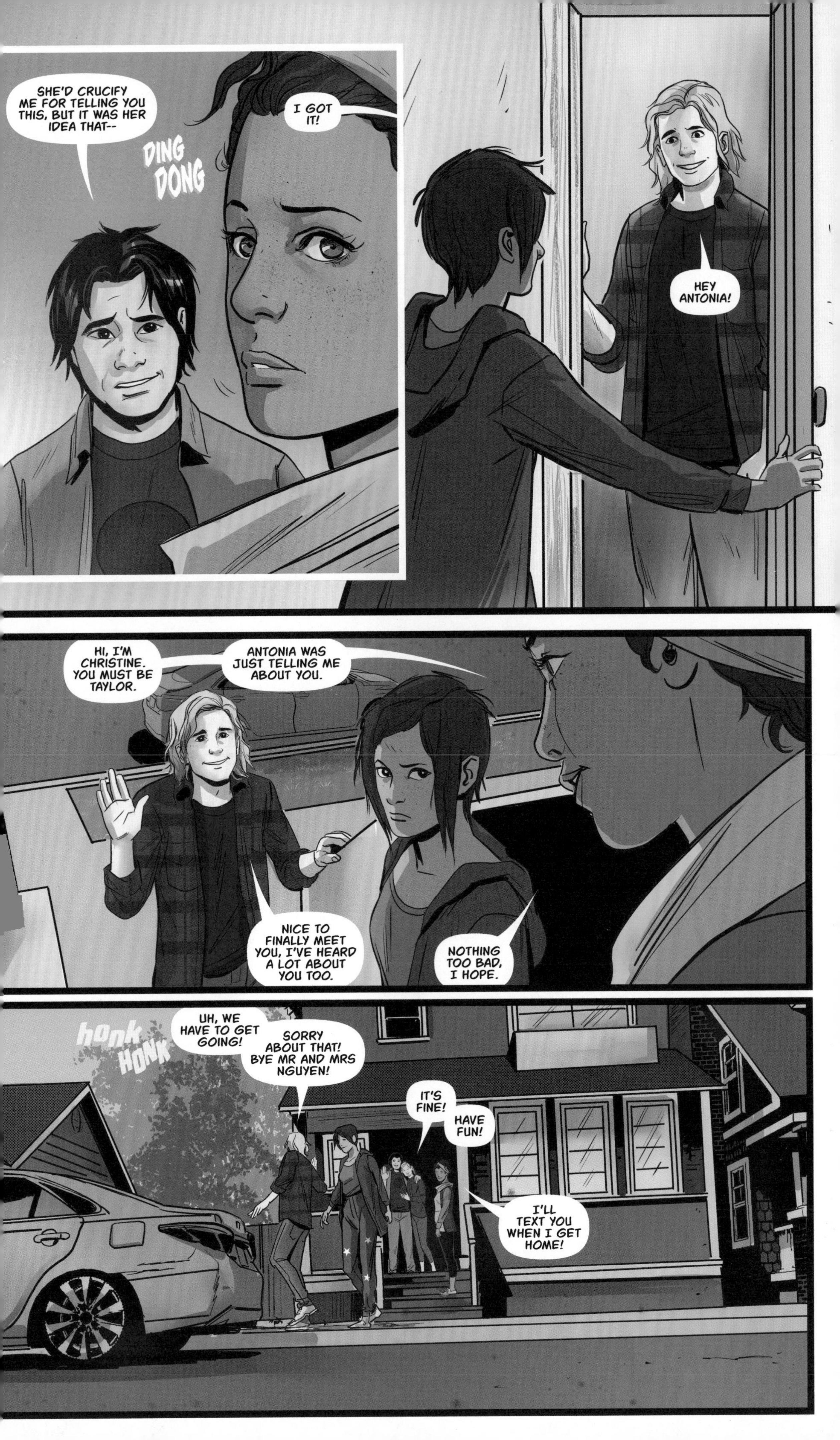
SHE'D CRUCIFY ME FOR TELLING YOU THIS, BUT IT WAS HER IDEA THAT--
DING DONG
I GOT IT!
HEY ANTONIA!
HI, I'M CHRISTINE. YOU MUST BE TAYLOR.
ANTONIA WAS JUST TELLING ME ABOUT YOU.
NICE TO FINALLY MEET YOU, I'VE HEARD A LOT ABOUT YOU TOO.
NOTHING TOO BAD, I HOPE.
honk HONK
UH, WE HAVE TO GET GOING!
SORRY ABOUT THAT! BYE MR AND MRS NGUYEN!
IT'S FINE!
HAVE FUN!
I'LL TEXT YOU WHEN I GET HOME!

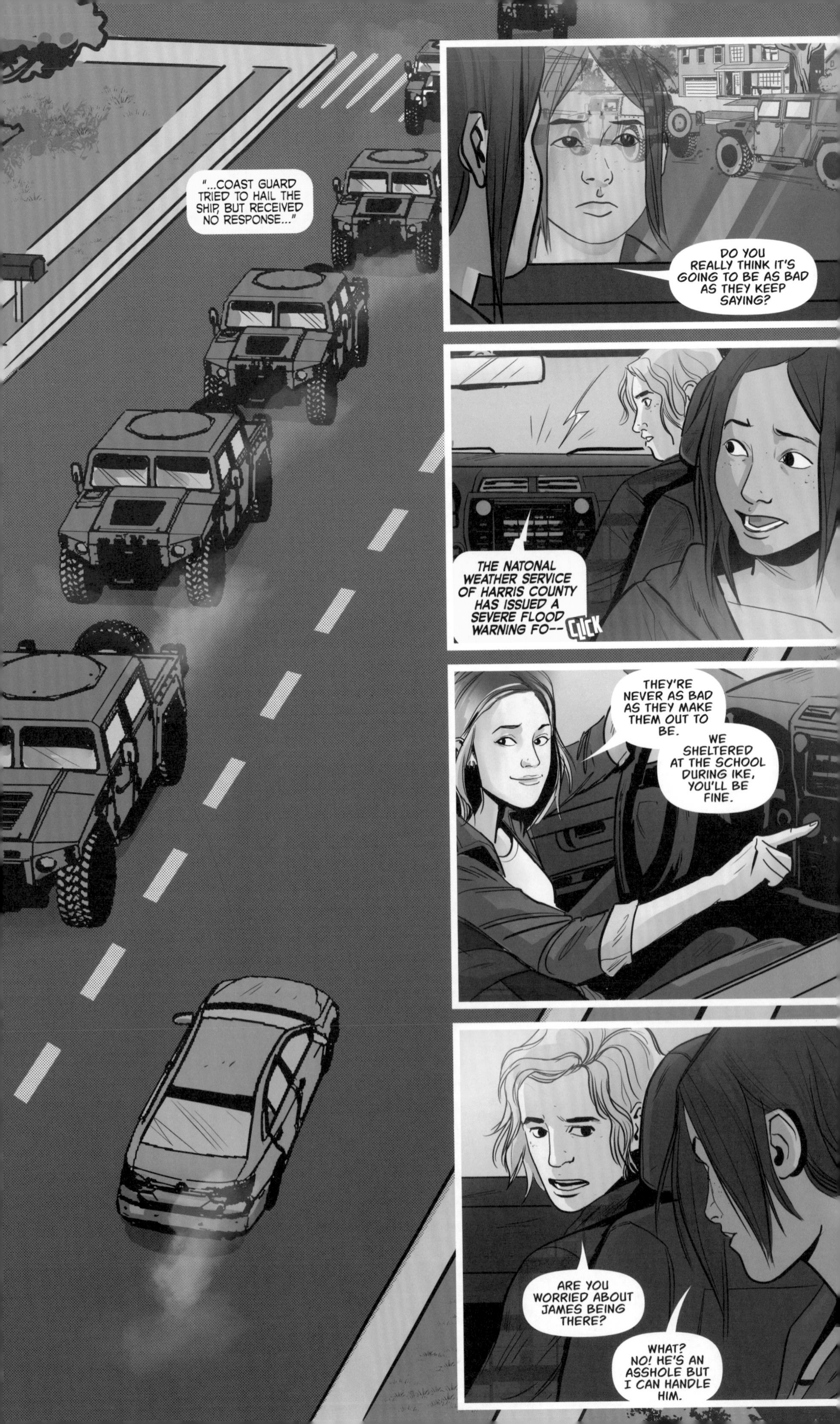
"...COAST GUARD TRIED TO HAIL THE SHIP, BUT RECEIVED NO RESPONSE..."
DO YOU REALLY THINK IT'S GOING TO BE AS BAD AS THEY KEEP SAYING?
THE NATONAL WEATHER SERVICE OF HARRIS COUNTY HAS ISSUED A SEVERE FLOOD WARNING FO--
CLICK
THEY'RE NEVER AS BAD AS THEY MAKE THEM OUT TO BE.
WE SHELTERED AT THE SCHOOL DURING IKE, YOU'LL BE FINE.
ARE YOU WORRIED ABOUT JAMES BEING THERE?
WHAT? NO! HE'S AN ASSHOLE BUT I CAN HANDLE HIM.

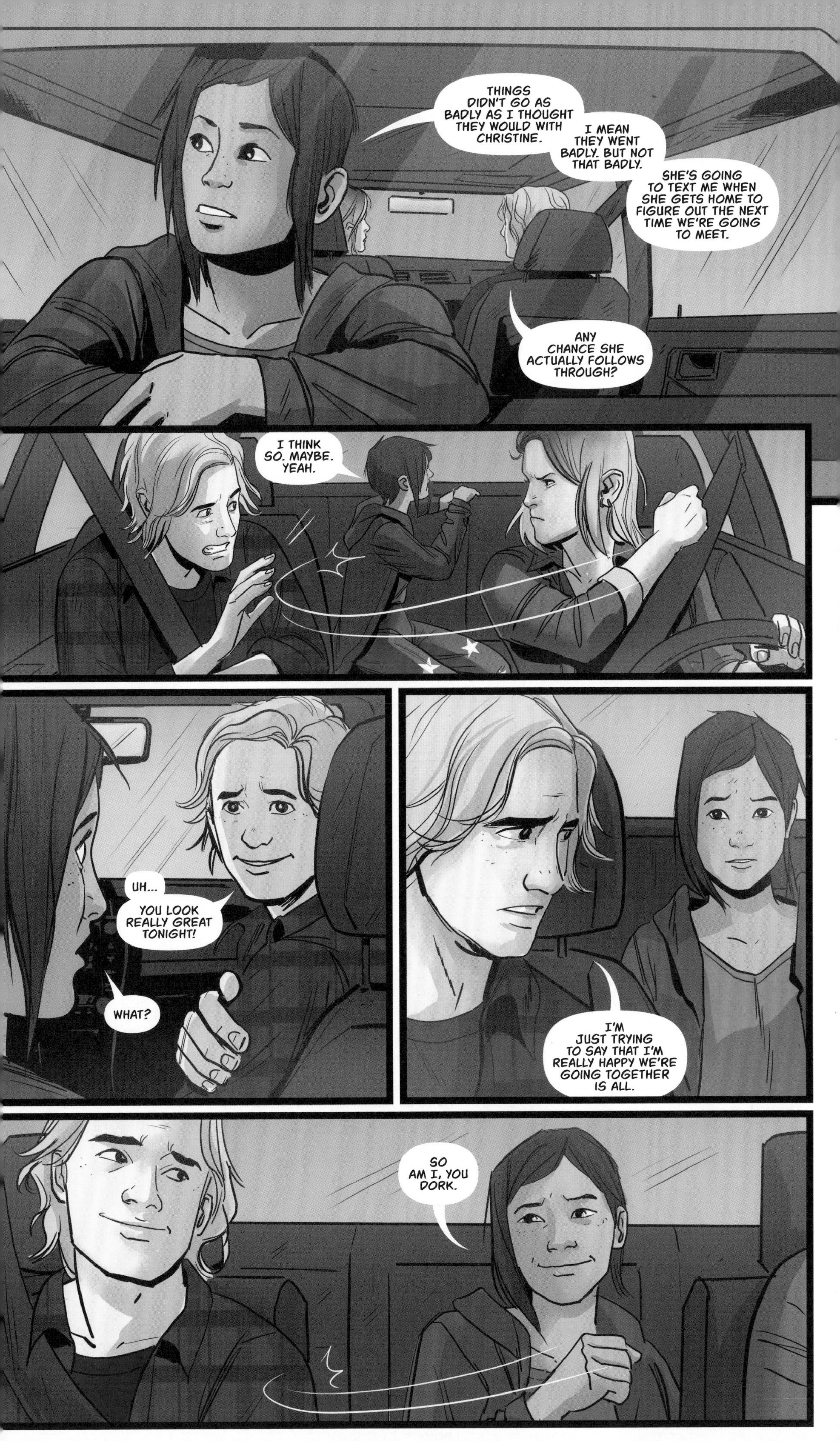
THINGS DIDN'T GO AS BADLY AS I THOUGHT THEY WOULD WITH CHRISTINE.
I MEAN THEY WENT BADLY. BUT NOT THAT BADLY.
SHE'S GOING TO TEXT ME WHEN SHE GETS HOME TO FIGURE OUT THE NEXT TIME WE'RE GOING TO MEET.
ANY CHANCE SHE ACTUALLY FOLLOWS THROUGH?
I THINK SO. MAYBE. YEAH.
UH...
YOU LOOK REALLY GREAT TONIGHT!
WHAT?
I'M JUST TRYING TO SAY THAT I'M REALLY HAPPY WE'RE GOING TOGETHER IS ALL.
SO AM I, YOU DORK.

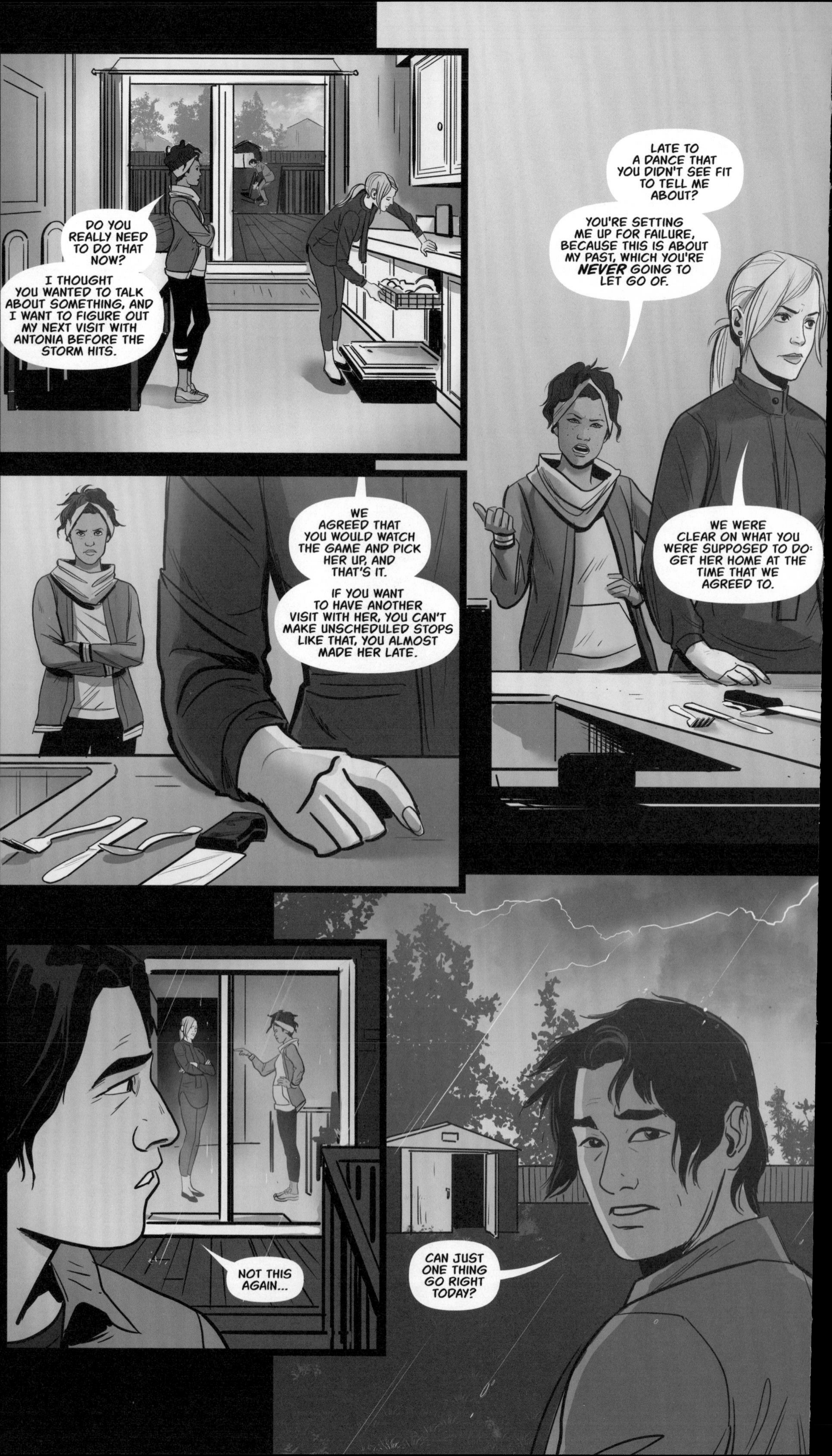
DO YOU REALLY NEED TO DO THAT NOW?
I THOUGHT YOU WANTED TO TALK ABOUT SOMETHING, AND I WANT TO FIGURE OUT MY NEXT VISIT WITH ANTONIA BEFORE THE STORM HITS.
WE AGREED THAT YOU WOULD WATCH THE GAME AND PICK HER UP, AND THAT'S IT.
IF YOU WANT TO HAVE ANOTHER VISIT WITH HER, YOU CAN'T MAKE UNSCHEDULED STOPS LIKE THAT, YOU ALMOST MADE HER LATE.
LATE TO A DANCE THAT YOU DIDN'T SEE FIT TO TELL ME ABOUT?
YOU'RE SETTING ME UP FOR FAILURE, BECAUSE THIS IS ABOUT MY PAST, WHICH YOU'RE ***NEVER*** GOING TO LET GO OF.
WE WERE CLEAR ON WHAT YOU WERE SUPPOSED TO DO: GET HER HOME AT THE TIME THAT WE AGREED TO.
NOT THIS AGAIN...
CAN JUST ONE THING GO RIGHT TODAY?

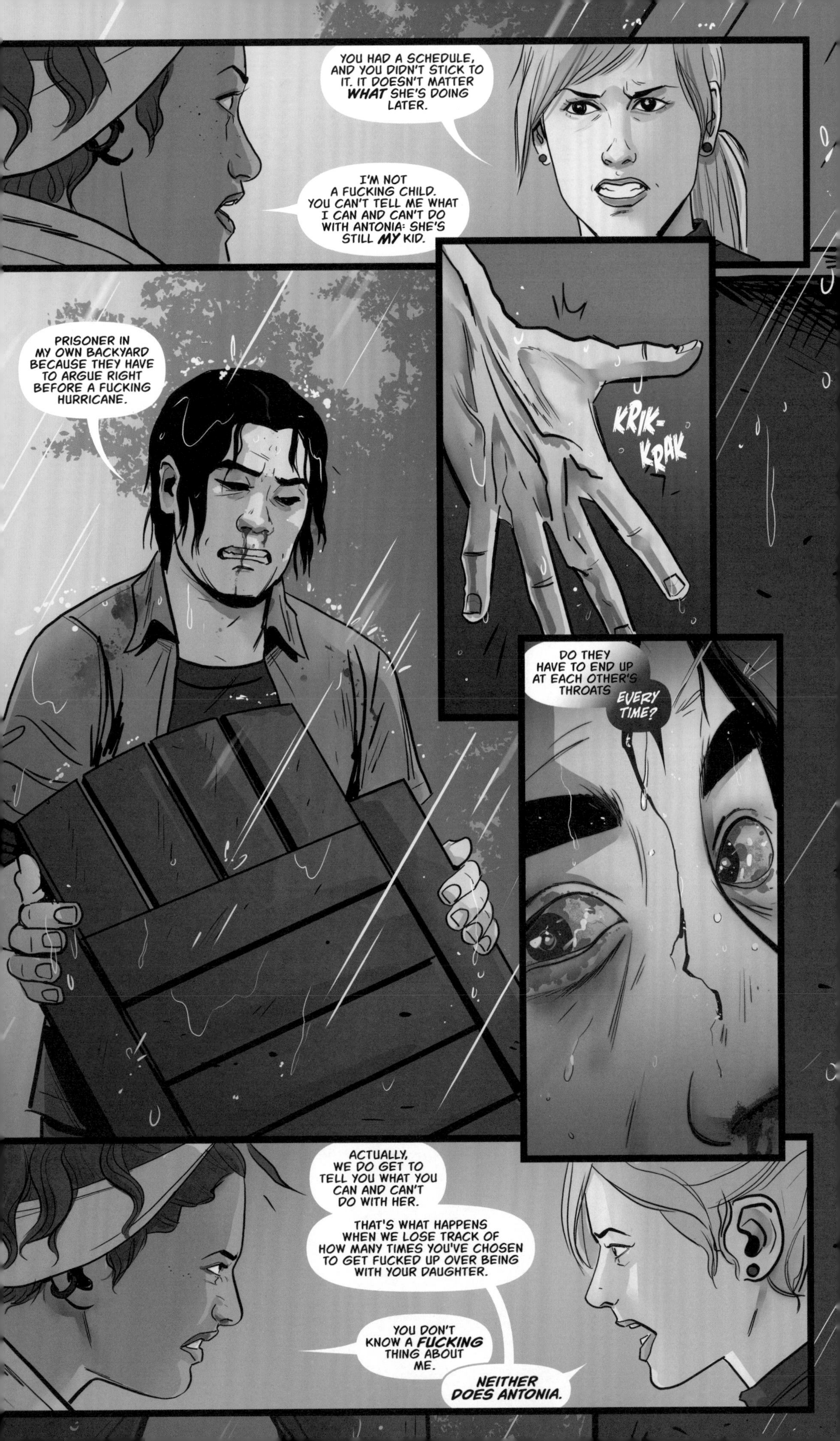

YOU HAD A SCHEDULE, AND YOU DIDN'T STICK TO IT. IT DOESN'T MATTER WHAT SHE'S DOING LATER.
I'M NOT A FUCKING CHILD. YOU CAN'T TELL ME WHAT I CAN AND CAN'T DO WITH ANTONIA: SHE'S STILL MY KID.
PRISONER IN MY OWN BACKYARD BECAUSE THEY HAVE TO ARGUE RIGHT BEFORE A FUCKING HURRICANE.
KRIK-KRAK
DO THEY HAVE TO END UP AT EACH OTHER'S THROATS
EVERY TIME?
ACTUALLY, WE DO GET TO TELL YOU WHAT YOU CAN AND CAN'T DO WITH HER.
THAT'S WHAT HAPPENS WHEN WE LOSE TRACK OF HOW MANY TIMES YOU'VE CHOSEN TO GET FUCKED UP OVER BEING WITH YOUR DAUGHTER.
YOU DON'T KNOW A FUCKING THING ABOUT ME.
NEITHER DOES ANTONIA.

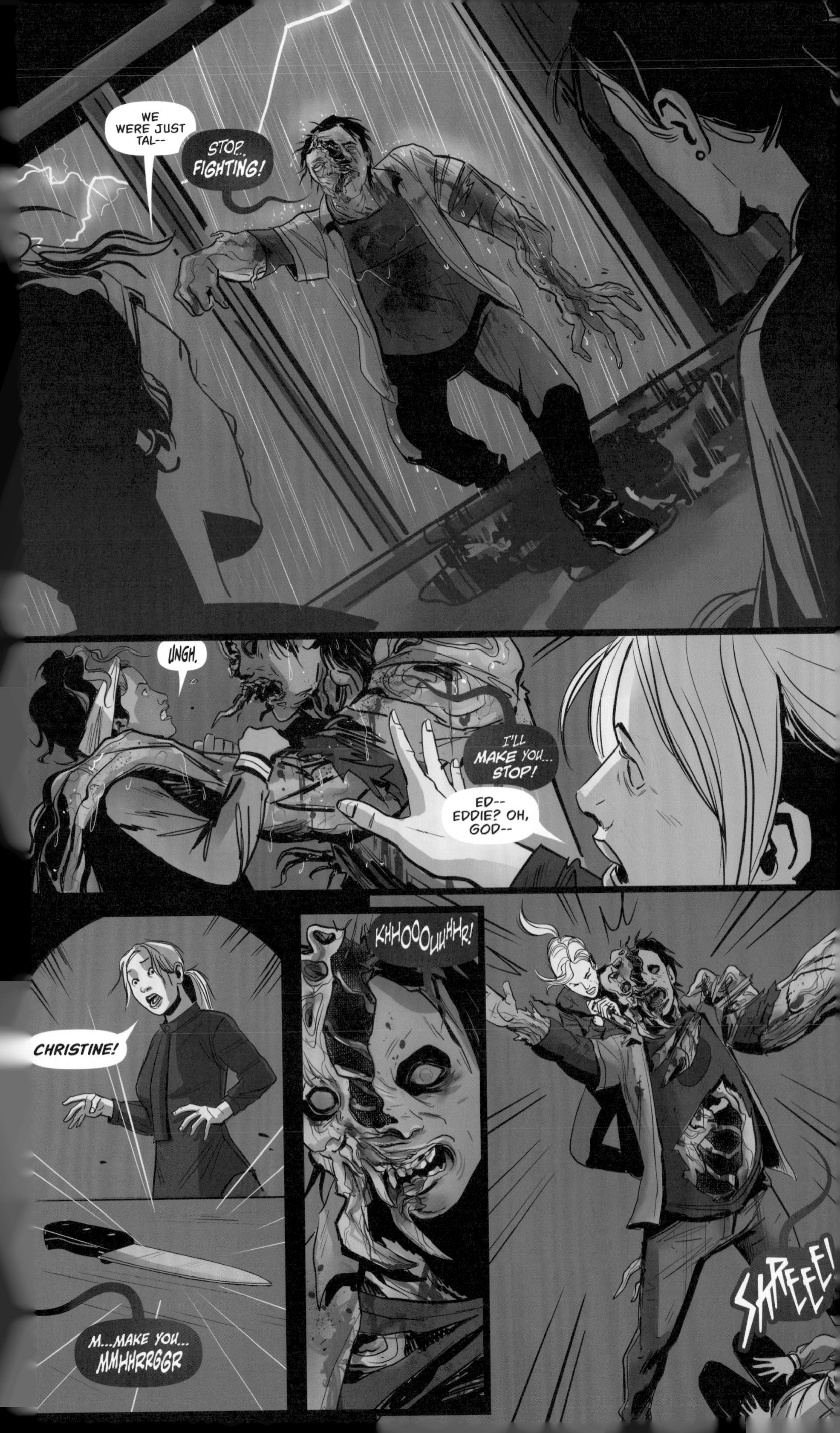
WE WERE JUST TAL--
STOP... FIGHTING!
UNGH.
I'LL MAKE YOU... STOP!
ED-- EDDIE? OH, GOD--
CHRISTINE!
M...MAKE YOU... MMHHRRGGR
KHHOOOUUHHHR!
SHREEE!

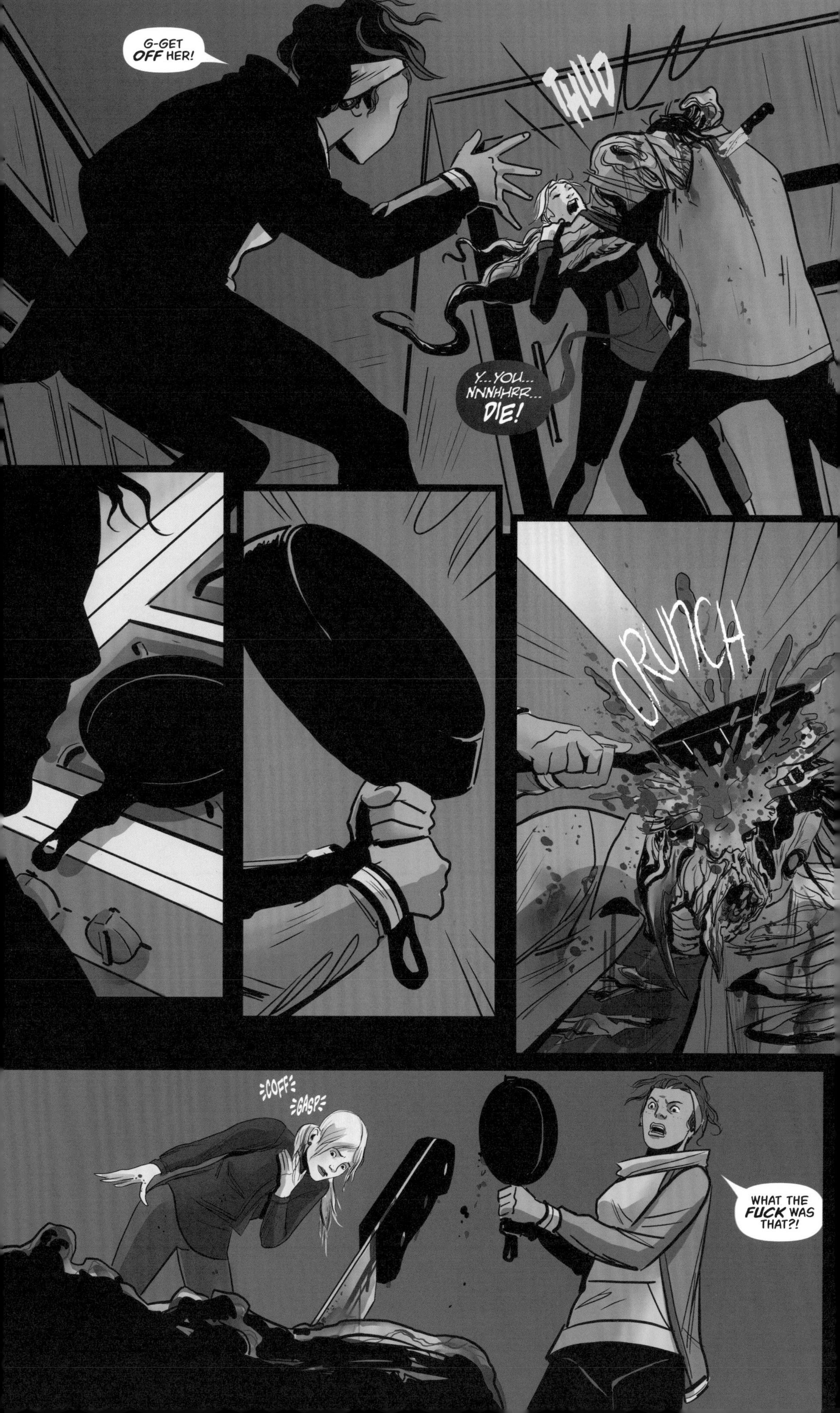
G-GET OFF HER!
THUD
Y... YOU... NNNHHRR... DIE!
CRUNCH!
COFF
GASP
WHAT THE FUCK WAS THAT?!

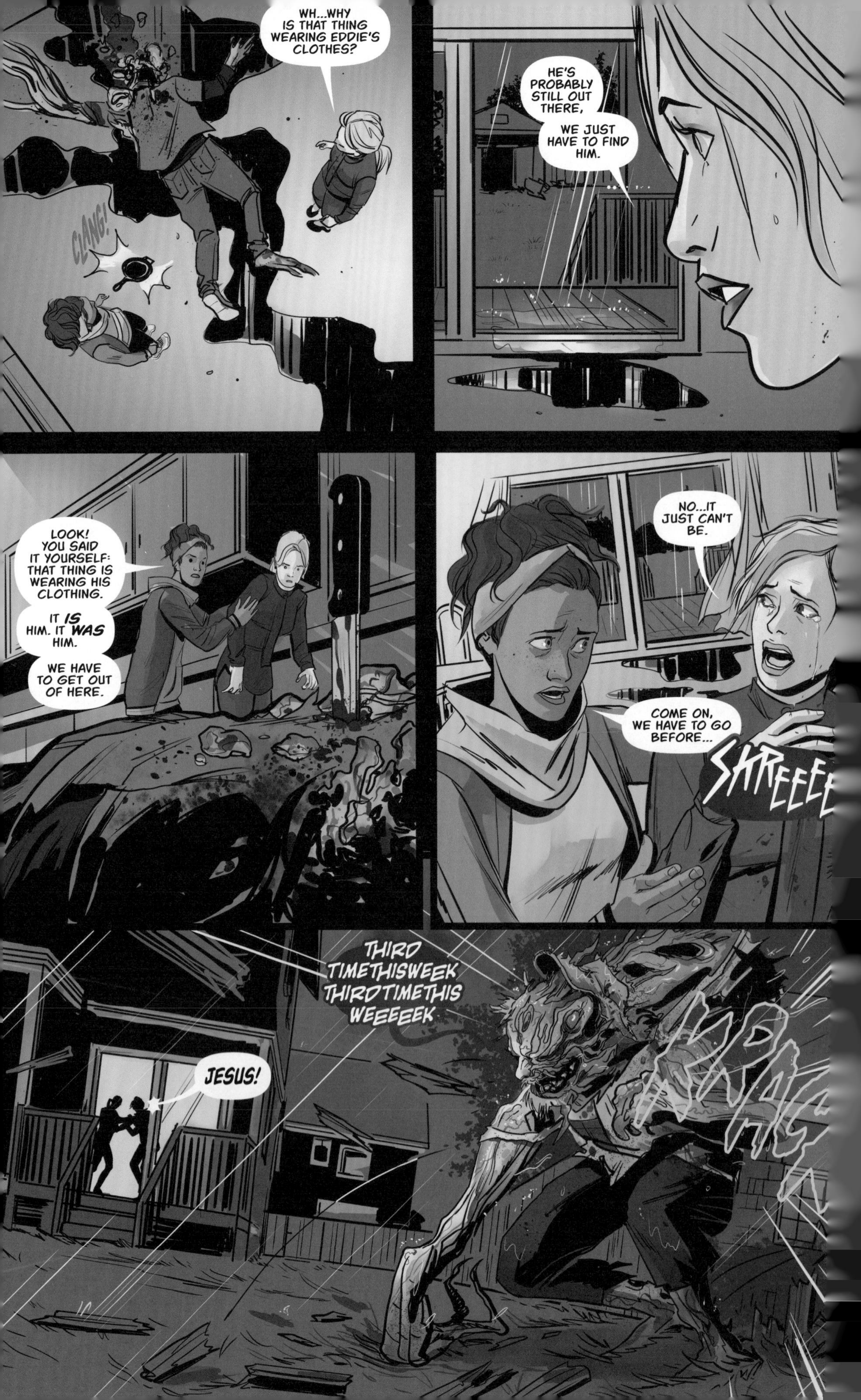
WH...WHY IS THAT THING WEARING EDDIE'S CLOTHES?
CLANG!
HE'S PROBABLY STILL OUT THERE,
WE JUST HAVE TO FIND HIM.
LOOK! YOU SAID IT YOURSELF: THAT THING IS WEARING HIS CLOTHING.
IT IS HIM. IT WAS HIM.
WE HAVE TO GET OUT OF HERE.
NO...IT JUST CAN'T BE.
COME ON, WE HAVE TO GO BEFORE...
SKREEEE
THIRD TIMETHISWEEK THIRDTIMETHIS WEEEEEK
JESUS!

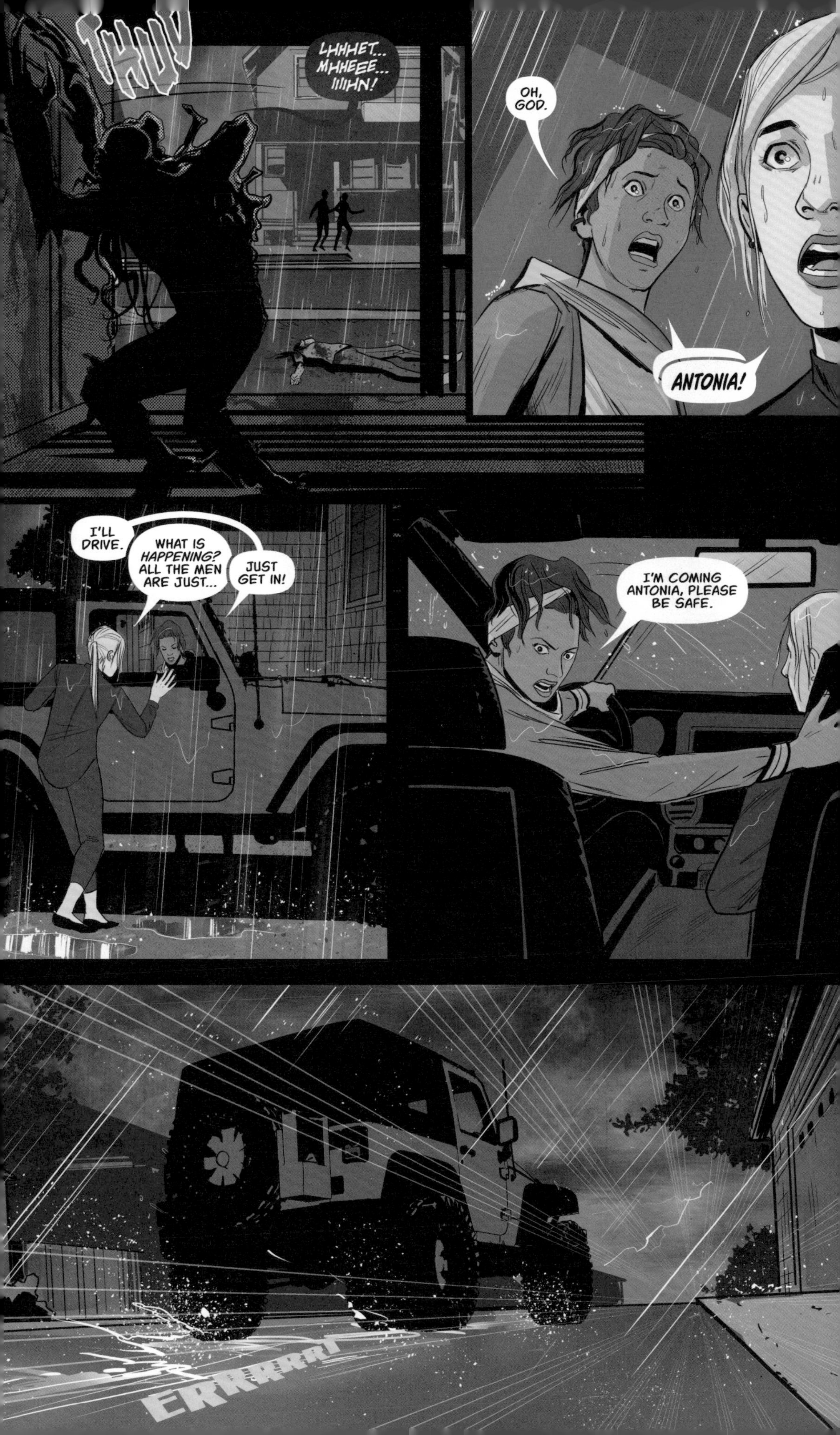
THUD
LHHHET... MHHEEE... IIIHN!
OH, GOD.
ANTONIA!
I'LL DRIVE.
WHAT IS HAPPENING? ALL THE MEN ARE JUST...
JUST GET IN!
I'M COMING ANTONIA, PLEASE BE SAFE.
ERRRRRT

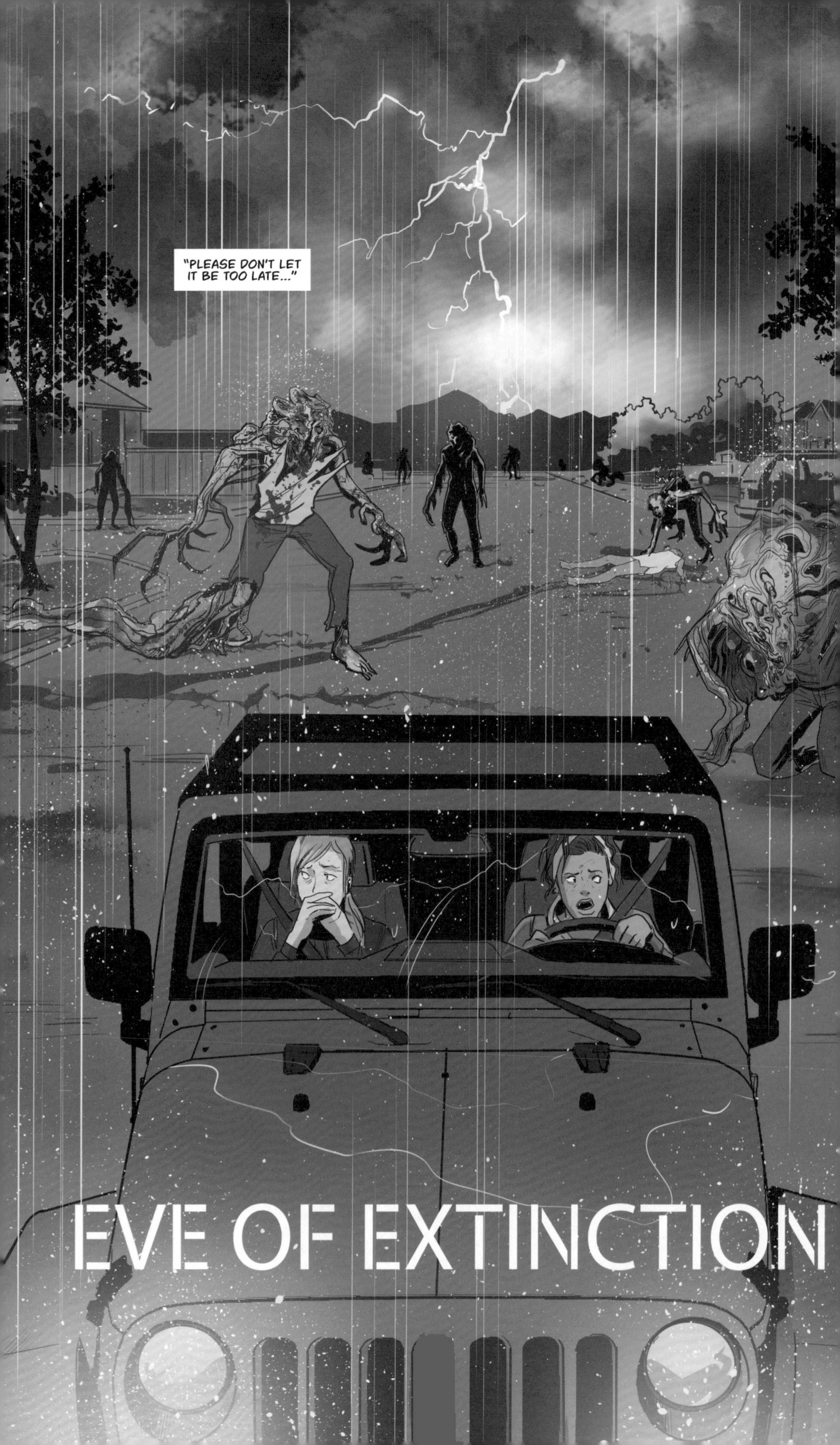
"PLEASE DON'T LET IT BE TOO LATE..."
EVE OF EXTINCTION

CHAPTER 2

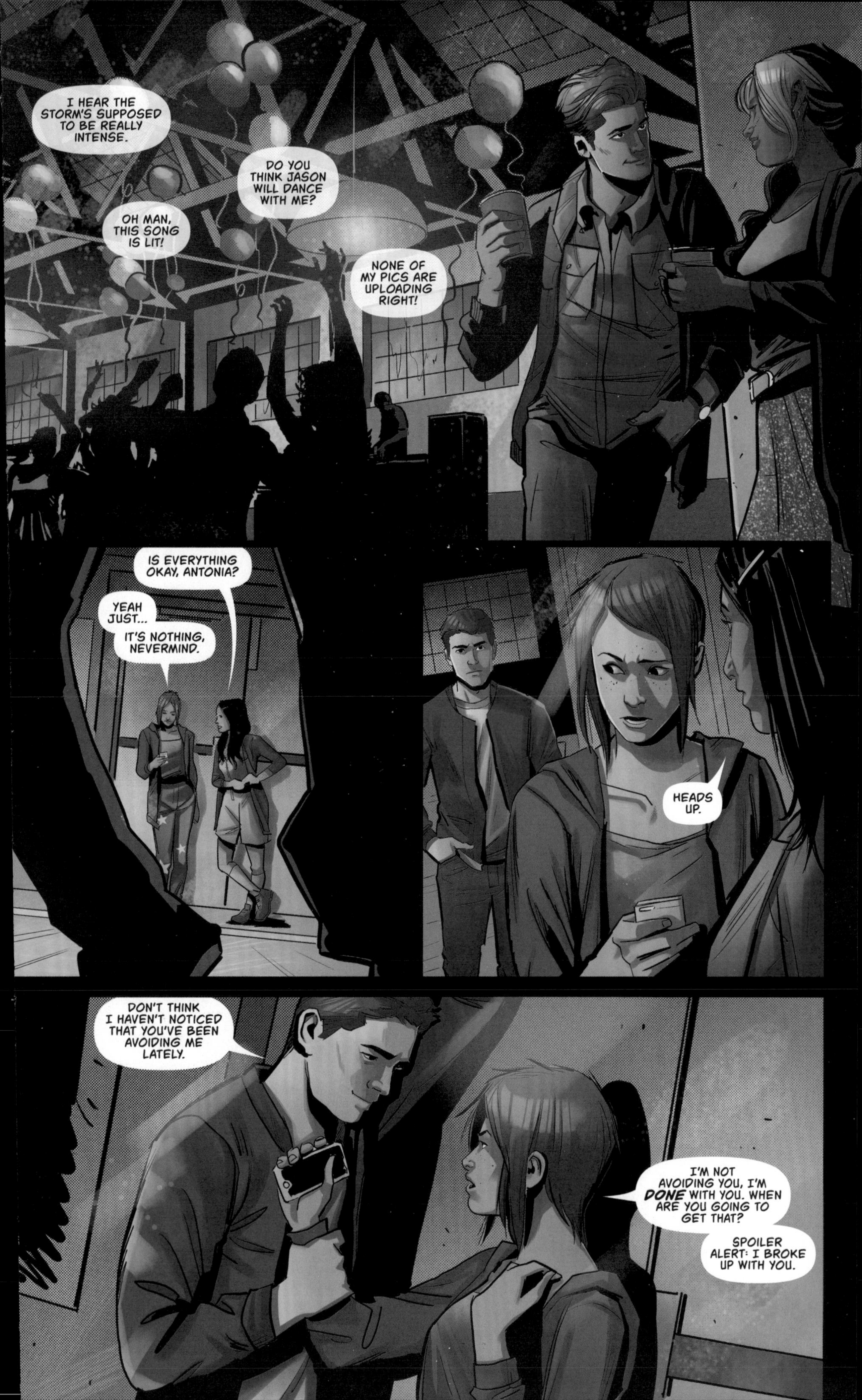
I HEAR THE STORM'S SUPPOSED TO BE REALLY INTENSE.
DO YOU THINK JASON WILL DANCE WITH ME?
OH MAN, THIS SONG IS LIT!
NONE OF MY PICS ARE UPLOADING RIGHT!
IS EVERYTHING OKAY, ANTONIA?
YEAH JUST...
IT'S NOTHING, NEVERMIND.
HEADS UP.
DON'T THINK I HAVEN'T NOTICED THAT YOU'VE BEEN AVOIDING ME LATELY.
I'M NOT AVOIDING YOU, I'M DONE WITH YOU. WHEN ARE YOU GOING TO GET THAT?
SPOILER ALERT: I BROKE UP WITH YOU.

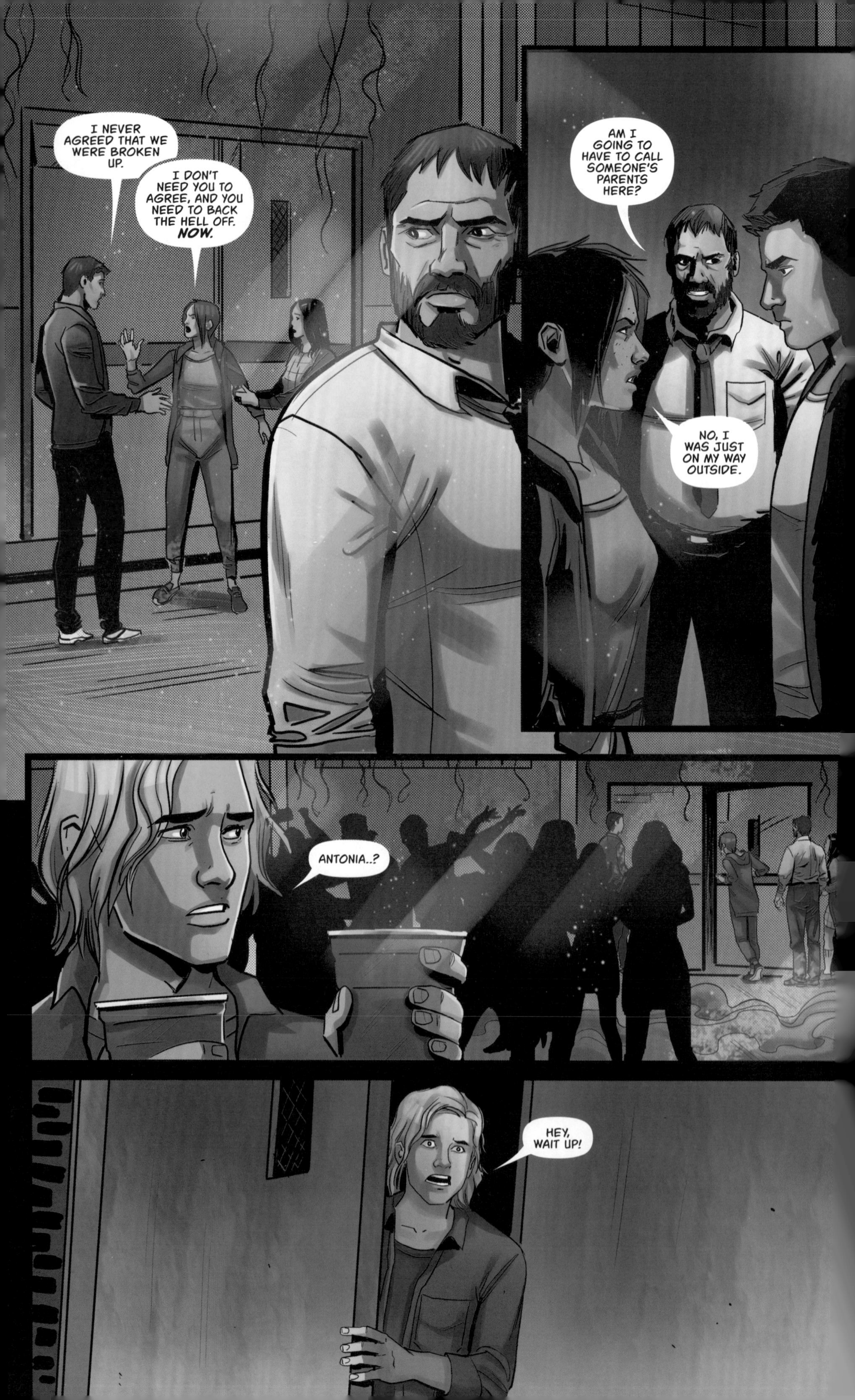
I NEVER AGREED THAT WE WERE BROKEN UP.
I DON'T NEED YOU TO AGREE, AND YOU NEED TO BACK THE HELL OFF. NOW.
AM I GOING TO HAVE TO CALL SOMEONE'S PARENTS HERE?
NO, I WAS JUST ON MY WAY OUTSIDE.
ANTONIA..?
HEY, WAIT UP!

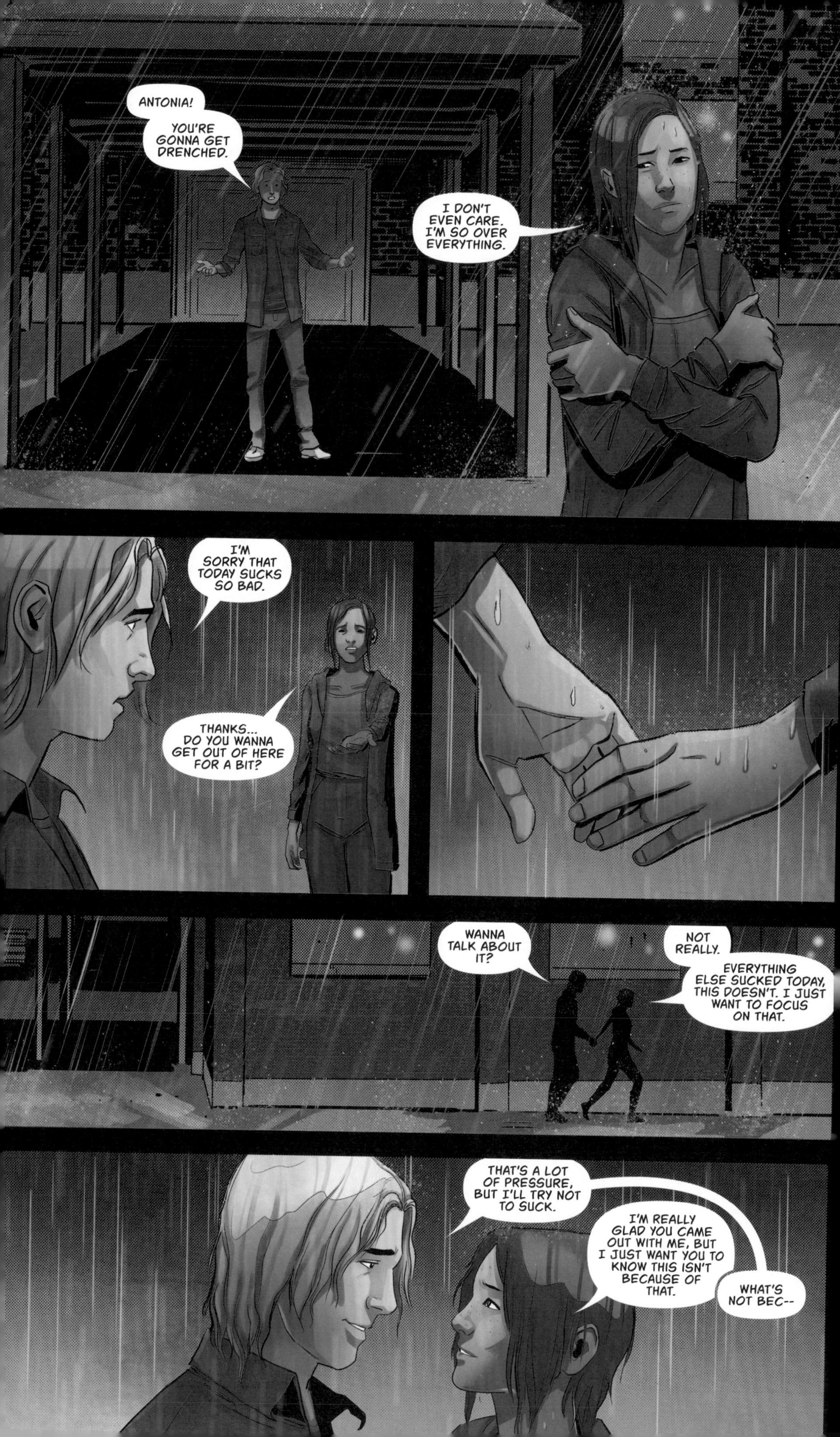
ANTONIA!
YOU'RE GONNA GET DRENCHED.
I DON'T EVEN CARE. I'M SO OVER EVERYTHING.
I'M SORRY THAT TODAY SUCKS SO BAD.
THANKS... DO YOU WANNA GET OUT OF HERE FOR A BIT?
WANNA TALK ABOUT IT?
NOT REALLY.
EVERYTHING ELSE SUCKED TODAY, THIS DOESN'T. I JUST WANT TO FOCUS ON THAT.
THAT'S A LOT OF PRESSURE, BUT I'LL TRY NOT TO SUCK.
I'M REALLY GLAD YOU CAME OUT WITH ME, BUT I JUST WANT YOU TO KNOW THIS ISN'T BECAUSE OF THAT.
WHAT'S NOT BEC--

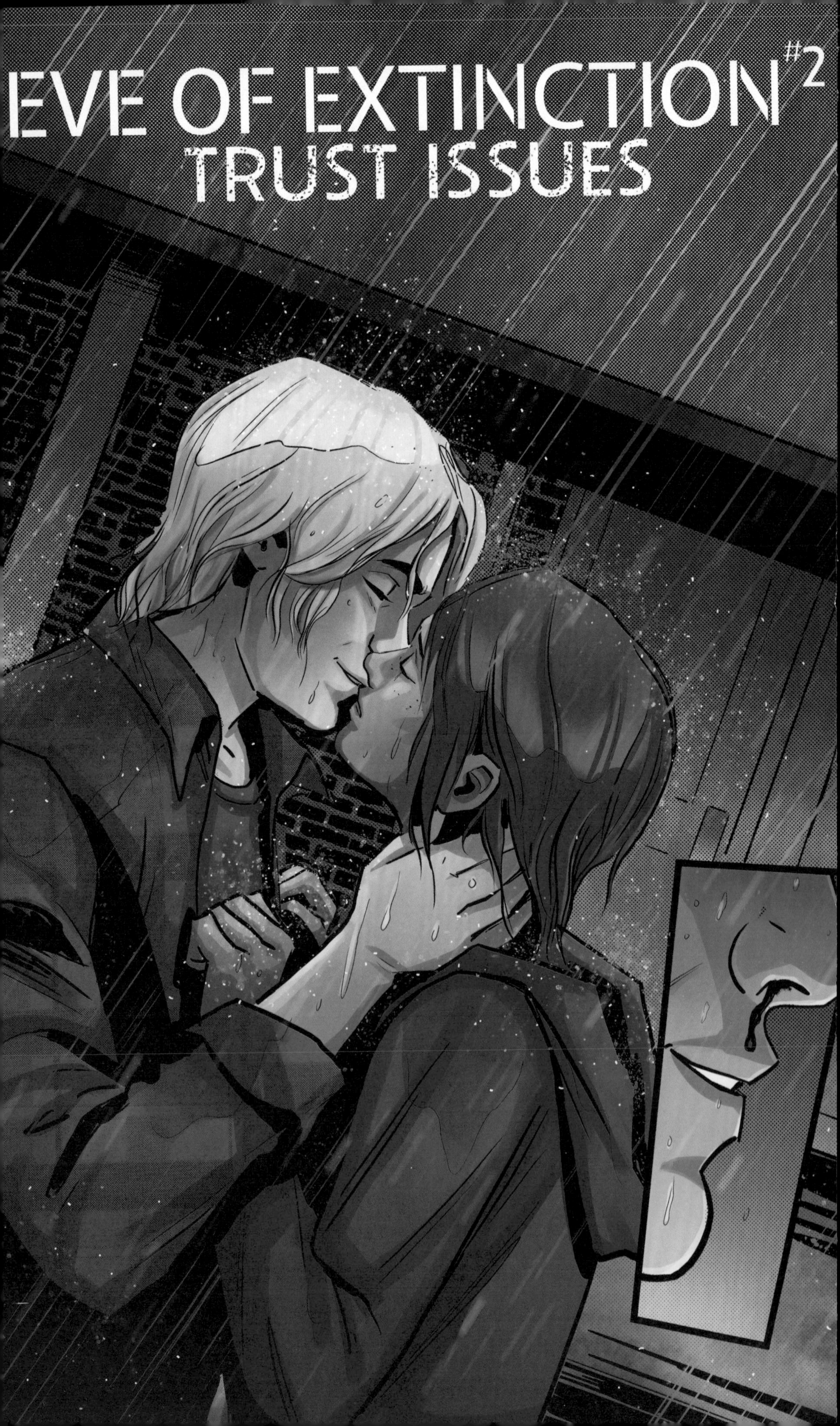
EVE OF EXTINCTION #2
TRUST ISSUES

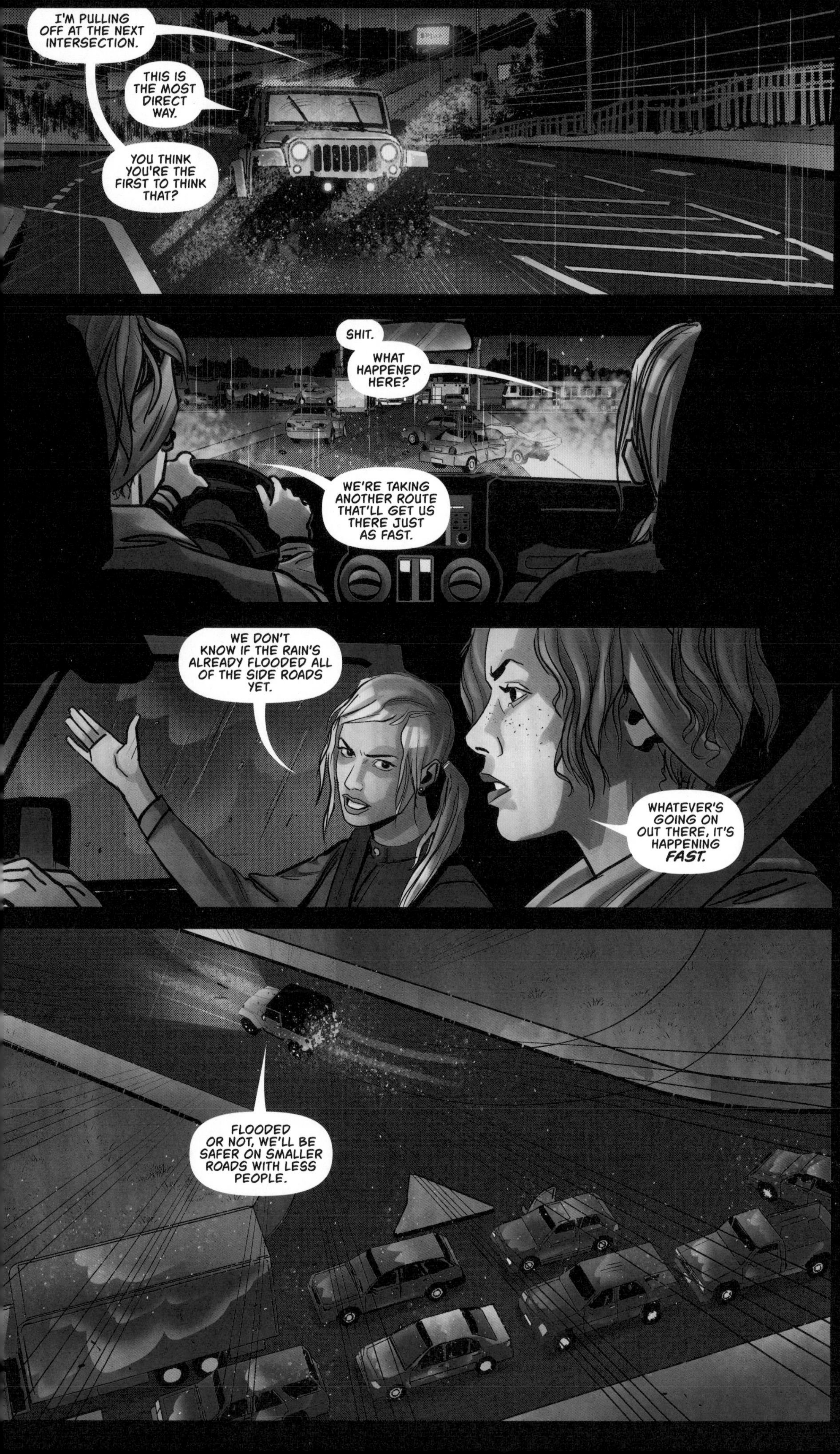
I'M PULLING OFF AT THE NEXT INTERSECTION.
THIS IS THE MOST DIRECT WAY.
YOU THINK YOU'RE THE FIRST TO THINK THAT?
SHIT.
WHAT HAPPENED HERE?
WE'RE TAKING ANOTHER ROUTE THAT'LL GET US THERE JUST AS FAST.
WE DON'T KNOW IF THE RAIN'S ALREADY FLOODED ALL OF THE SIDE ROADS YET.
WHATEVER'S GOING ON OUT THERE, IT'S HAPPENING *FAST.*
FLOODED OR NOT, WE'LL BE SAFER ON SMALLER ROADS WITH LESS PEOPLE.

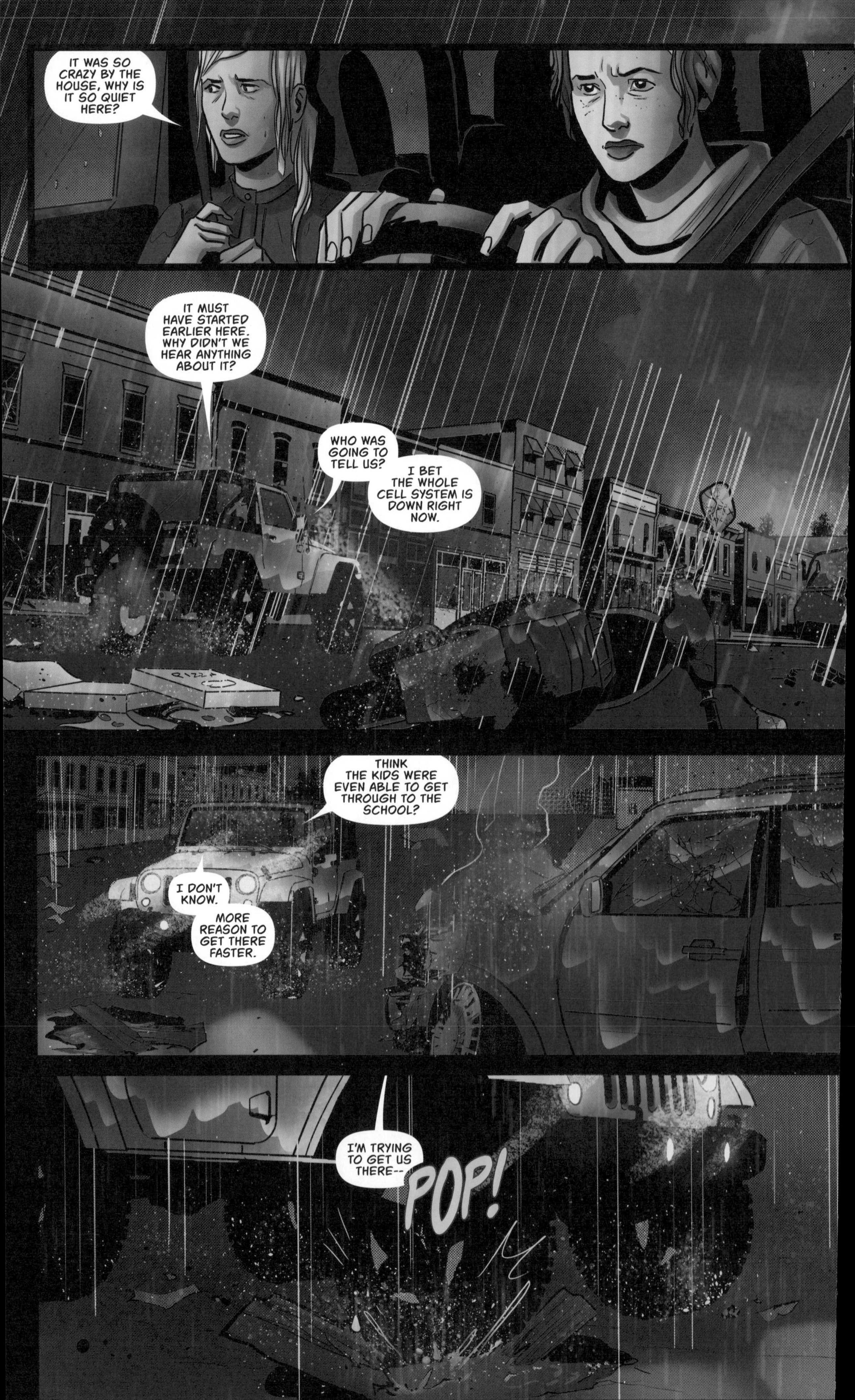
IT WAS SO CRAZY BY THE HOUSE, WHY IS IT SO QUIET HERE?
IT MUST HAVE STARTED EARLIER HERE. WHY DIDN'T WE HEAR ANYTHING ABOUT IT?
WHO WAS GOING TO TELL US?
I BET THE WHOLE CELL SYSTEM IS DOWN RIGHT NOW.
THINK THE KIDS WERE EVEN ABLE TO GET THROUGH TO THE SCHOOL?
I DON'T KNOW.
MORE REASON TO GET THERE FASTER.
I'M TRYING TO GET US THERE--
POP!

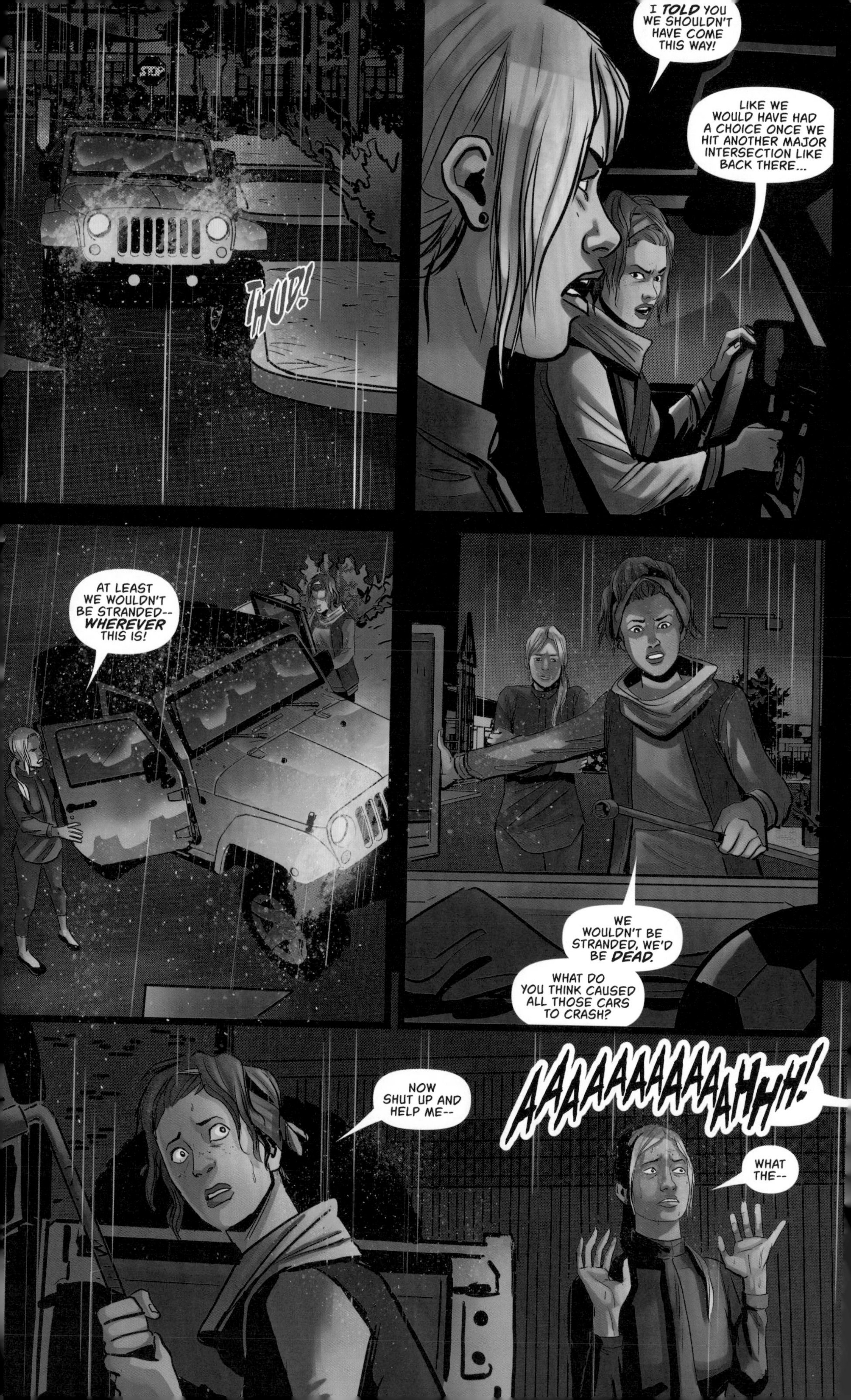
THUD!
I TOLD YOU WE SHOULDN'T HAVE COME THIS WAY!
LIKE WE WOULD HAVE HAD A CHOICE ONCE WE HIT ANOTHER MAJOR INTERSECTION LIKE BACK THERE...
AT LEAST WE WOULDN'T BE STRANDED-- WHEREVER THIS IS!
WE WOULDN'T BE STRANDED, WE'D BE DEAD.
WHAT DO YOU THINK CAUSED ALL THOSE CARS TO CRASH?
NOW SHUT UP AND HELP ME--
AAAAAAAAAAHHH!
WHAT THE--

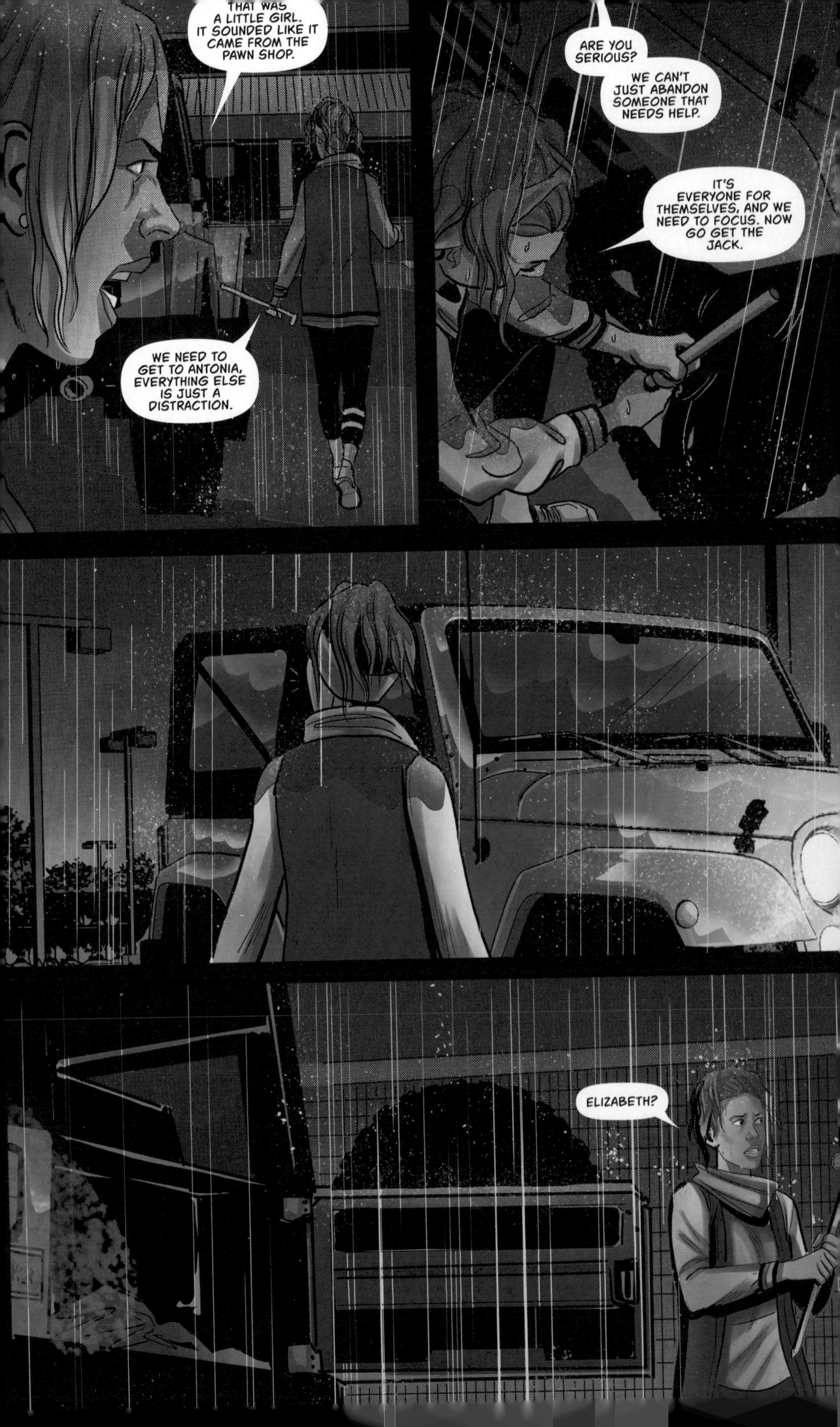
THAT WAS A LITTLE GIRL. IT SOUNDED LIKE IT CAME FROM THE PAWN SHOP.
WE NEED TO GET TO ANTONIA, EVERYTHING ELSE IS JUST A DISTRACTION.
ARE YOU SERIOUS?
WE CAN'T JUST ABANDON SOMEONE THAT NEEDS HELP.
IT'S EVERYONE FOR THEMSELVES, AND WE NEED TO FOCUS. NOW GO GET THE JACK.
ELIZABETH?

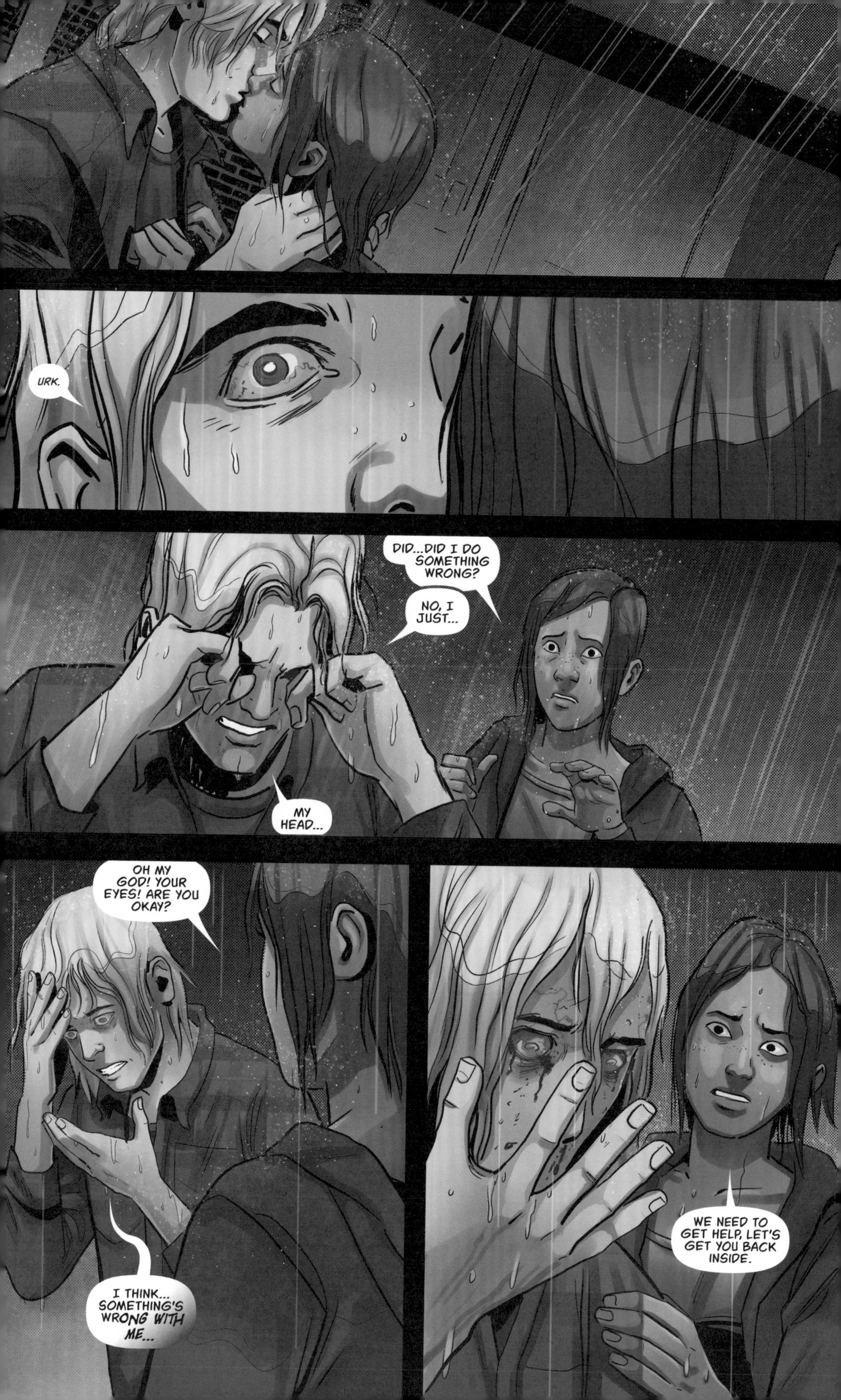
URK.
DID...DID I DO SOMETHING WRONG?
NO, I JUST...
MY HEAD...
OH MY GOD! YOUR EYES! ARE YOU OKAY?
I THINK... SOMETHING'S WRONG WITH ME...
WE NEED TO GET HELP, LET'S GET YOU BACK INSIDE.

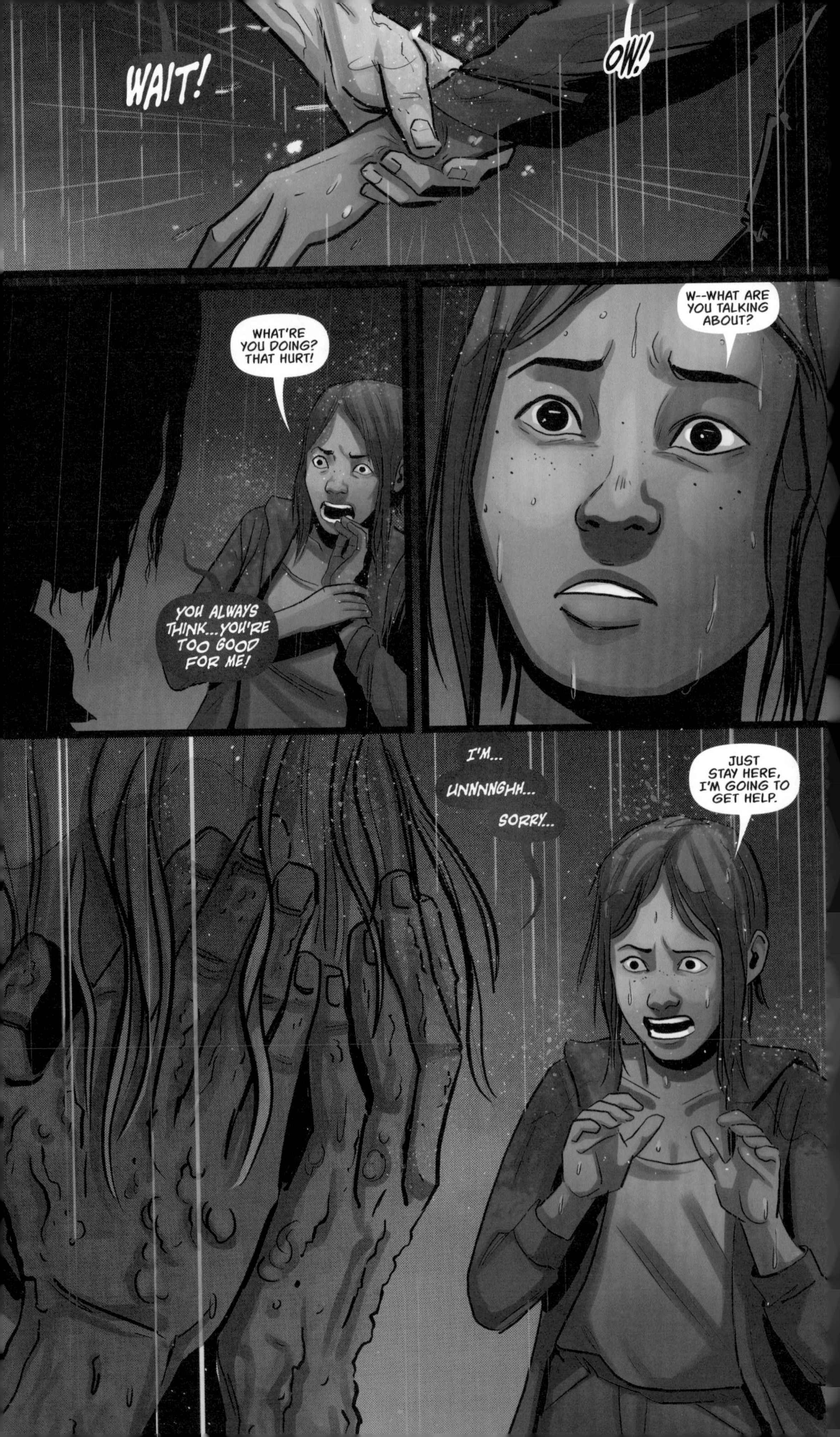
WAIT!
OW!
WHAT'RE YOU DOING? THAT HURT!
YOU ALWAYS THINK...YOU'RE TOO GOOD FOR ME!
W--WHAT ARE YOU TALKING ABOUT?
I'M...
UNNNNGHH...
SORRY...
JUST STAY HERE, I'M GOING TO GET HELP.

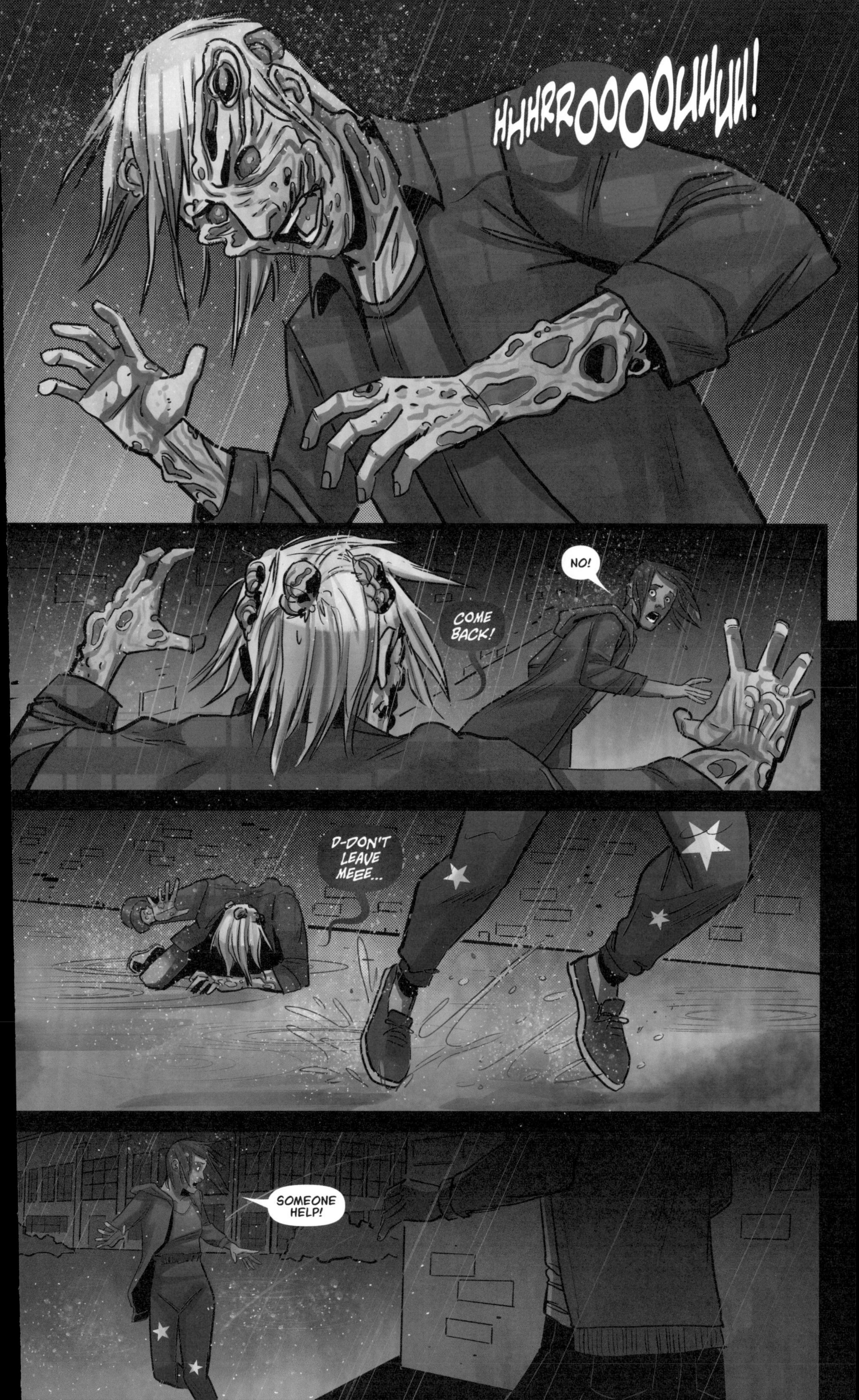
HHHRROOOOUUUUU!
NO!
COME BACK!
D-DON'T LEAVE MEEE...
SOMEONE HELP!

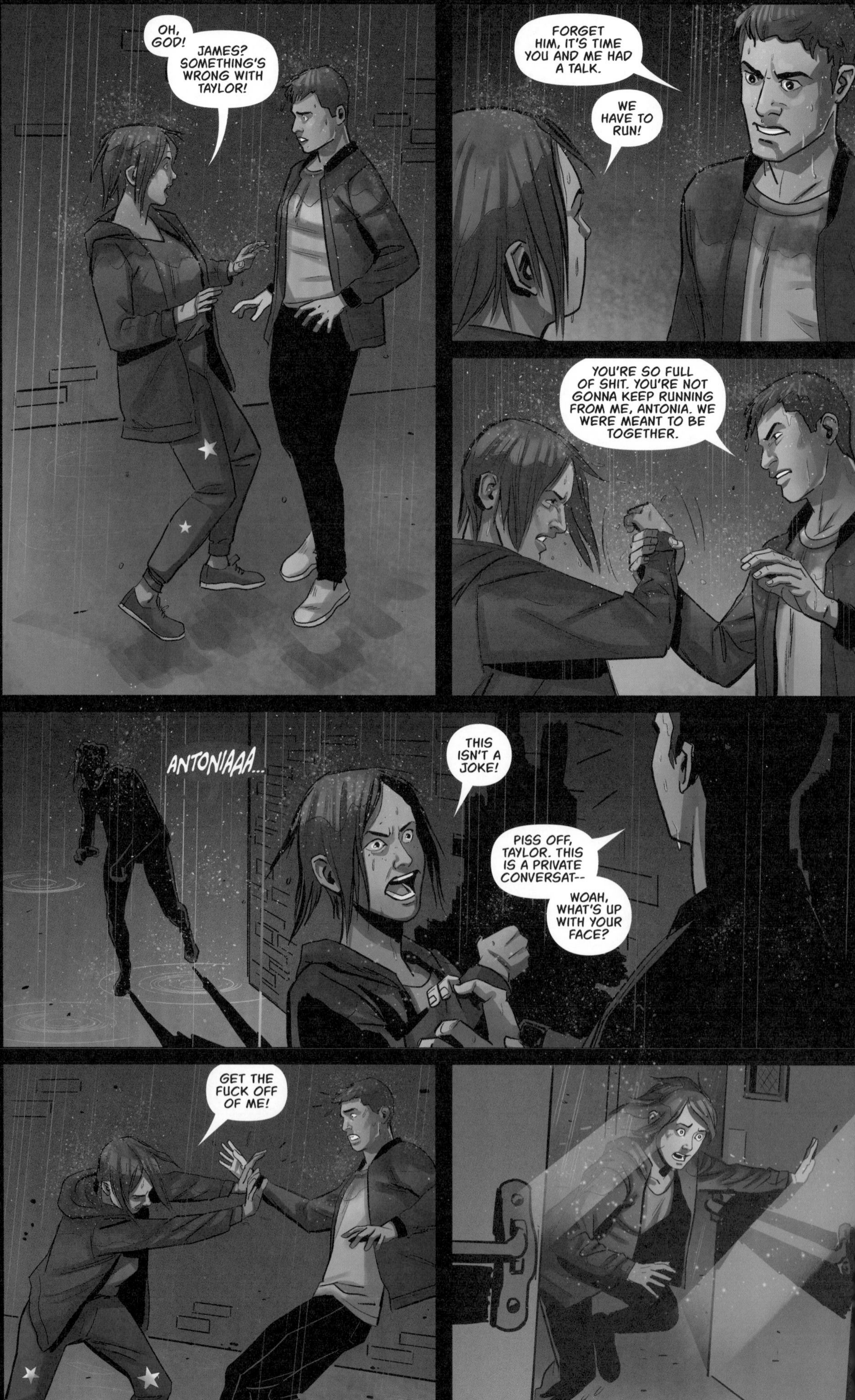

OH, GOD!
JAMES? SOMETHING'S WRONG WITH TAYLOR!
FORGET HIM, IT'S TIME YOU AND ME HAD A TALK.
WE HAVE TO RUN!
YOU'RE SO FULL OF SHIT. YOU'RE NOT GONNA KEEP RUNNING FROM ME, ANTONIA. WE WERE MEANT TO BE TOGETHER.
ANTONIAAA...
THIS ISN'T A JOKE!
PISS OFF, TAYLOR. THIS IS A PRIVATE CONVERSAT--
WOAH, WHAT'S UP WITH YOUR FACE?
GET THE FUCK OFF OF ME!

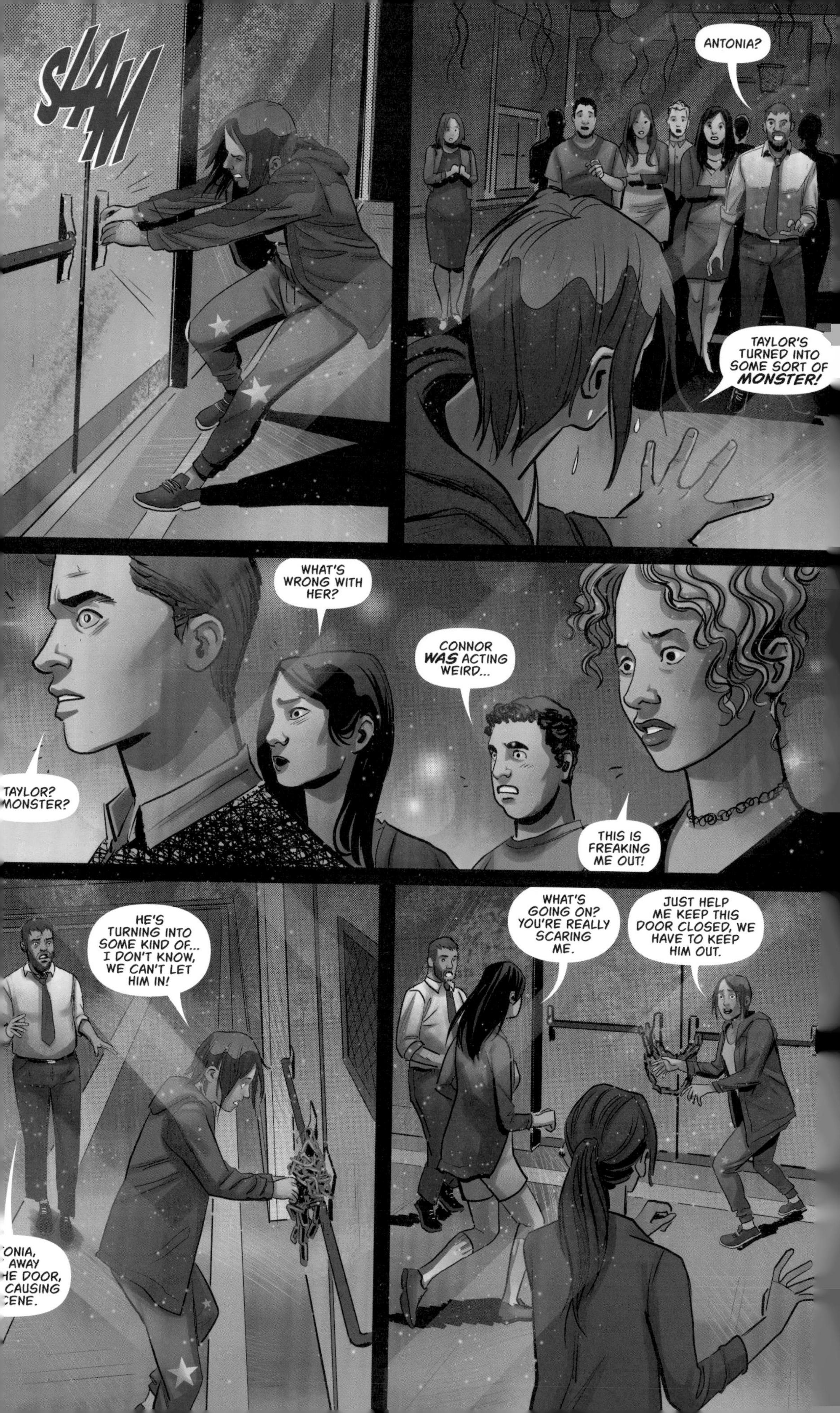
SLAM
ANTONIA?
TAYLOR'S TURNED INTO SOME SORT OF **MONSTER!**
WHAT'S WRONG WITH HER?
CONNOR **WAS** ACTING WEIRD...
TAYLOR? MONSTER?
THIS IS FREAKING ME OUT!
HE'S TURNING INTO SOME KIND OF... I DON'T KNOW, WE CAN'T LET HIM IN!
ONIA, AWAY HE DOOR, CAUSING CENE.
WHAT'S GOING ON? YOU'RE REALLY SCARING ME.
JUST HELP ME KEEP THIS DOOR CLOSED, WE HAVE TO KEEP HIM OUT.

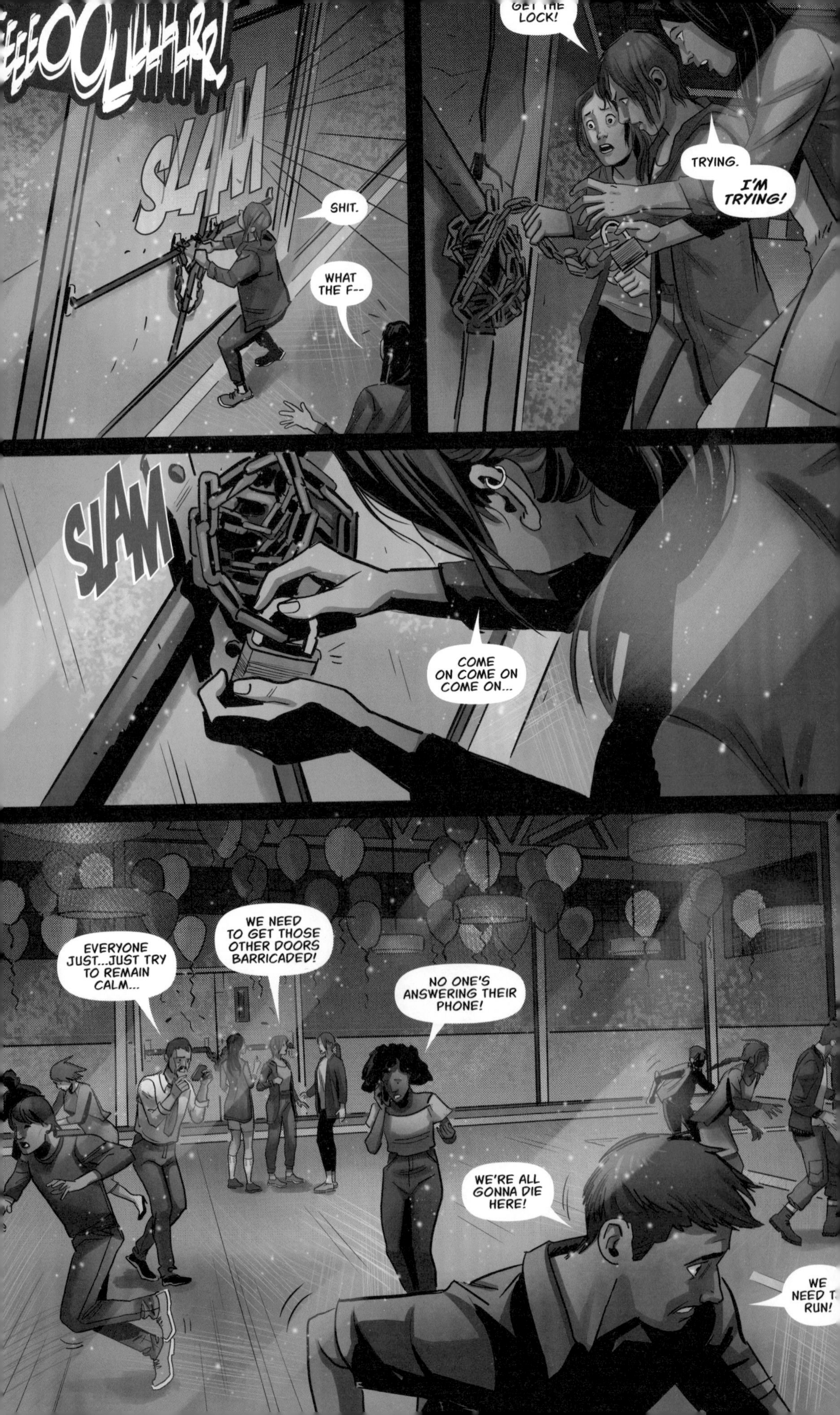
EEEOOLLHHRR!
SLAM
SHIT.
WHAT THE F--
GET THE LOCK!
TRYING.
I'M TRYING!
SLAM
COME ON COME ON COME ON...
EVERYONE JUST...JUST TRY TO REMAIN CALM...
WE NEED TO GET THOSE OTHER DOORS BARRICADED!
NO ONE'S ANSWERING THEIR PHONE!
WE'RE ALL GONNA DIE HERE!
WE NEED T RUN!

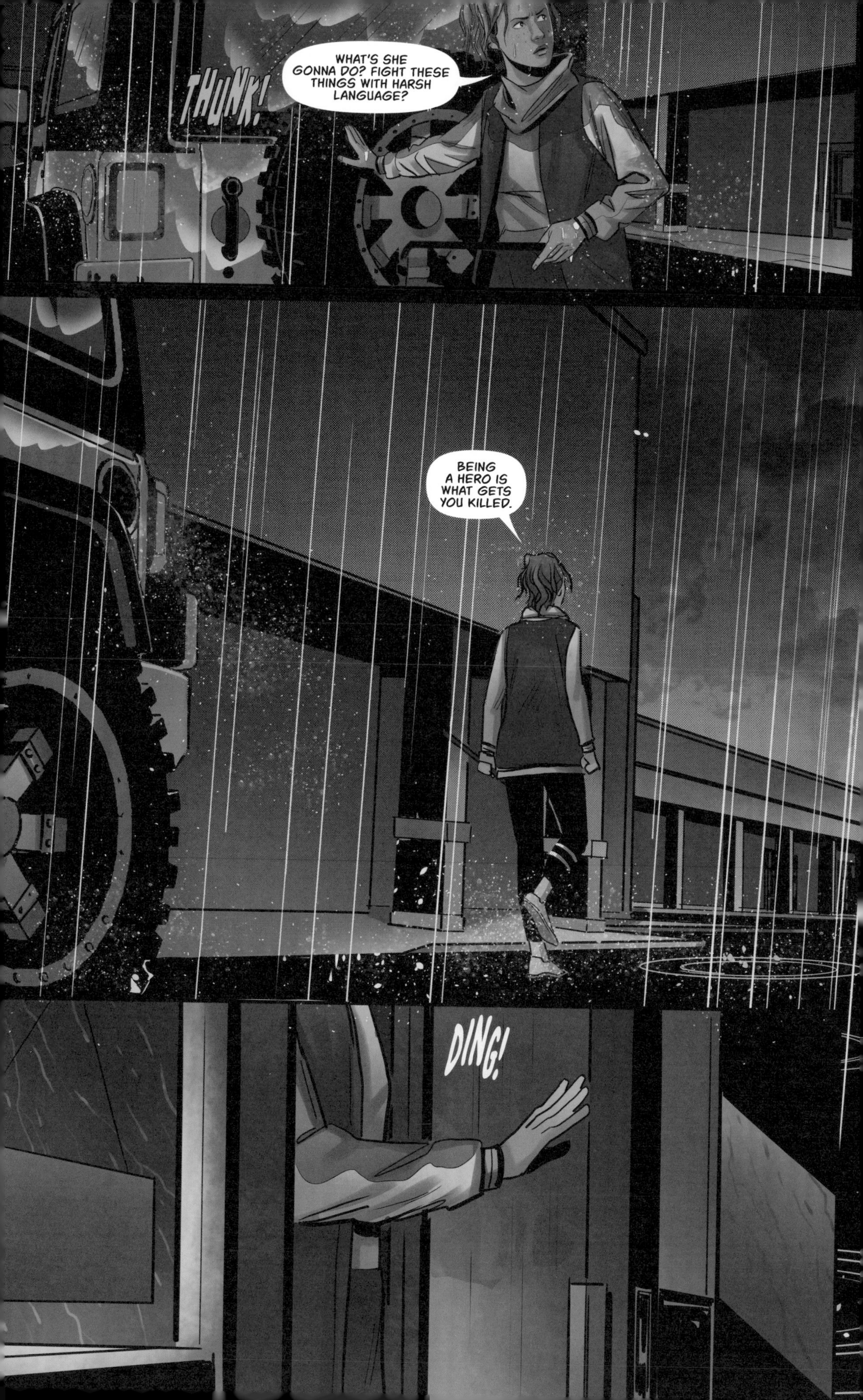
THUNK!
WHAT'S SHE GONNA DO? FIGHT THESE THINGS WITH HARSH LANGUAGE?
BEING A HERO IS WHAT GETS YOU KILLED.
DING!

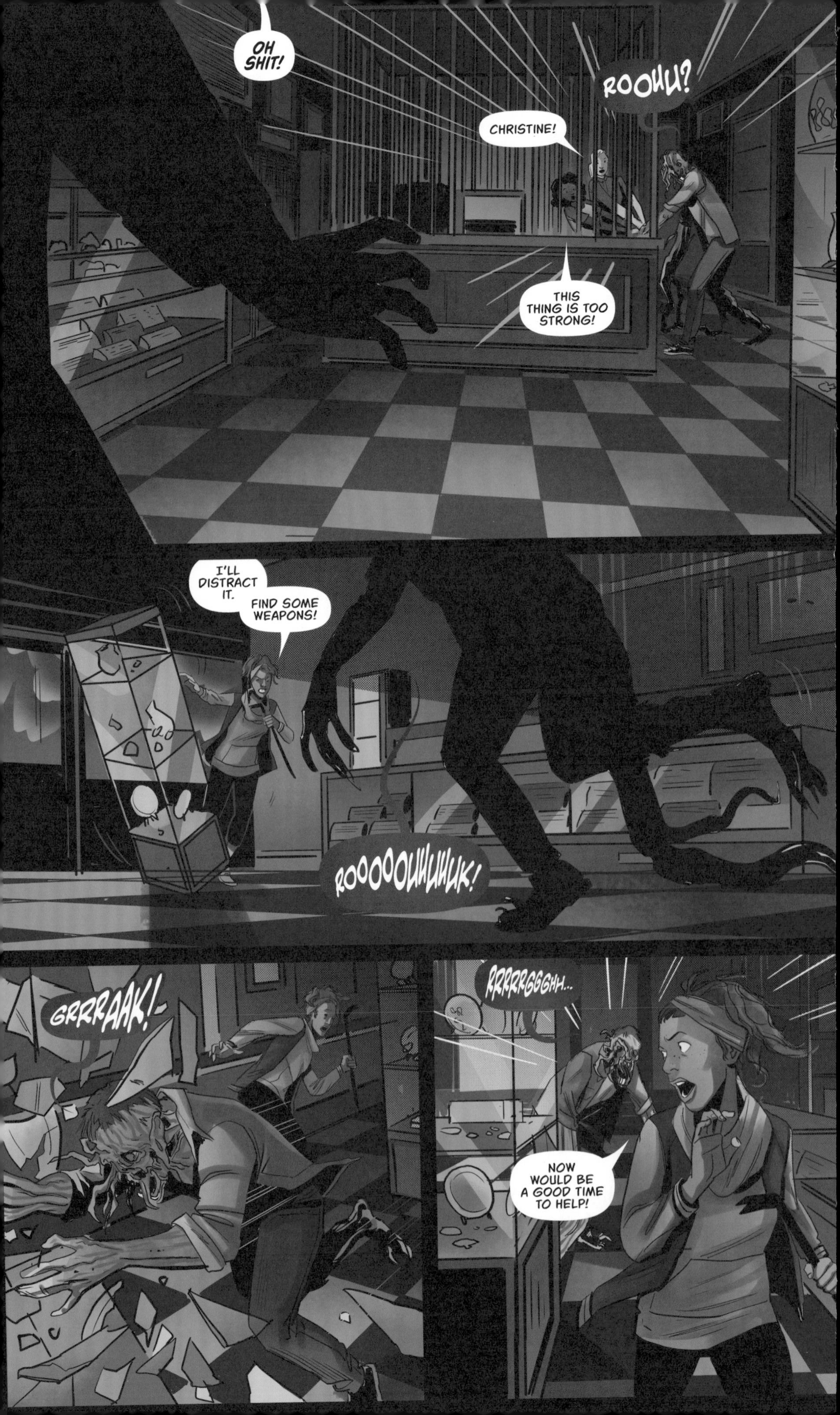
OH SHIT!
ROOHU?
CHRISTINE!
THIS THING IS TOO STRONG!
I'LL DISTRACT IT.
FIND SOME WEAPONS!
ROOOOOUHUHUK!
GRRRAAK!
RRRRRGGGHH...
NOW WOULD BE A GOOD TIME TO HELP!

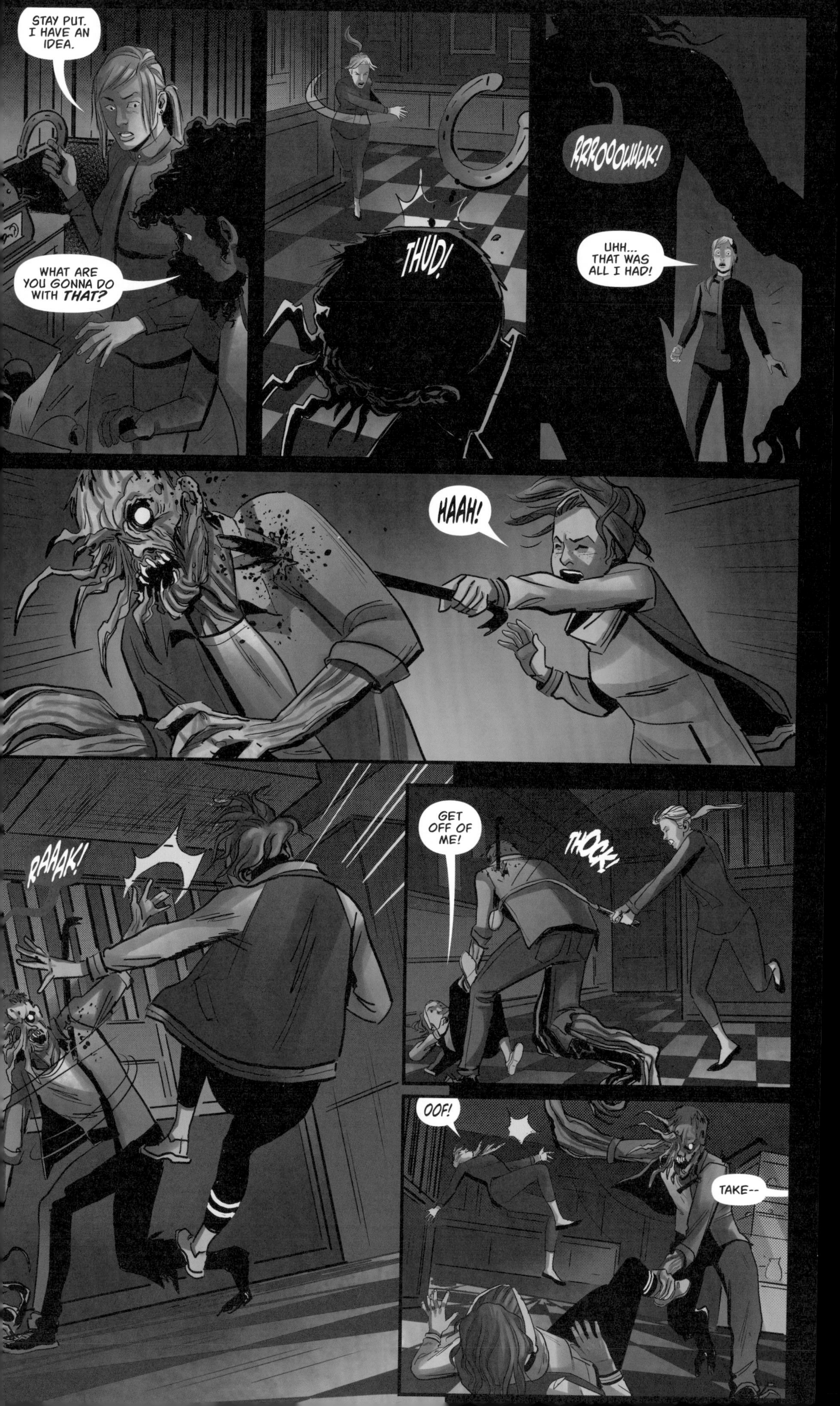
STAY PUT. I HAVE AN IDEA.
WHAT ARE YOU GONNA DO WITH THAT?
THUD!
RRRROOOUUUK!
UHH... THAT WAS ALL I HAD!
HAAH!
RAAAK!
GET OFF OF ME!
THOCK!
OOF!
TAKE--

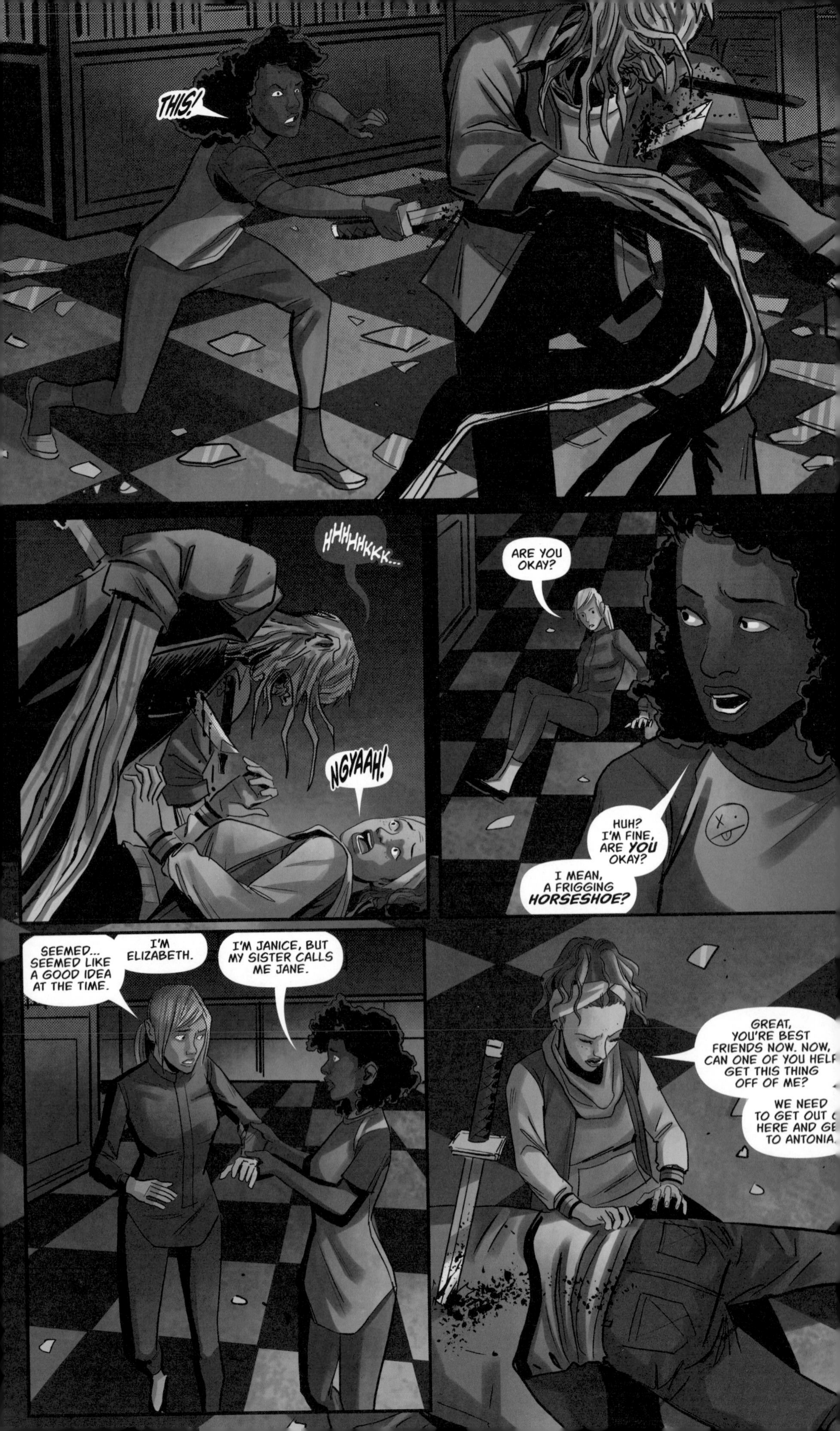
THIS!
HHHHHKKK...
NGYAAH!
ARE YOU OKAY?
HUH? I'M FINE, ARE YOU OKAY?
I MEAN, A FRIGGING HORSESHOE?
SEEMED... SEEMED LIKE A GOOD IDEA AT THE TIME.
I'M ELIZABETH.
I'M JANICE, BUT MY SISTER CALLS ME JANE.
GREAT, YOU'RE BEST FRIENDS NOW. NOW, CAN ONE OF YOU HELP GET THIS THING OFF OF ME?
WE NEED TO GET OUT OF HERE AND GET TO ANTONIA.

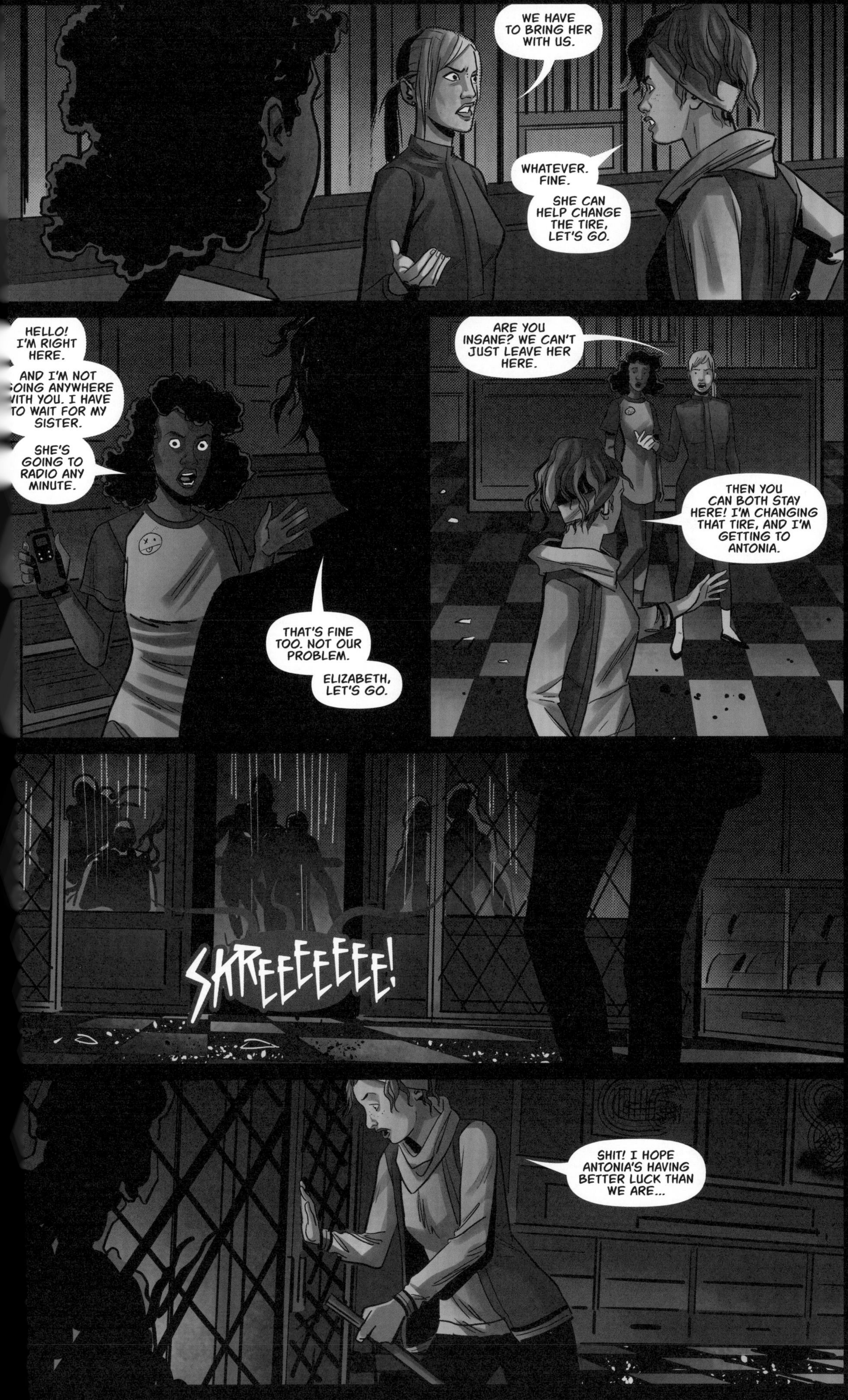
WE HAVE TO BRING HER WITH US.
WHATEVER. FINE.
SHE CAN HELP CHANGE THE TIRE, LET'S GO.
HELLO! I'M RIGHT HERE.
AND I'M NOT GOING ANYWHERE WITH YOU. I HAVE TO WAIT FOR MY SISTER.
SHE'S GOING TO RADIO ANY MINUTE.
THAT'S FINE TOO. NOT OUR PROBLEM.
ELIZABETH, LET'S GO.
ARE YOU INSANE? WE CAN'T JUST LEAVE HER HERE.
THEN YOU CAN BOTH STAY HERE! I'M CHANGING THAT TIRE, AND I'M GETTING TO ANTONIA.
SKREEEEEEE!
SHIT! I HOPE ANTONIA'S HAVING BETTER LUCK THAN WE ARE...

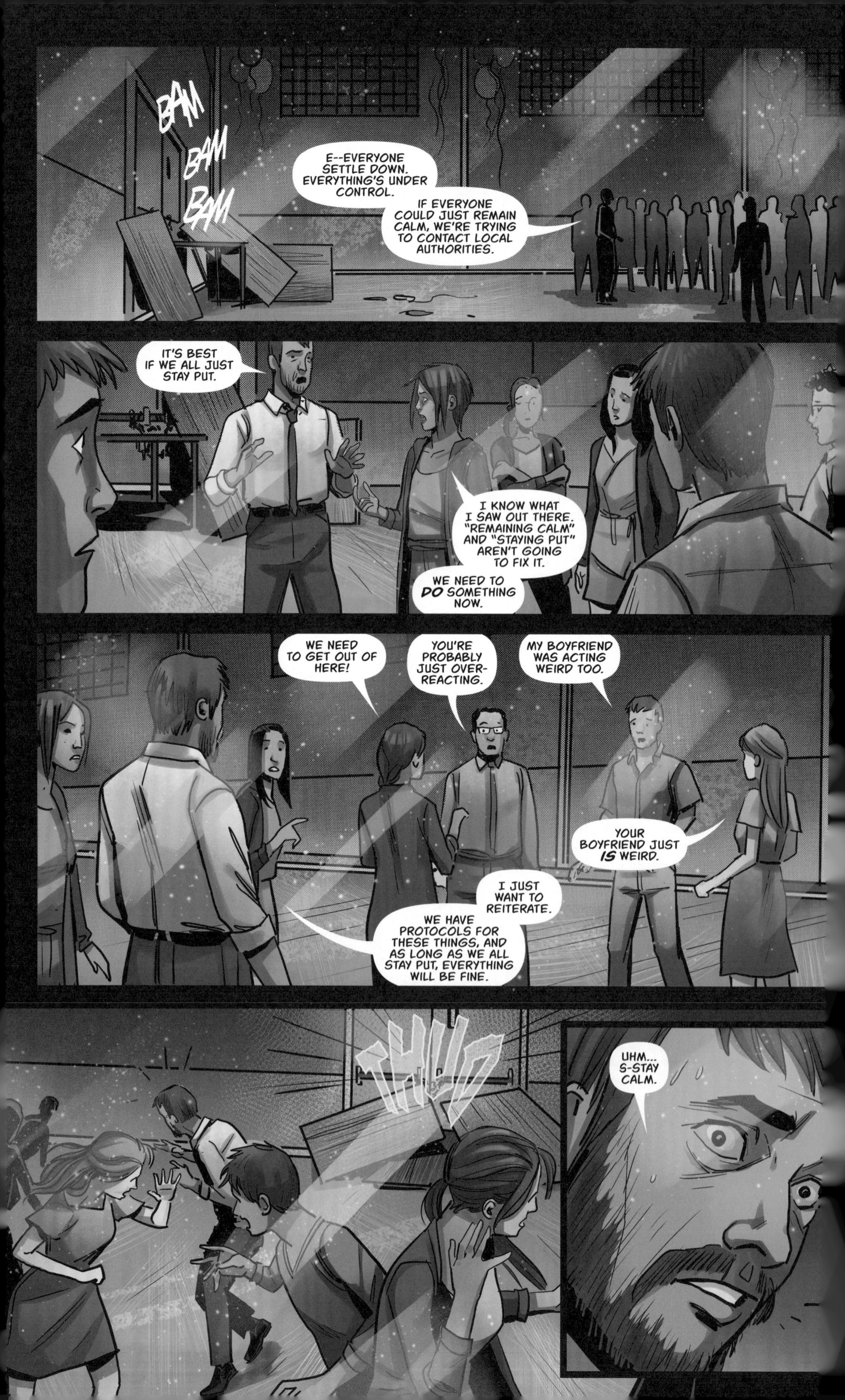
BAM
BAM
BAM
E--EVERYONE SETTLE DOWN. EVERYTHING'S UNDER CONTROL.
IF EVERYONE COULD JUST REMAIN CALM, WE'RE TRYING TO CONTACT LOCAL AUTHORITIES.
IT'S BEST IF WE ALL JUST STAY PUT.
I KNOW WHAT I SAW OUT THERE. "REMAINING CALM" AND "STAYING PUT" AREN'T GOING TO FIX IT.
WE NEED TO **DO** SOMETHING NOW.
WE NEED TO GET OUT OF HERE!
YOU'RE PROBABLY JUST OVER-REACTING.
MY BOYFRIEND WAS ACTING WEIRD TOO.
YOUR BOYFRIEND JUST ***IS*** WEIRD.
I JUST WANT TO REITERATE.
WE HAVE PROTOCOLS FOR THESE THINGS, AND AS LONG AS WE ALL STAY PUT, EVERYTHING WILL BE FINE.
THUD
UHM... S-STAY CALM.

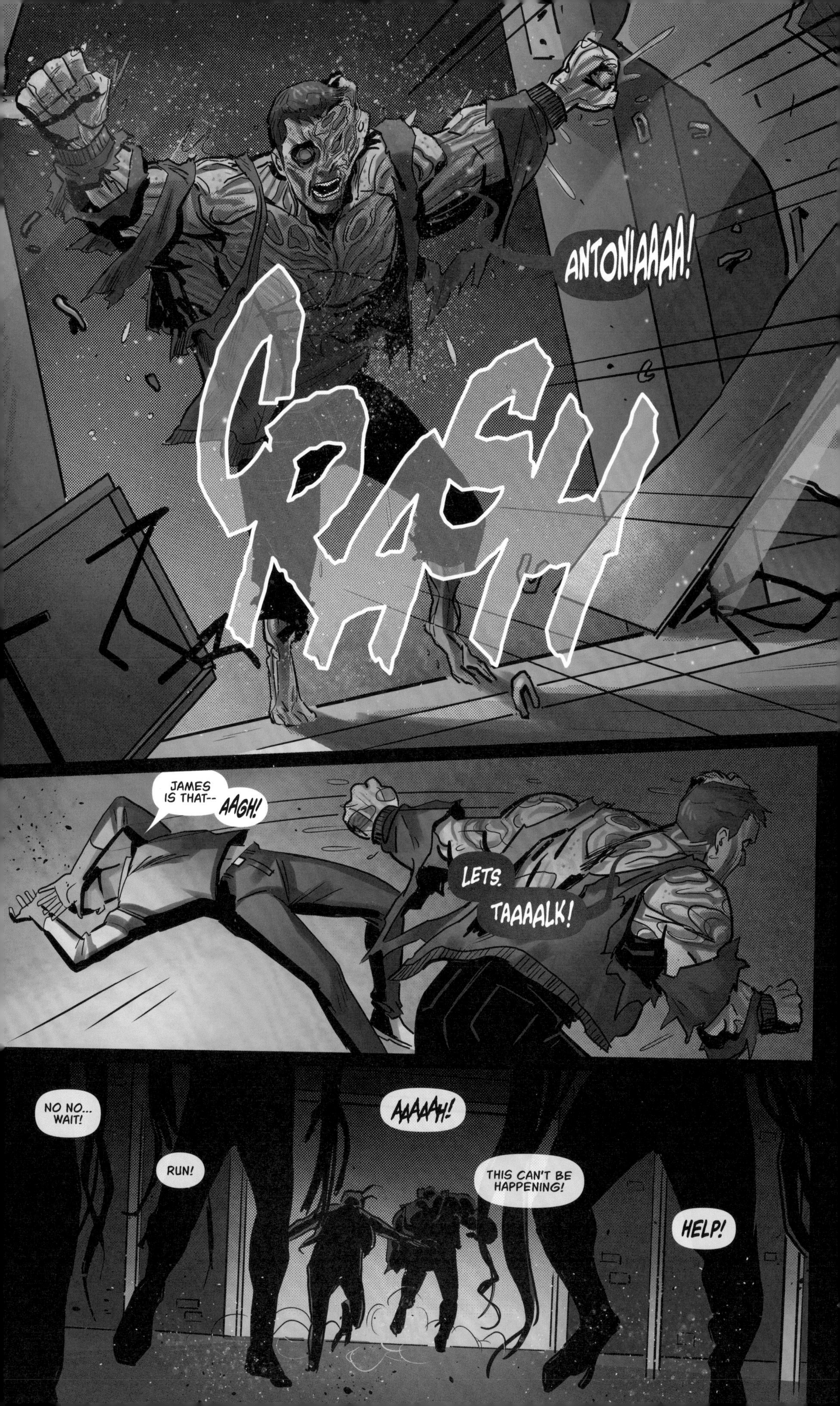
ANTONIAAAA!
CRASH
JAMES IS THAT-- AAGH!
LETS. TAAAALK!
NO NO... WAIT!
AAAAAH!
RUN!
THIS CAN'T BE HAPPENING!
HELP!

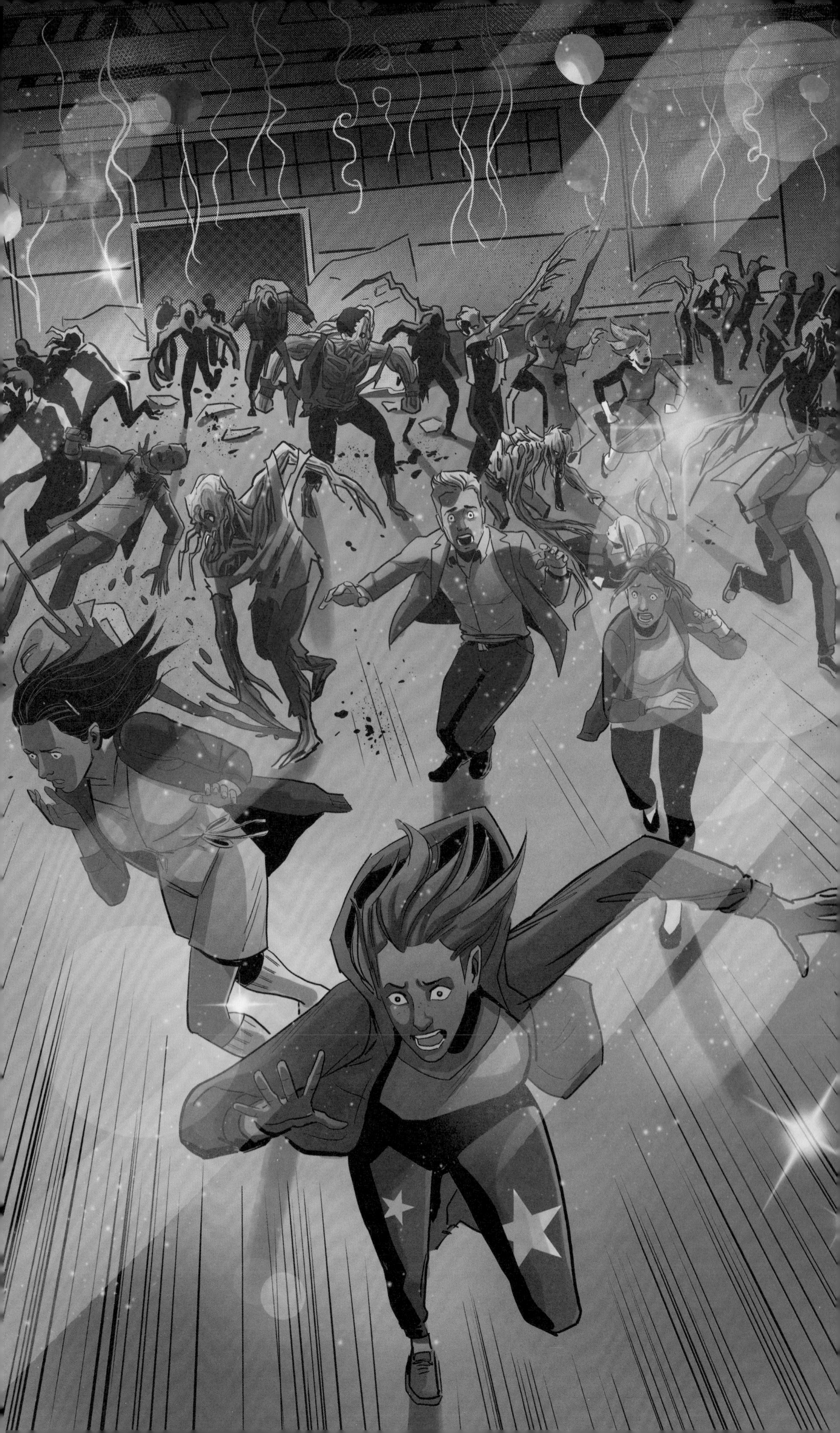

CHAPTER 3

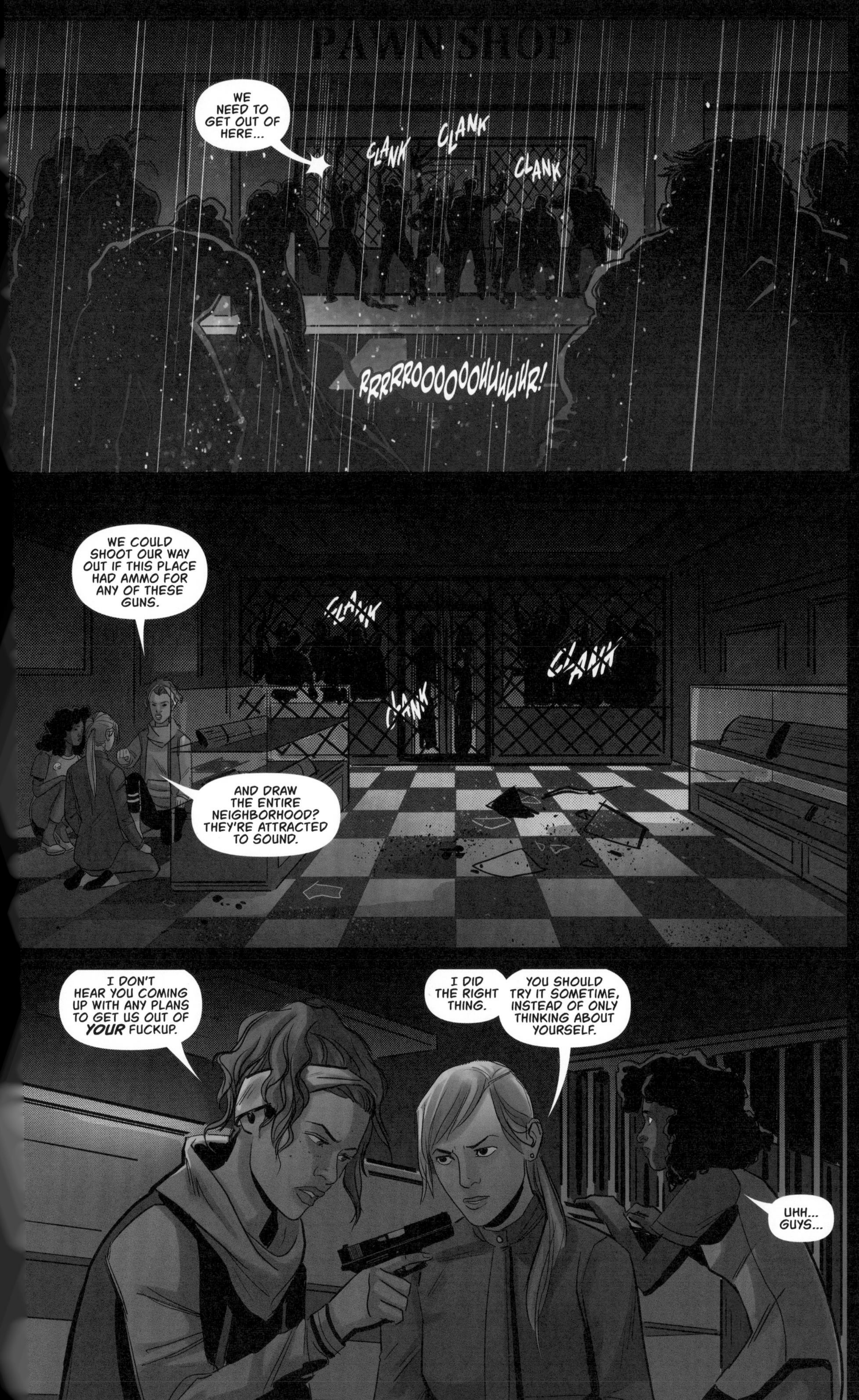
PAWN SHOP
WE NEED TO GET OUT OF HERE...
CLANK
CLANK
CLANK
RRRRROOOOOOHUUUUR!
WE COULD SHOOT OUR WAY OUT IF THIS PLACE HAD AMMO FOR ANY OF THESE GUNS.
CLANK
CLANK
CLANK
AND DRAW THE ENTIRE NEIGHBORHOOD? THEY'RE ATTRACTED TO SOUND.
I DON'T HEAR YOU COMING UP WITH ANY PLANS TO GET US OUT OF YOUR FUCKUP.
I DID THE RIGHT THING.
YOU SHOULD TRY IT SOMETIME, INSTEAD OF ONLY THINKING ABOUT YOURSELF.
UHH... GUYS...

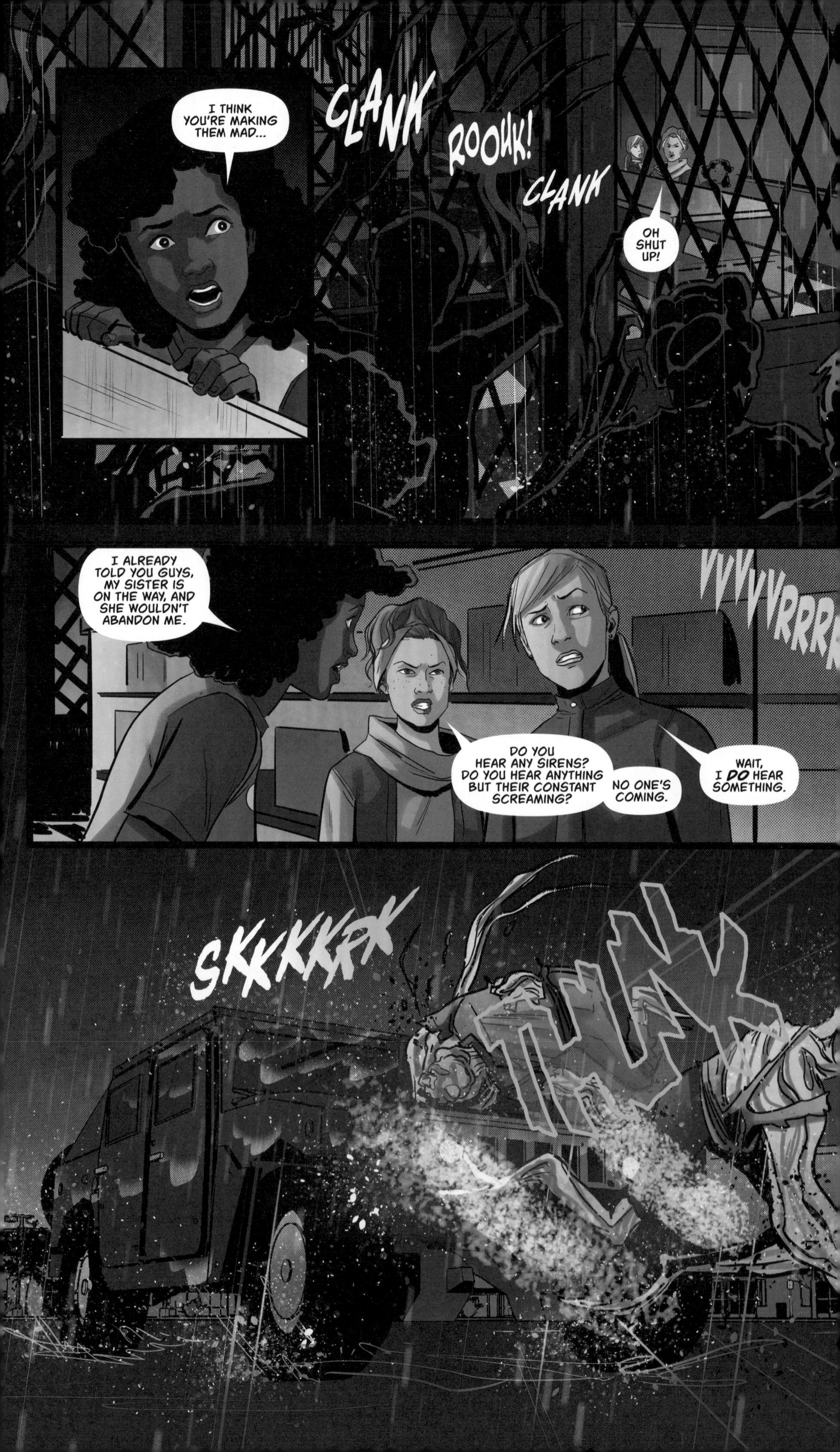
I THINK YOU'RE MAKING THEM MAD...
CLANK
ROOUK!
CLANK
OH SHUT UP!
I ALREADY TOLD YOU GUYS, MY SISTER IS ON THE WAY, AND SHE WOULDN'T ABANDON ME.
VVVVVRRRR
DO YOU HEAR ANY SIRENS? DO YOU HEAR ANYTHING BUT THEIR CONSTANT SCREAMING?
NO ONE'S COMING.
WAIT, I **DO** HEAR SOMETHING.
SKKKRK
THUK

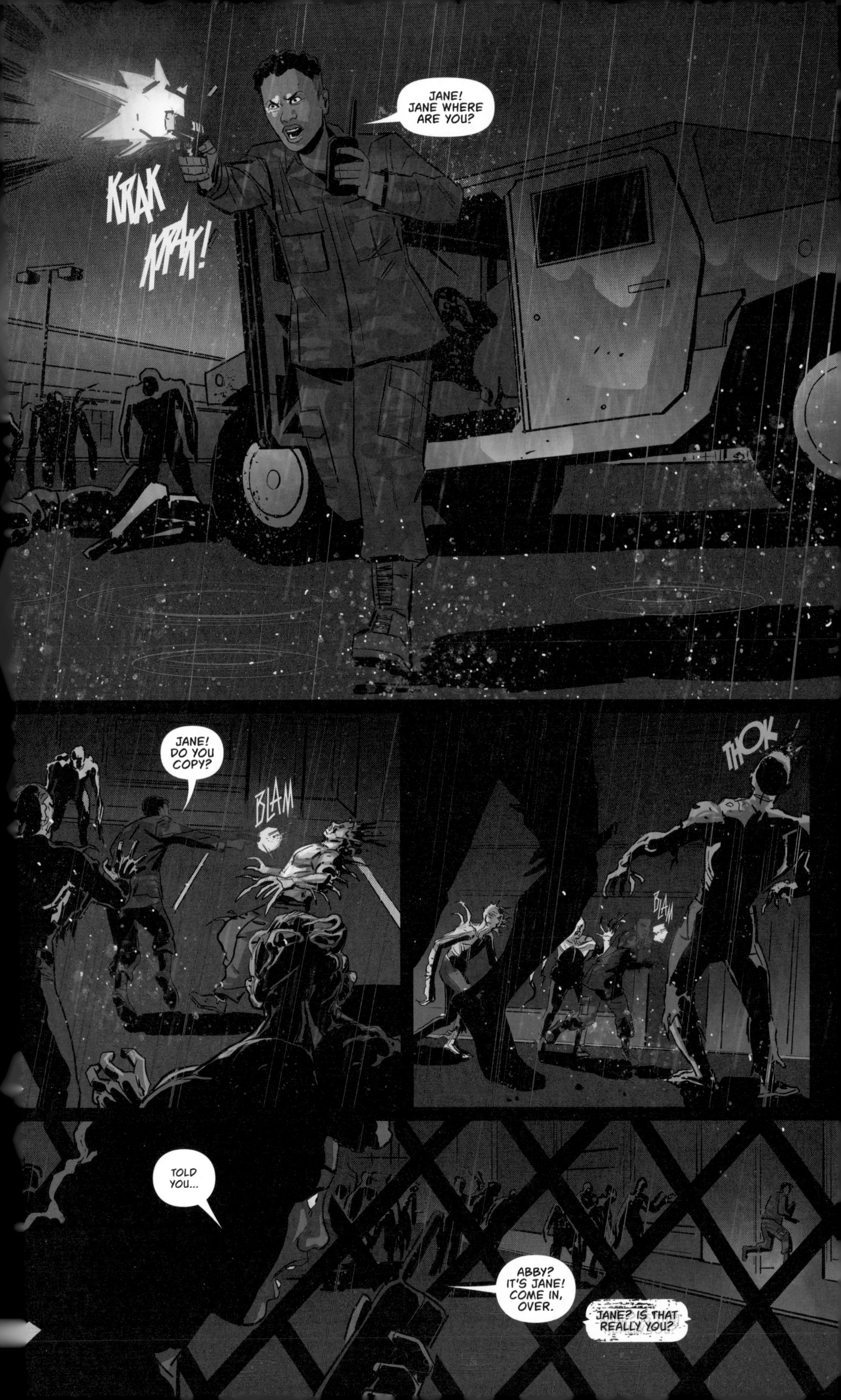
JANE! JANE WHERE ARE YOU?
KRAK
KRAK!
JANE! DO YOU COPY?
BLAM
THOK
BLAM
TOLD YOU...
ABBY? IT'S JANE! COME IN, OVER.
JANE? IS THAT REALLY YOU?

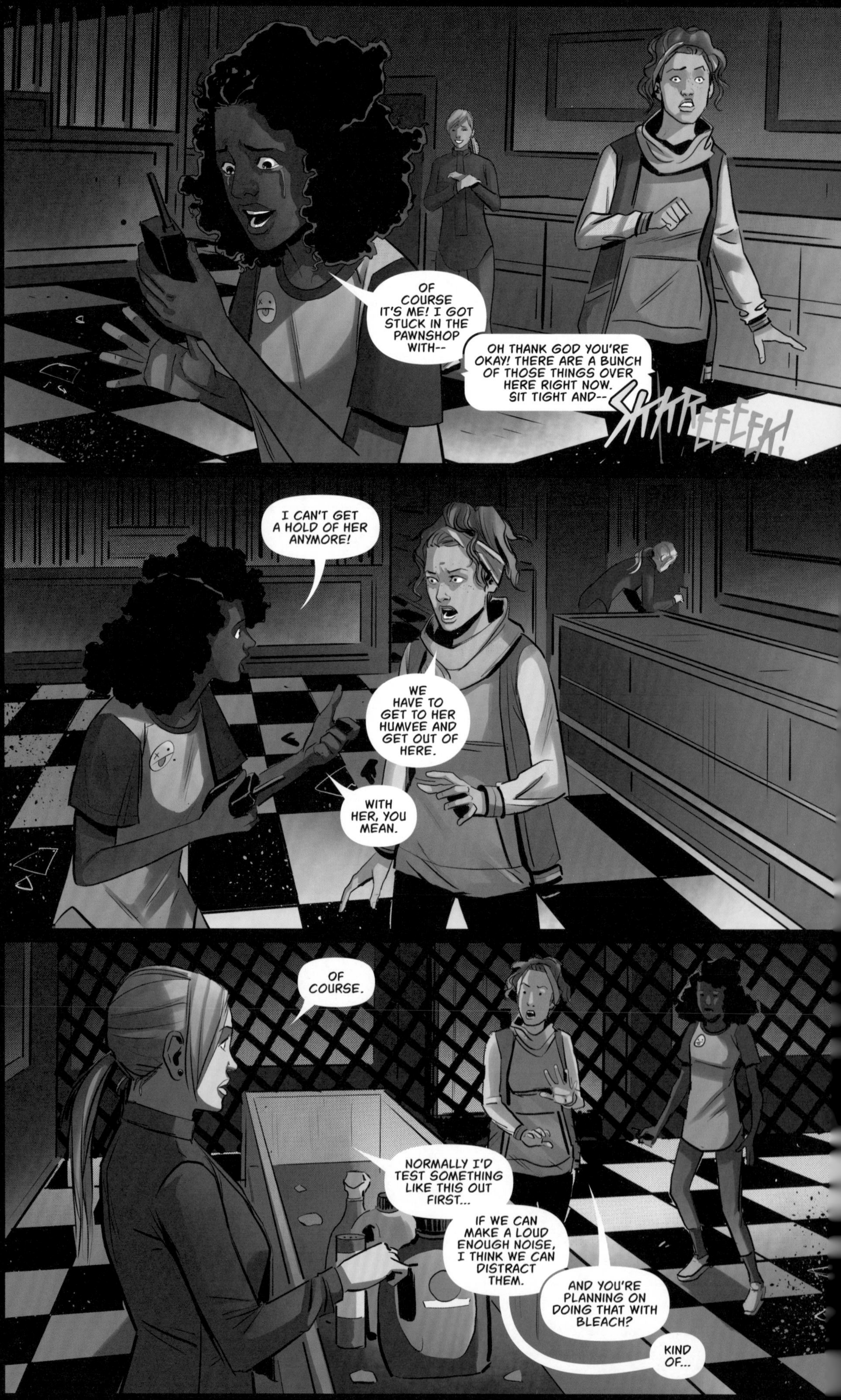

OF COURSE IT'S ME! I GOT STUCK IN THE PAWNSHOP WITH--
OH THANK GOD YOU'RE OKAY! THERE ARE A BUNCH OF THOSE THINGS OVER HERE RIGHT NOW. SIT TIGHT AND--
SKKREEEEK!
I CAN'T GET A HOLD OF HER ANYMORE!
WE HAVE TO GET TO HER HUMVEE AND GET OUT OF HERE.
WITH HER, YOU MEAN.
OF COURSE.
NORMALLY I'D TEST SOMETHING LIKE THIS OUT FIRST...
IF WE CAN MAKE A LOUD ENOUGH NOISE, I THINK WE CAN DISTRACT THEM.
AND YOU'RE PLANNING ON DOING THAT WITH BLEACH?
KIND OF...

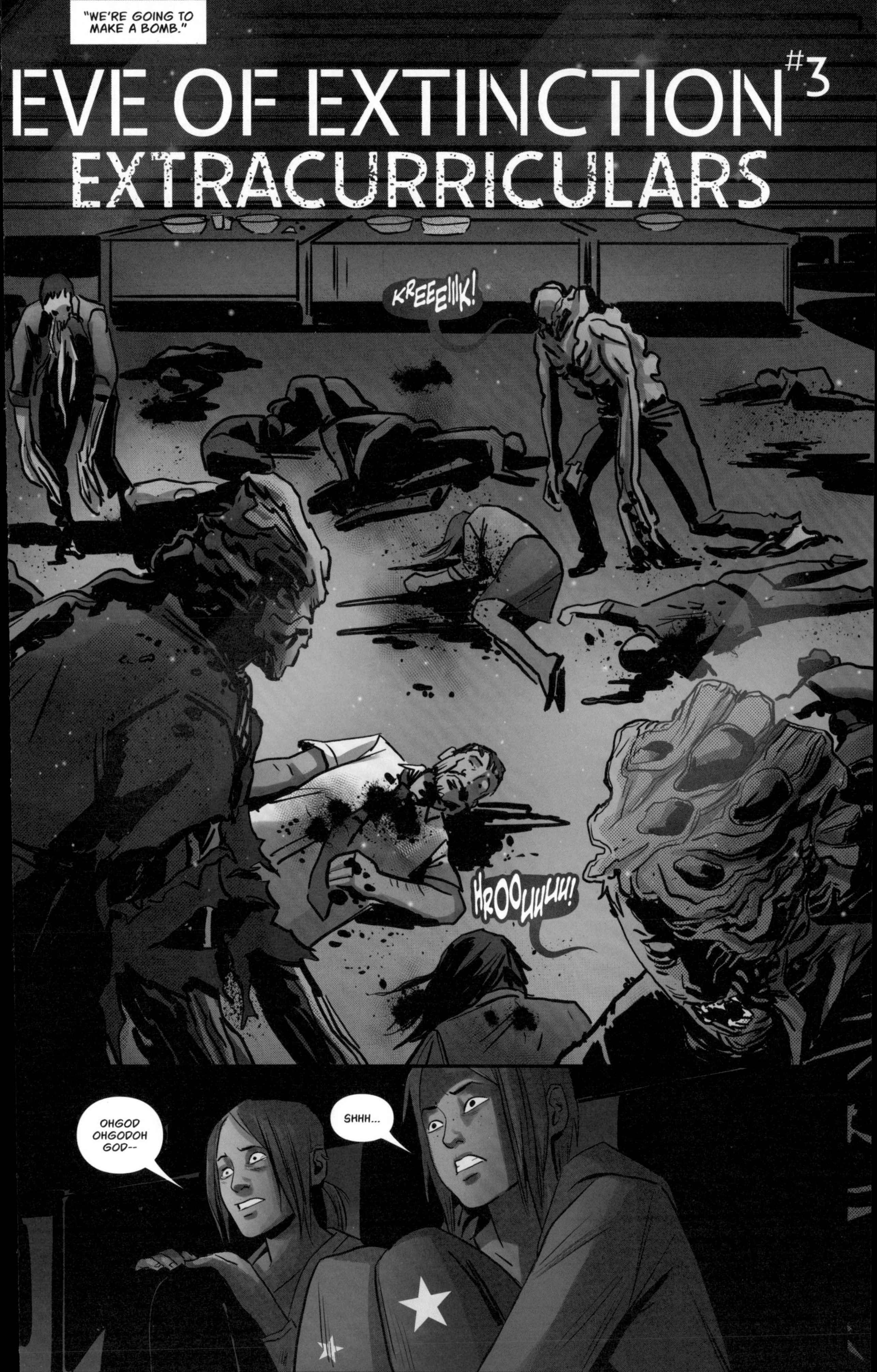
"WE'RE GOING TO MAKE A BOMB."
EVE OF EXTINCTION #3
EXTRACURRICULARS
KREEEIIIK!
HROOUUUU!
OHGOD OHGODOH GOD--
SHHH...

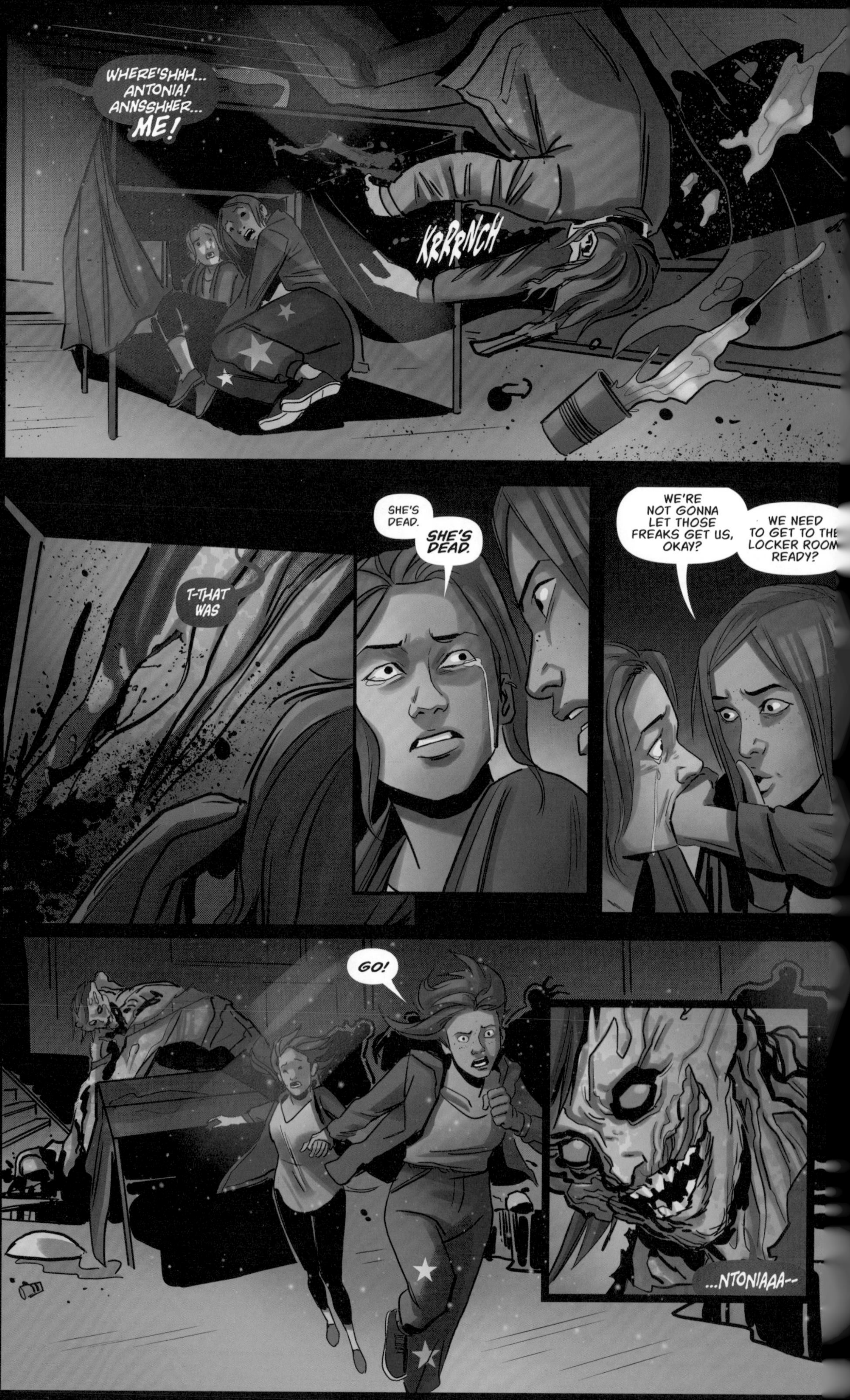
WHERE'SHHH... ANTONIA! ANNSSHHER... ME!
KRRRNCH
T-THAT WAS
SHE'S DEAD.
SHE'S DEAD.
WE'RE NOT GONNA LET THOSE FREAKS GET US, OKAY?
WE NEED TO GET TO THE LOCKER ROOM. READY?
GO!
...NTONIAAA--

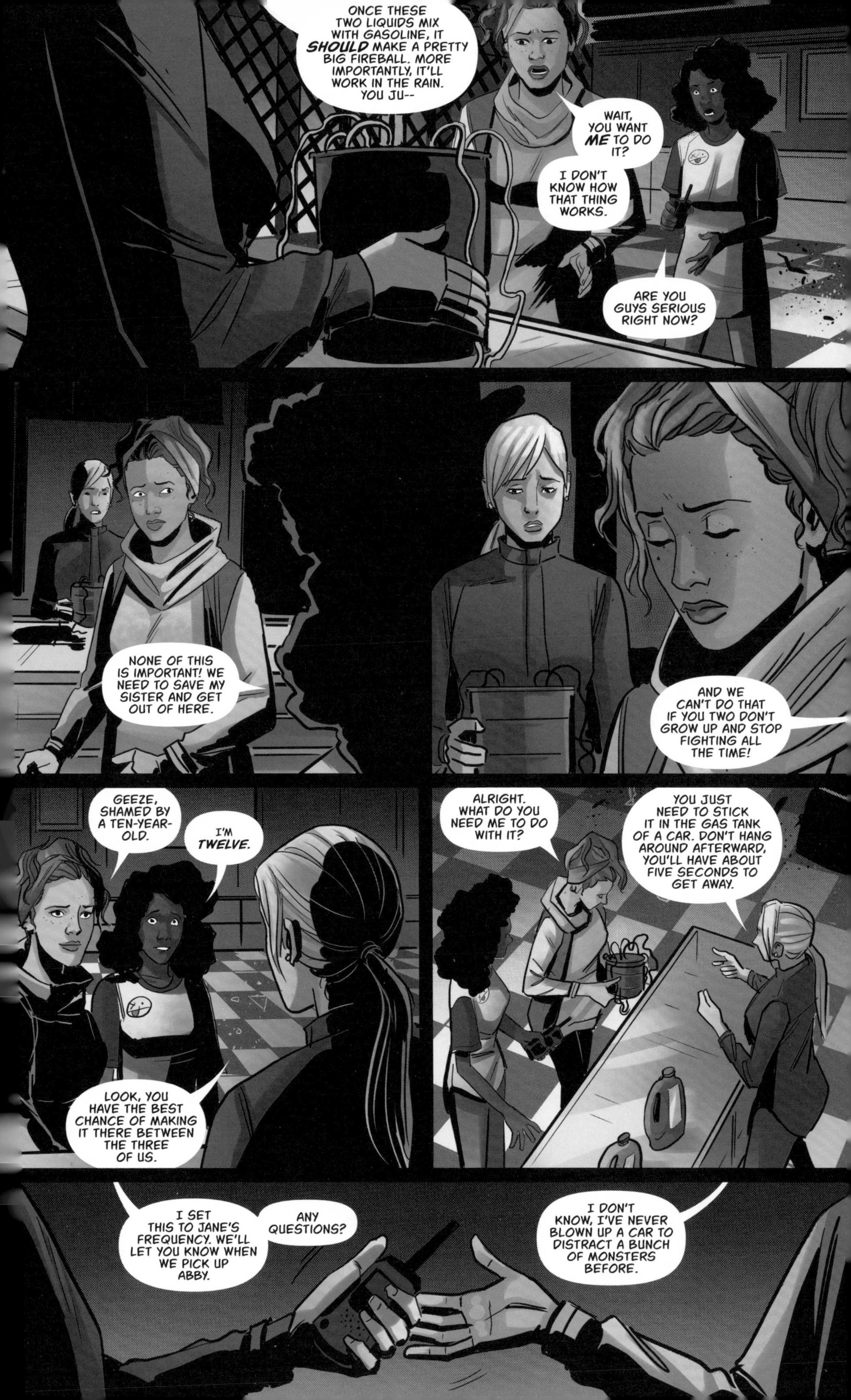
ONCE THESE TWO LIQUIDS MIX WITH GASOLINE, IT SHOULD MAKE A PRETTY BIG FIREBALL. MORE IMPORTANTLY, IT'LL WORK IN THE RAIN. YOU JU--
WAIT, YOU WANT ME TO DO IT?
I DON'T KNOW HOW THAT THING WORKS.
ARE YOU GUYS SERIOUS RIGHT NOW?
NONE OF THIS IS IMPORTANT! WE NEED TO SAVE MY SISTER AND GET OUT OF HERE.
AND WE CAN'T DO THAT IF YOU TWO DON'T GROW UP AND STOP FIGHTING ALL THE TIME!
GEEZE, SHAMED BY A TEN-YEAR-OLD.
I'M TWELVE.
LOOK, YOU HAVE THE BEST CHANCE OF MAKING IT THERE BETWEEN THE THREE OF US.
ALRIGHT. WHAT DO YOU NEED ME TO DO WITH IT?
YOU JUST NEED TO STICK IT IN THE GAS TANK OF A CAR. DON'T HANG AROUND AFTERWARD, YOU'LL HAVE ABOUT FIVE SECONDS TO GET AWAY.
I SET THIS TO JANE'S FREQUENCY. WE'LL LET YOU KNOW WHEN WE PICK UP ABBY.
ANY QUESTIONS?
I DON'T KNOW, I'VE NEVER BLOWN UP A CAR TO DISTRACT A BUNCH OF MONSTERS BEFORE.

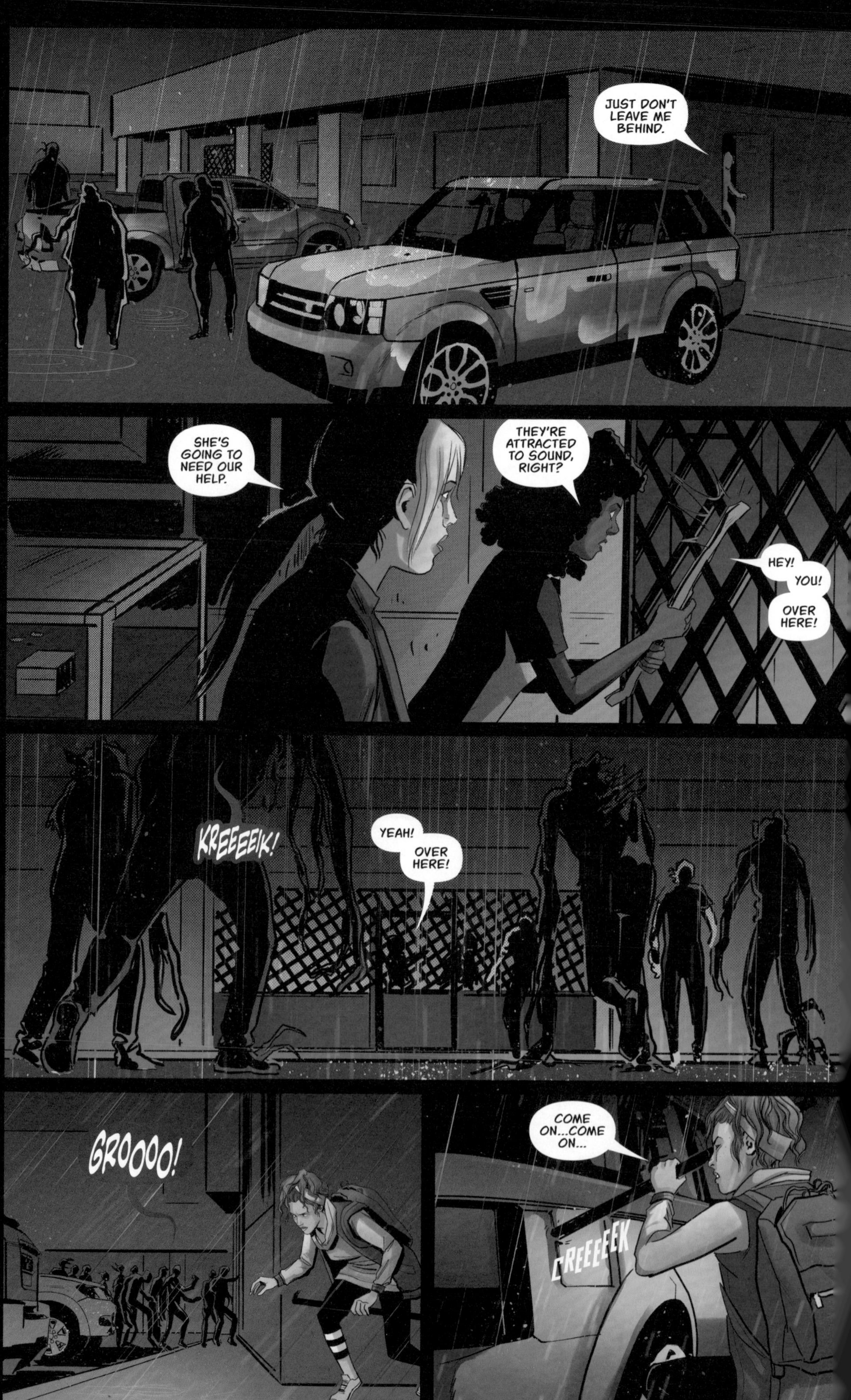
JUST DON'T LEAVE ME BEHIND.
SHE'S GOING TO NEED OUR HELP.
THEY'RE ATTRACTED TO SOUND, RIGHT?
HEY!
YOU!
OVER HERE!
KREEEEIK!
YEAH!
OVER HERE!
GROOOO!
COME ON...COME ON...
CREEEEEK

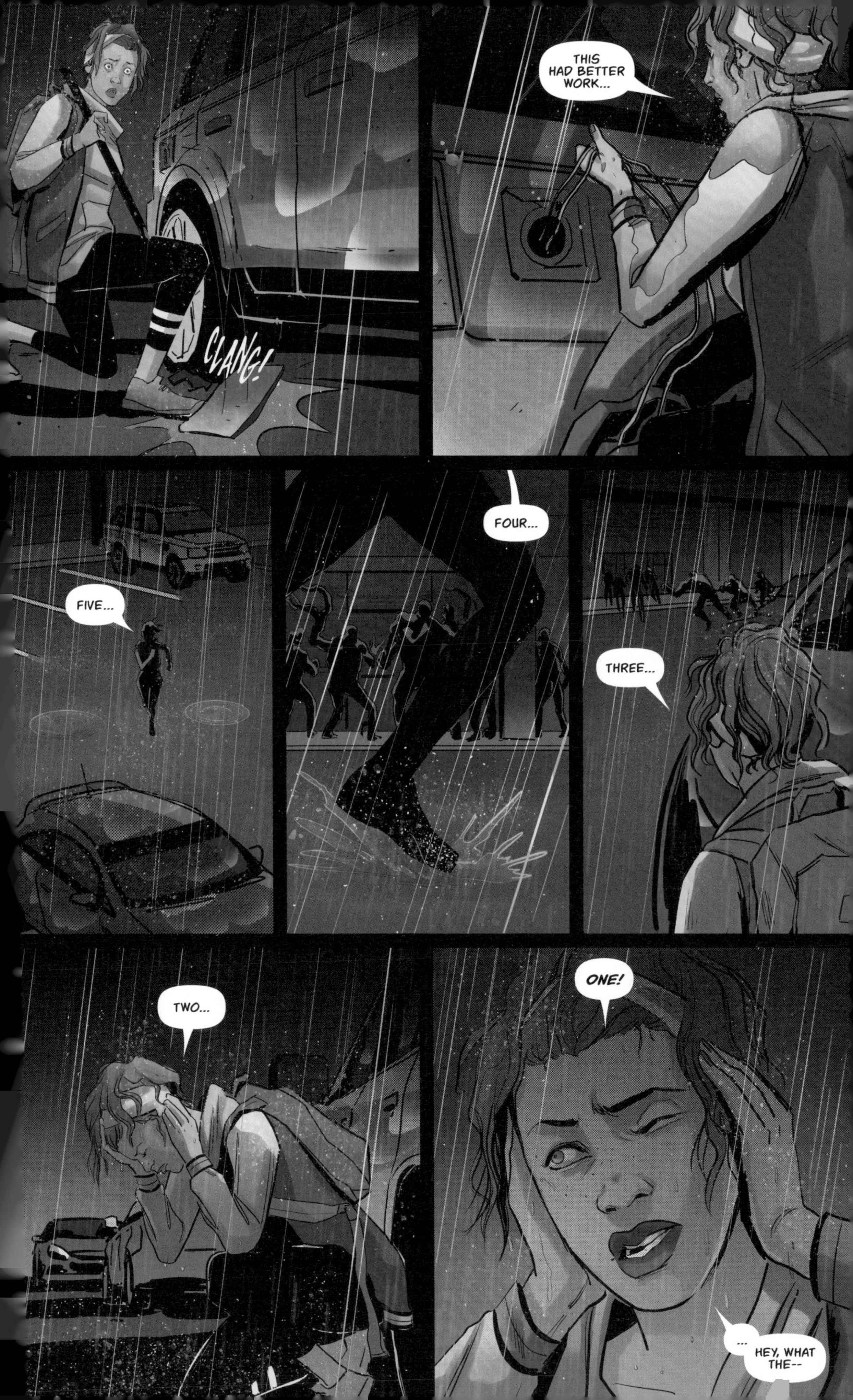
CLANG!
THIS HAD BETTER WORK...
FIVE...
FOUR...
THREE...
TWO...
ONE!
... HEY, WHAT THE--

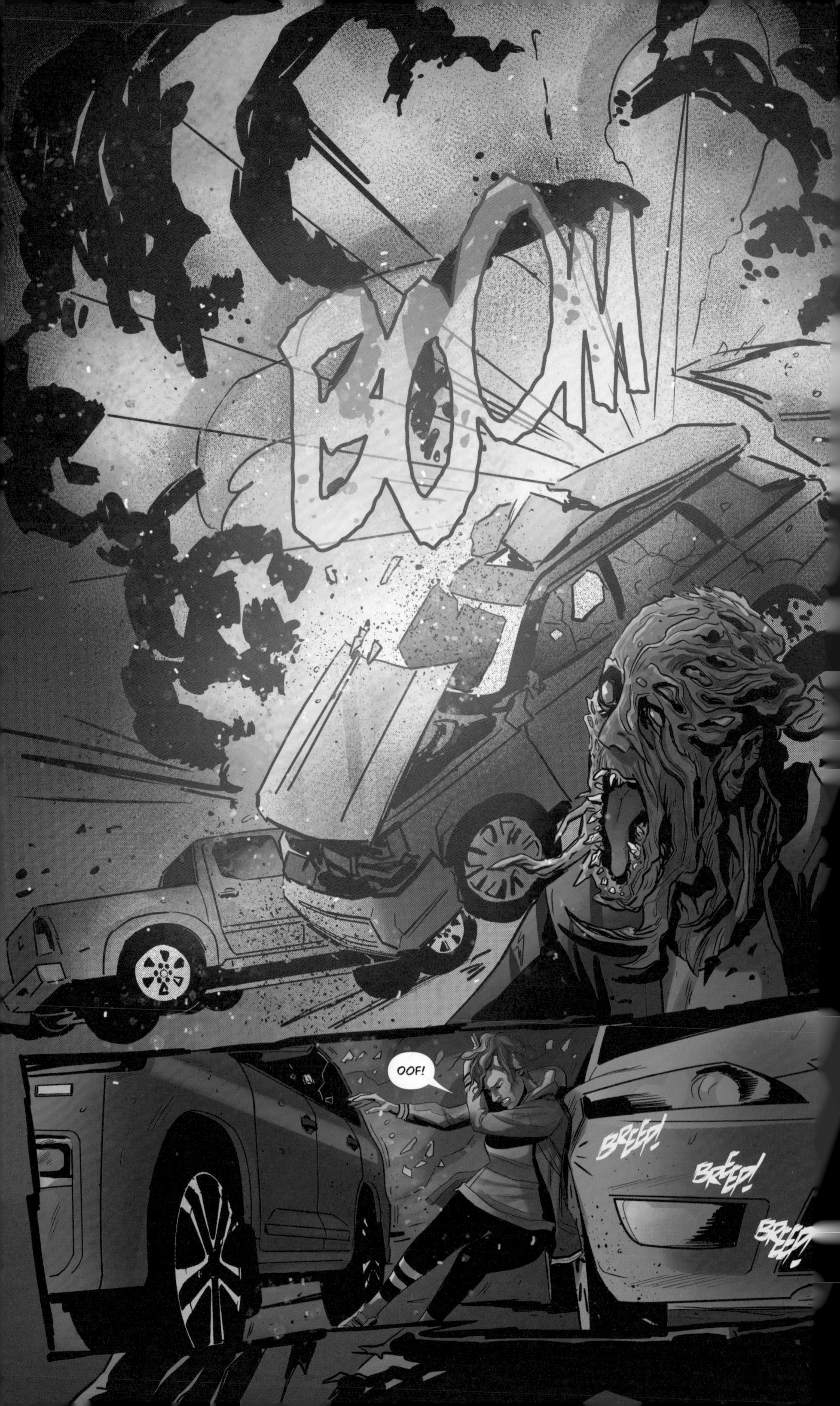
BOOM
OOF!
BREEP!
BREEP!
BREEP!

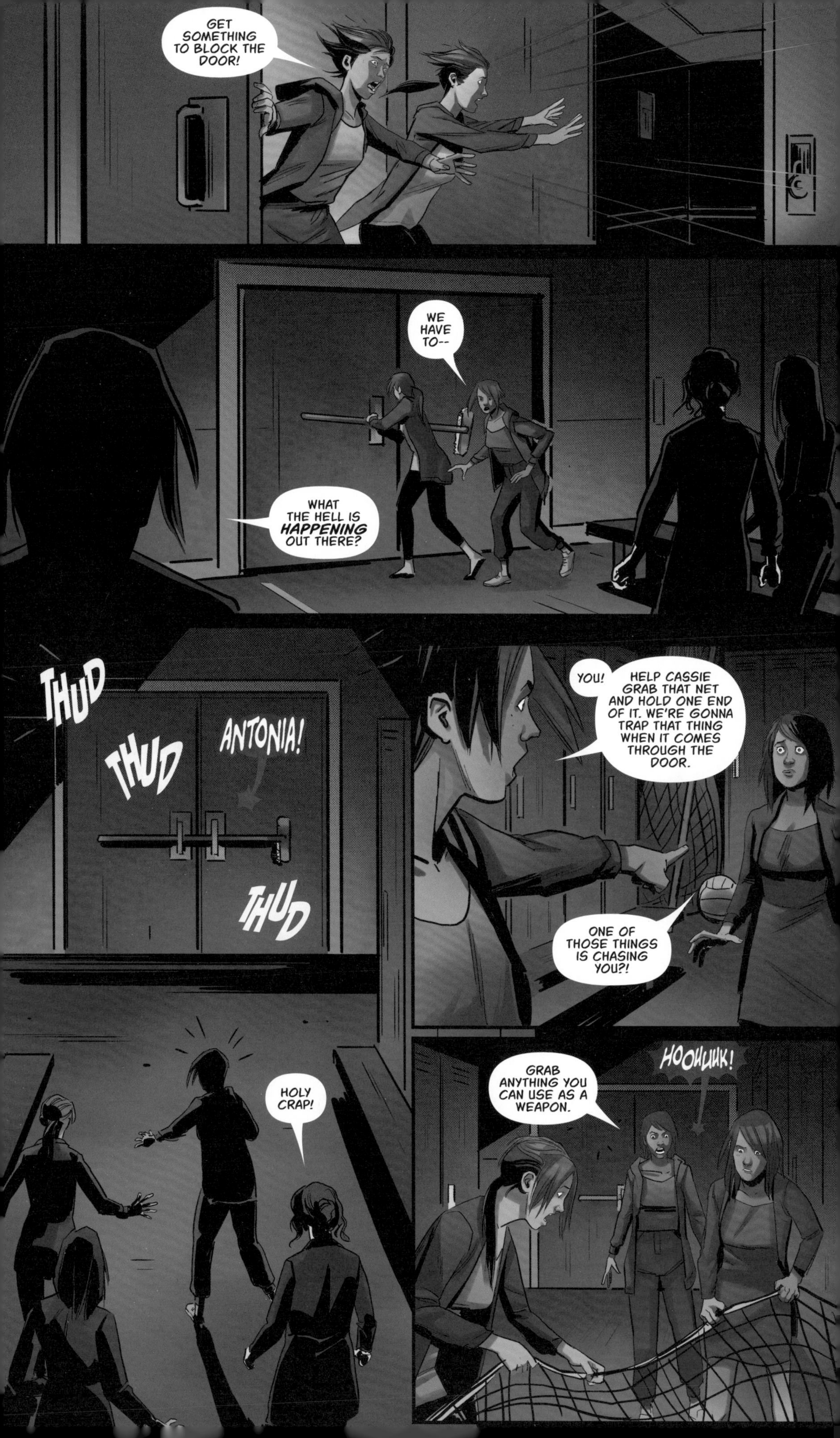
GET SOMETHING TO BLOCK THE DOOR!
WE HAVE TO--
WHAT THE HELL IS **HAPPENING** OUT THERE?
THUD
THUD
ANTONIA!
THUD
YOU!
HELP CASSIE GRAB THAT NET AND HOLD ONE END OF IT. WE'RE GONNA TRAP THAT THING WHEN IT COMES THROUGH THE DOOR.
ONE OF THOSE THINGS IS CHASING YOU?!
HOLY CRAP!
GRAB ANYTHING YOU CAN USE AS A WEAPON.
HOOHUUK!

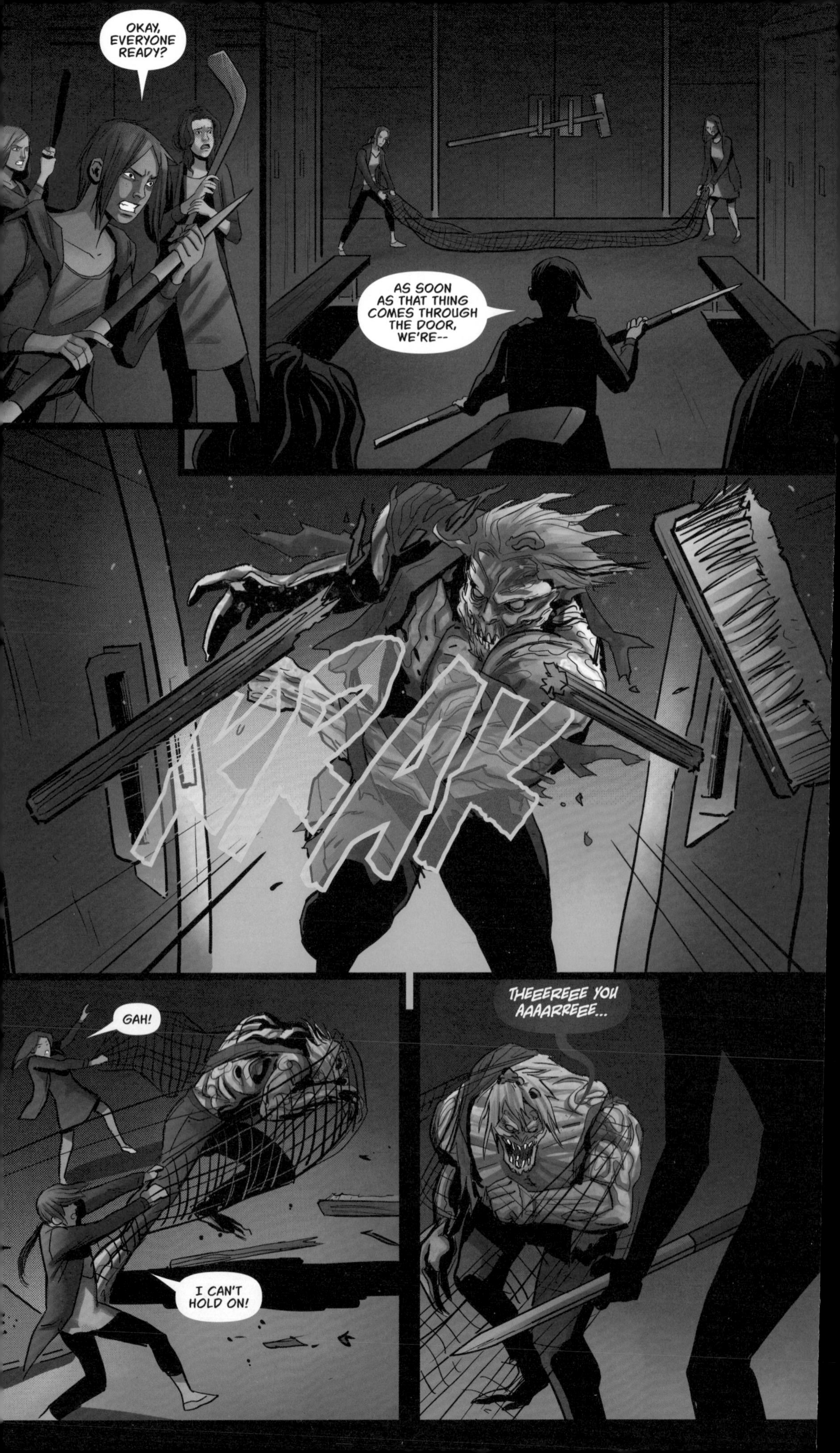
OKAY, EVERYONE READY?
AS SOON AS THAT THING COMES THROUGH THE DOOR, WE'RE--
KRAK
GAH!
I CAN'T HOLD ON!
THEEEREEE YOU AAAARREEE...

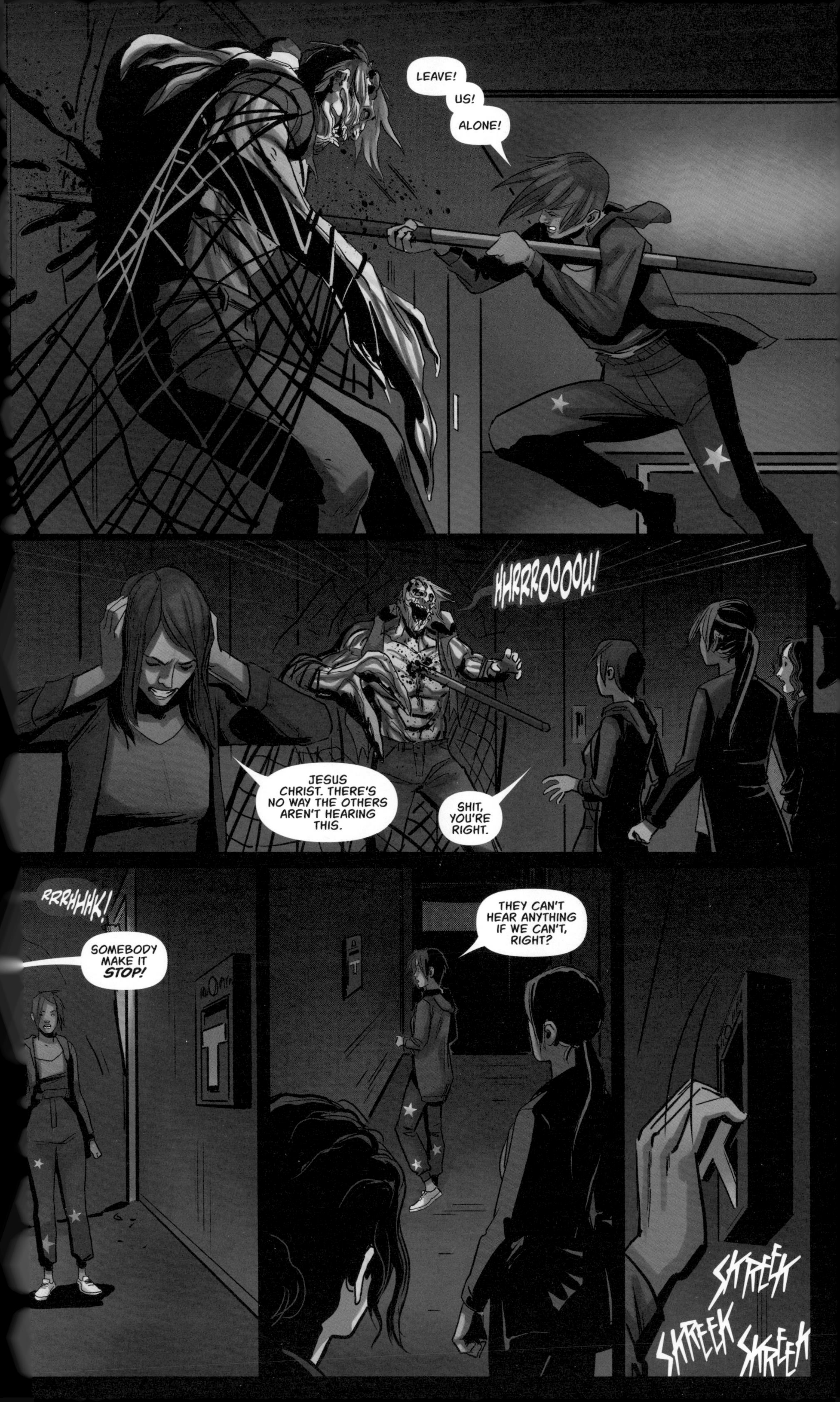
LEAVE!
US!
ALONE!
HHRRROOOOOU!
JESUS CHRIST. THERE'S NO WAY THE OTHERS AREN'T HEARING THIS.
SHIT, YOU'RE RIGHT.
RRRHHHK!
SOMEBODY MAKE IT STOP!
THEY CAN'T HEAR ANYTHING IF WE CAN'T, RIGHT?
SKREEK
SKREEK
SKREEK

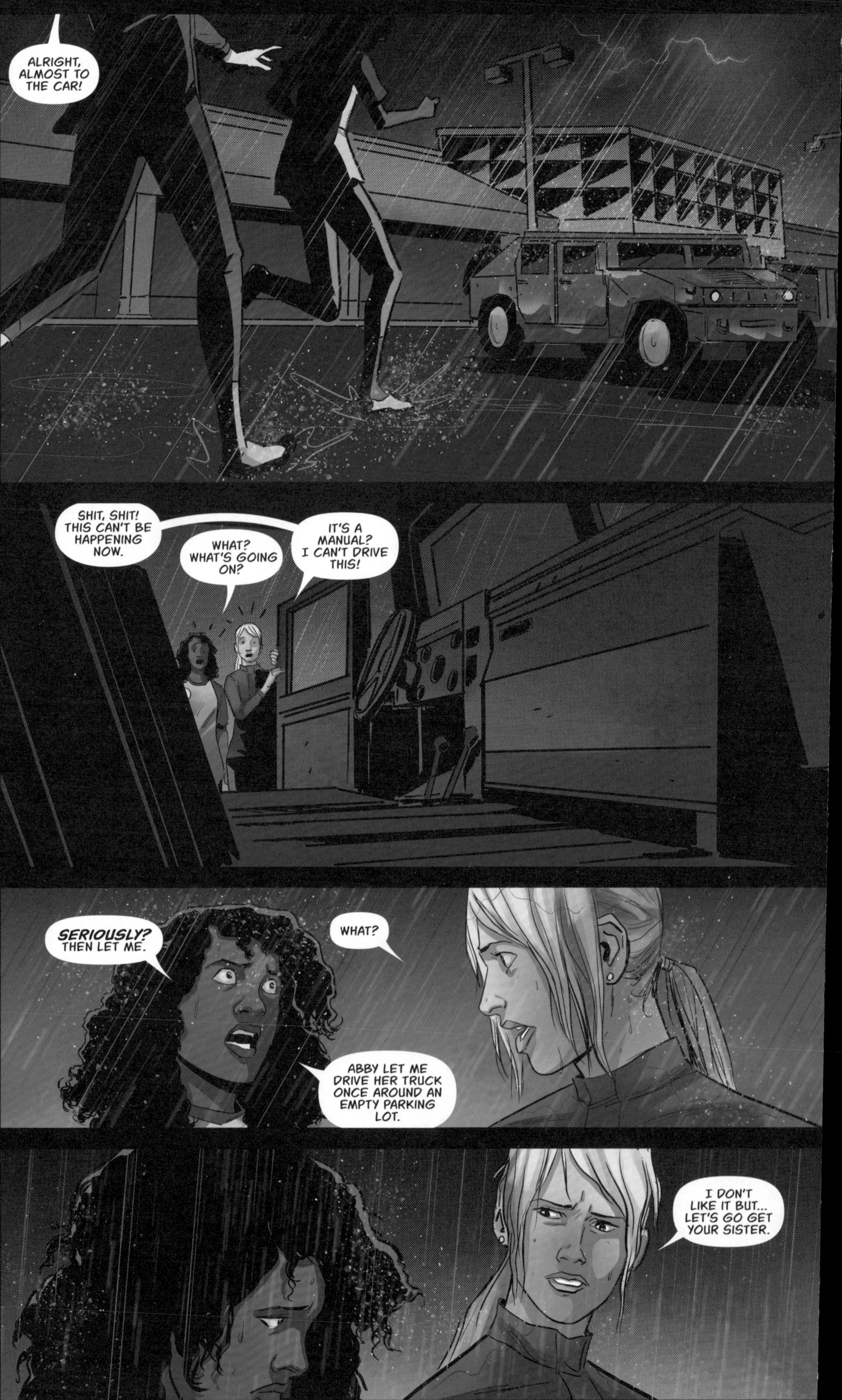
ALRIGHT, ALMOST TO THE CAR!
SHIT, SHIT! THIS CAN'T BE HAPPENING NOW.
WHAT? WHAT'S GOING ON?
IT'S A MANUAL? I CAN'T DRIVE THIS!
SERIOUSLY? THEN LET ME.
WHAT?
ABBY LET ME DRIVE HER TRUCK ONCE AROUND AN EMPTY PARKING LOT.
I DON'T LIKE IT BUT... LET'S GO GET YOUR SISTER.

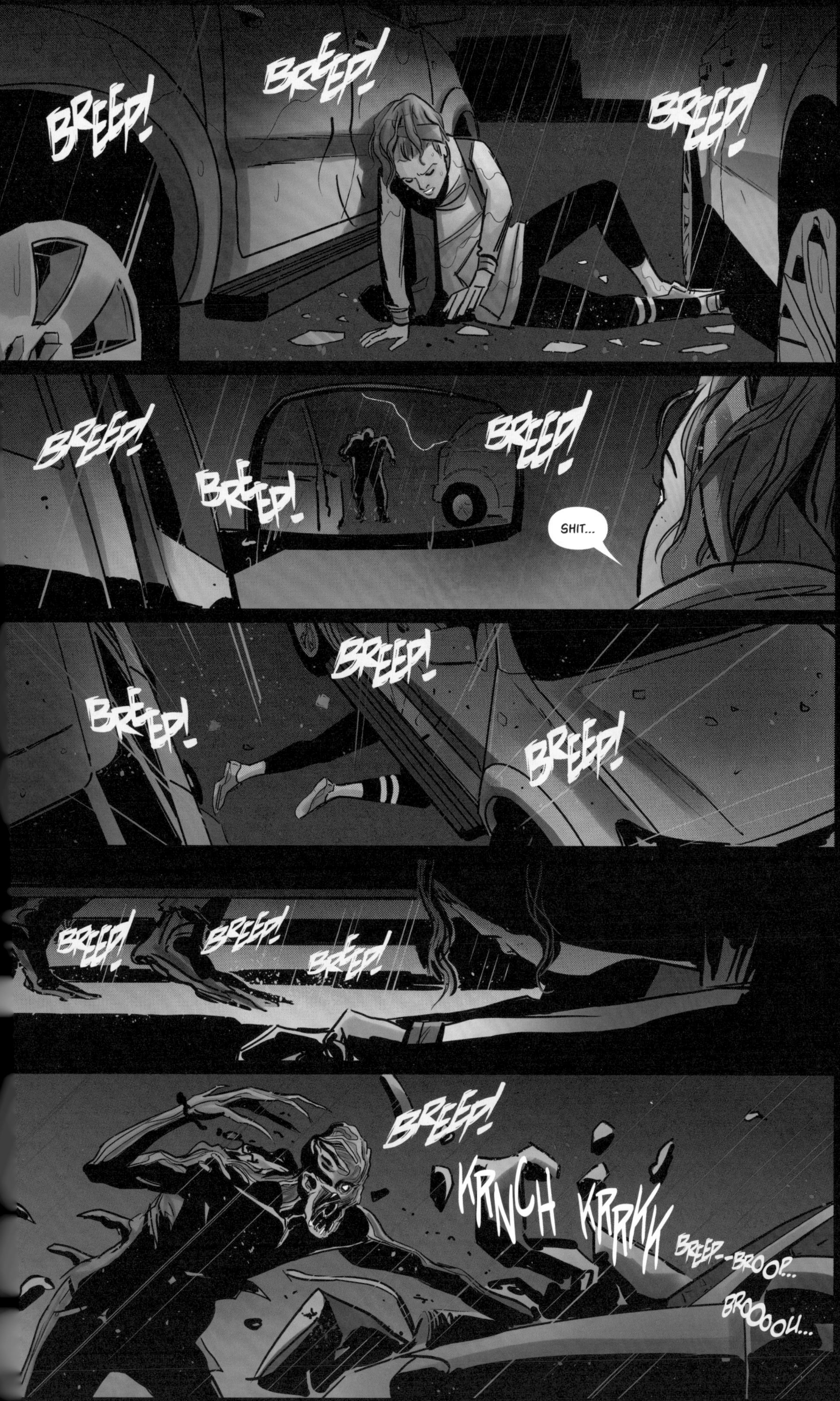
BREEP!
BREEP!
BREEP!
BREEP!
BREEP!
BREEP!
SHIT...
BREEP!
BREEP!
BREEP!
BREEP!
BREEP!
BREEP!
BREEP!
KRNCH KRRKK
BREEP--BROOP...
BROOOOU...

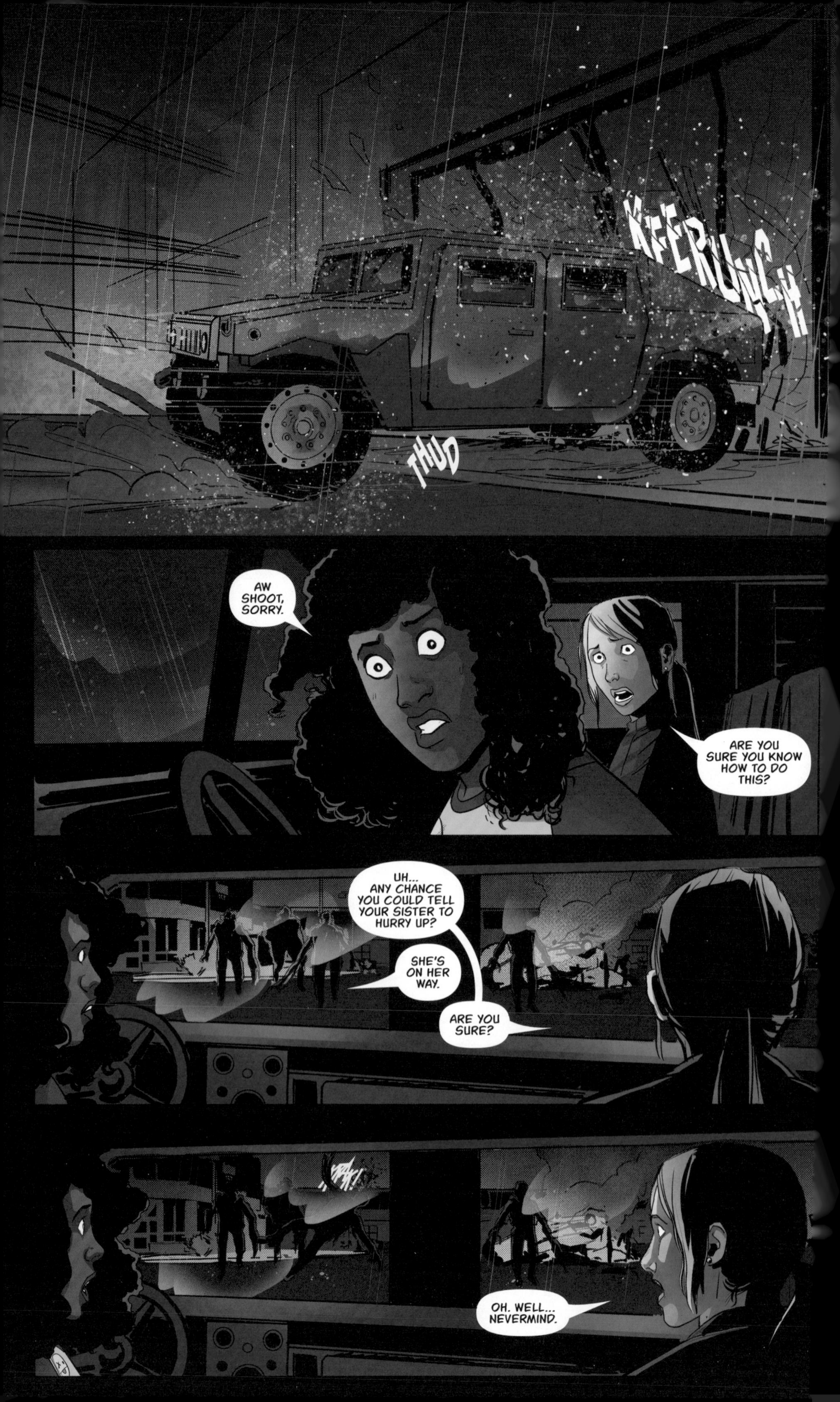

THUD
AW SHOOT, SORRY.
ARE YOU SURE YOU KNOW HOW TO DO THIS?
UH... ANY CHANCE YOU COULD TELL YOUR SISTER TO HURRY UP?
SHE'S ON HER WAY.
ARE YOU SURE?
OH. WELL... NEVERMIND.

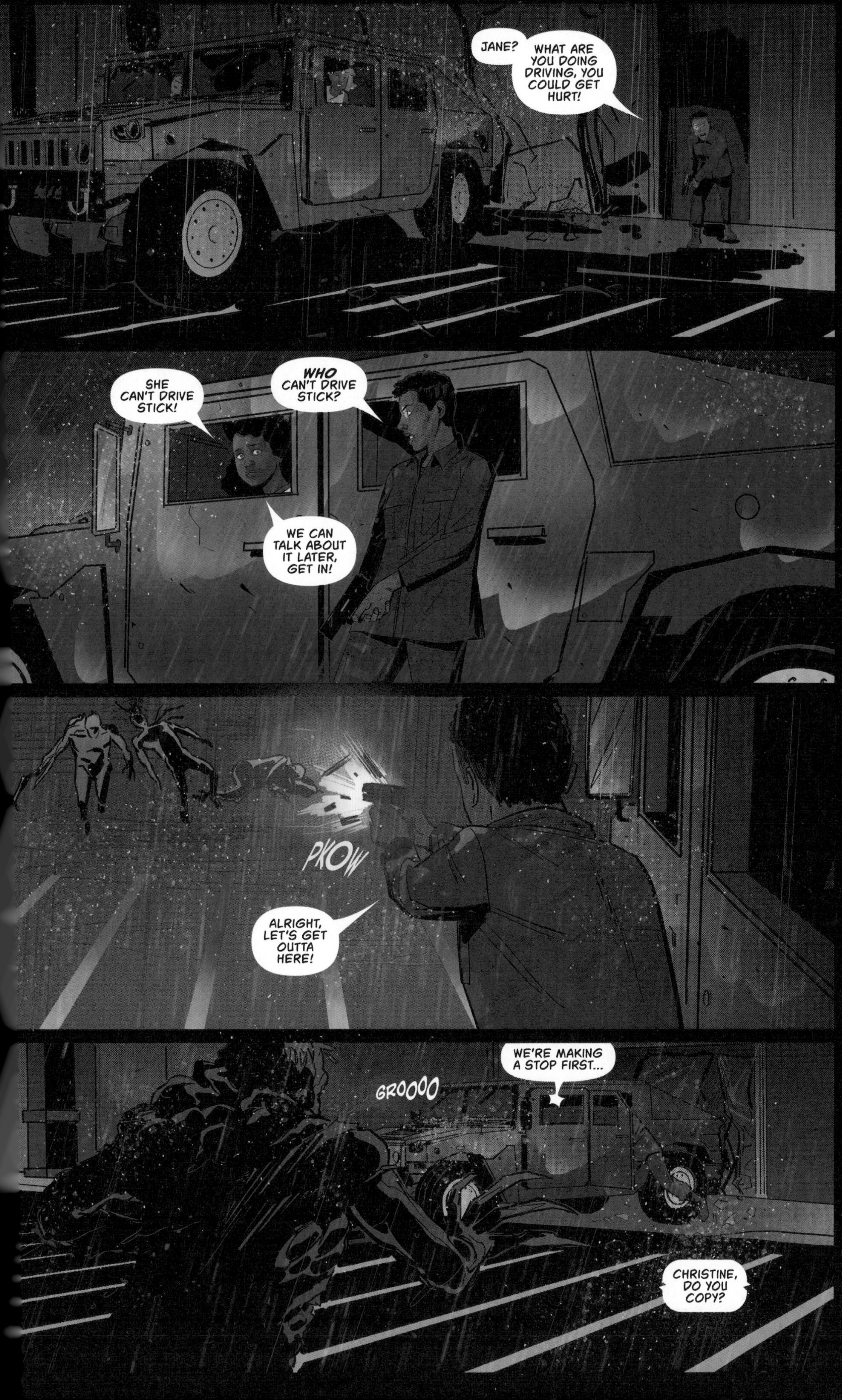
JANE?
WHAT ARE YOU DOING DRIVING, YOU COULD GET HURT!
SHE CAN'T DRIVE STICK!
WHO CAN'T DRIVE STICK?
WE CAN TALK ABOUT IT LATER, GET IN!
PKOW
ALRIGHT, LET'S GET OUTTA HERE!
GROOOO
WE'RE MAKING A STOP FIRST...
CHRISTINE, DO YOU COPY?

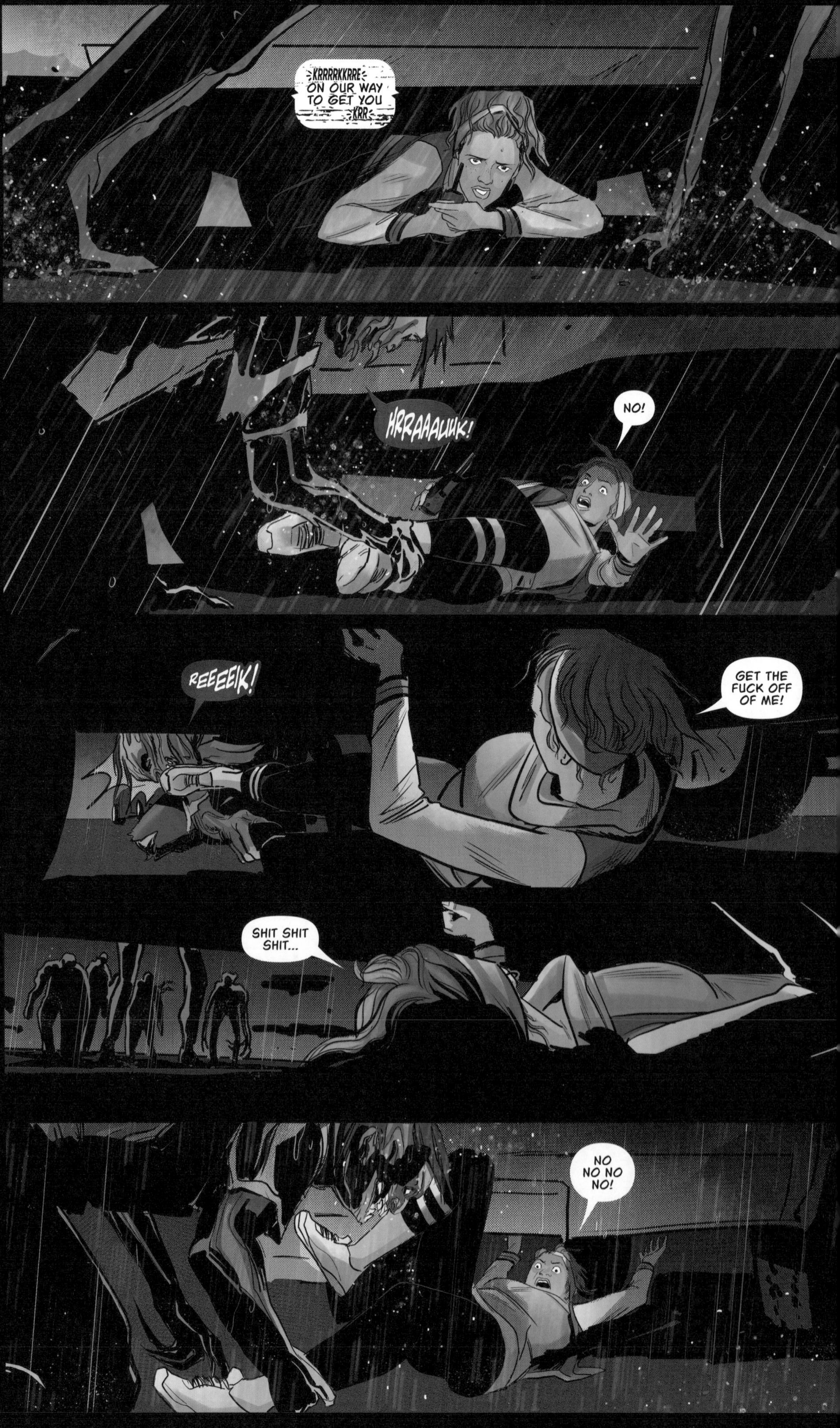

KRRRRKKRRE ON OUR WAY TO GET YOU KRR
HRRAAAUUK!
NO!
REEEEIK!
GET THE FUCK OFF OF ME!
SHIT SHIT SHIT...
NO NO NO NO!

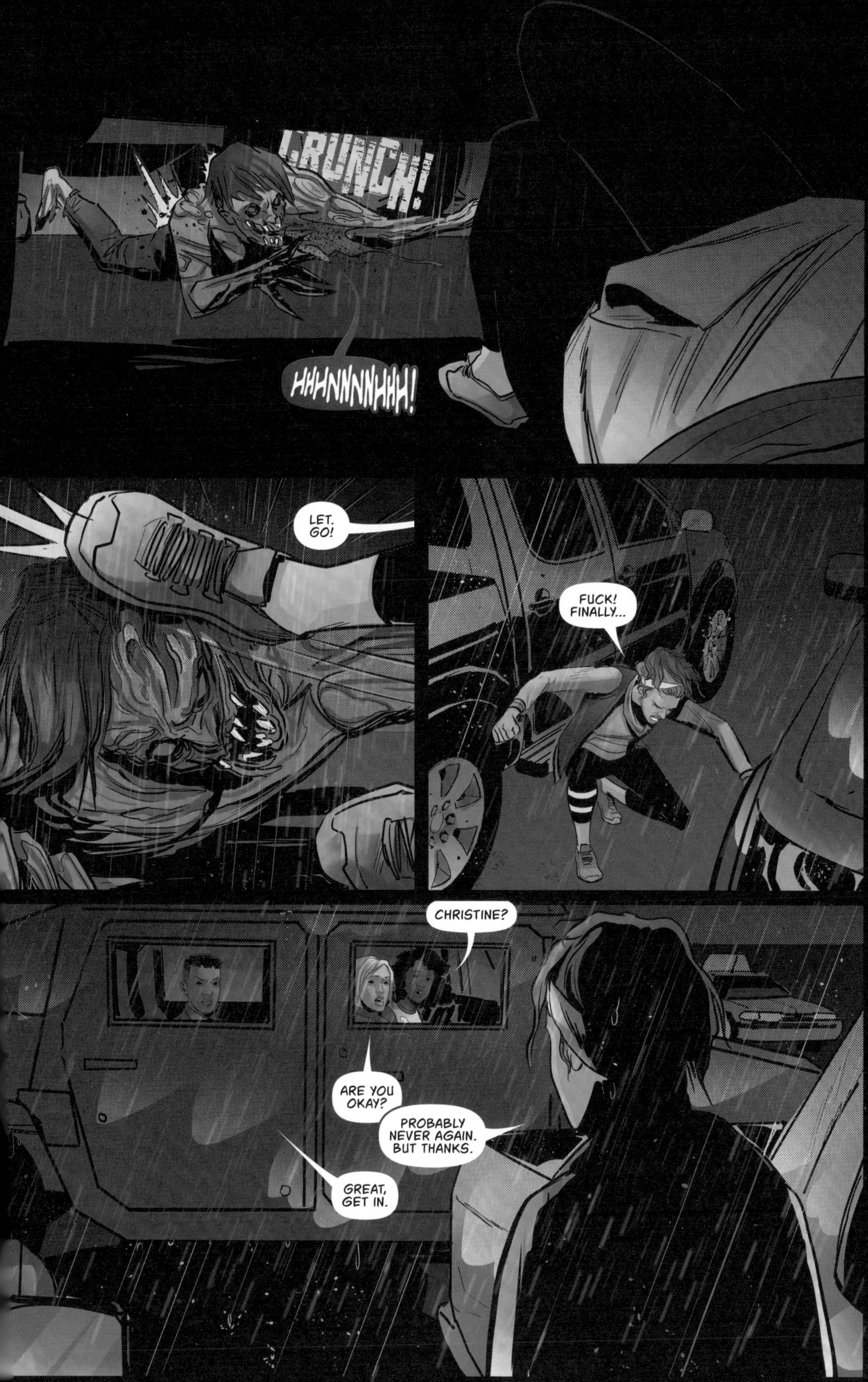
CRUNCH!
HHHNNNNHHH!
LET. GO!
FUCK! FINALLY...
CHRISTINE?
ARE YOU OKAY?
PROBABLY NEVER AGAIN. BUT THANKS.
GREAT, GET IN.

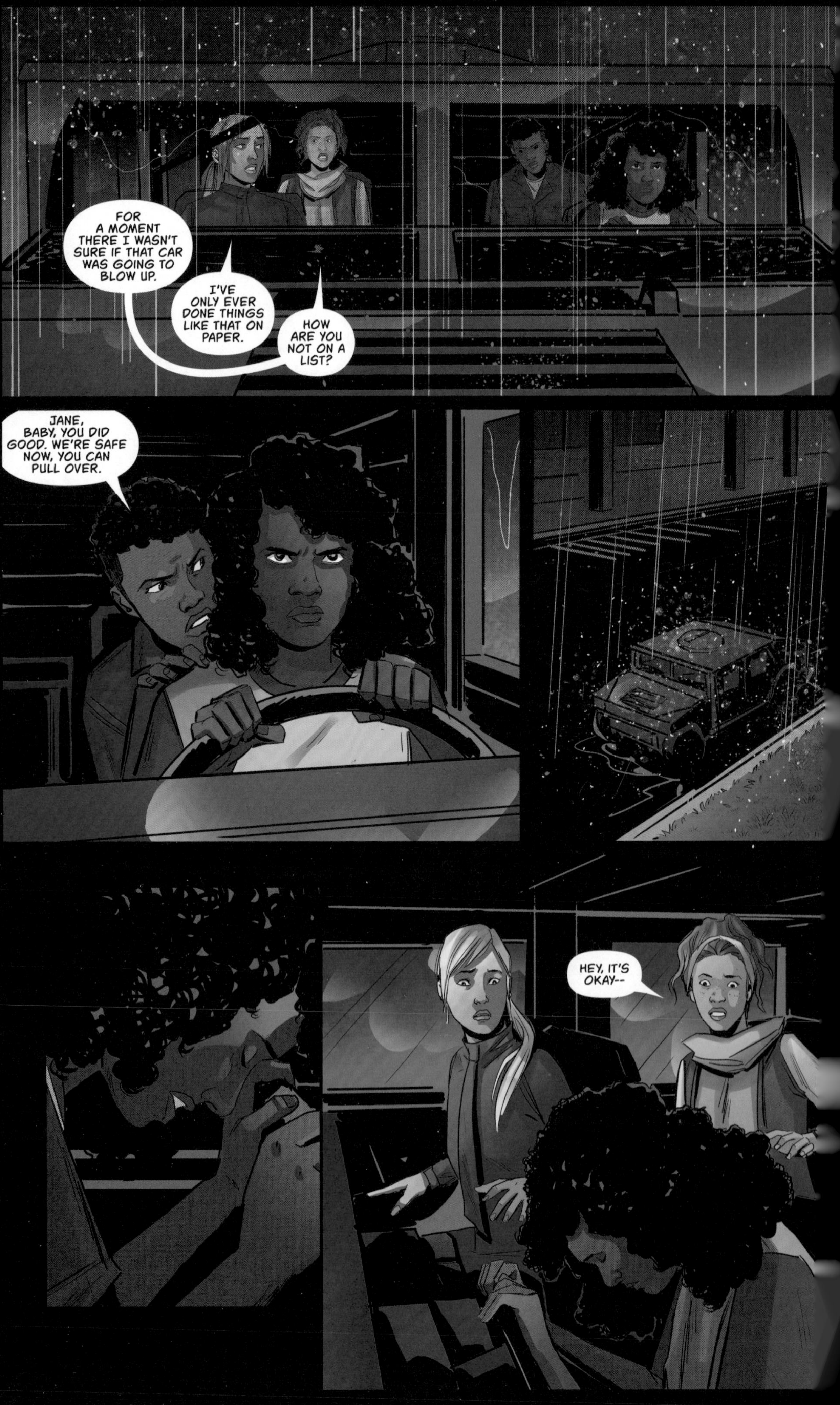
FOR A MOMENT THERE I WASN'T SURE IF THAT CAR WAS GOING TO BLOW UP.
I'VE ONLY EVER DONE THINGS LIKE THAT ON PAPER.
HOW ARE YOU NOT ON A LIST?
JANE, BABY, YOU DID GOOD. WE'RE SAFE NOW, YOU CAN PULL OVER.
HEY, IT'S OKAY--

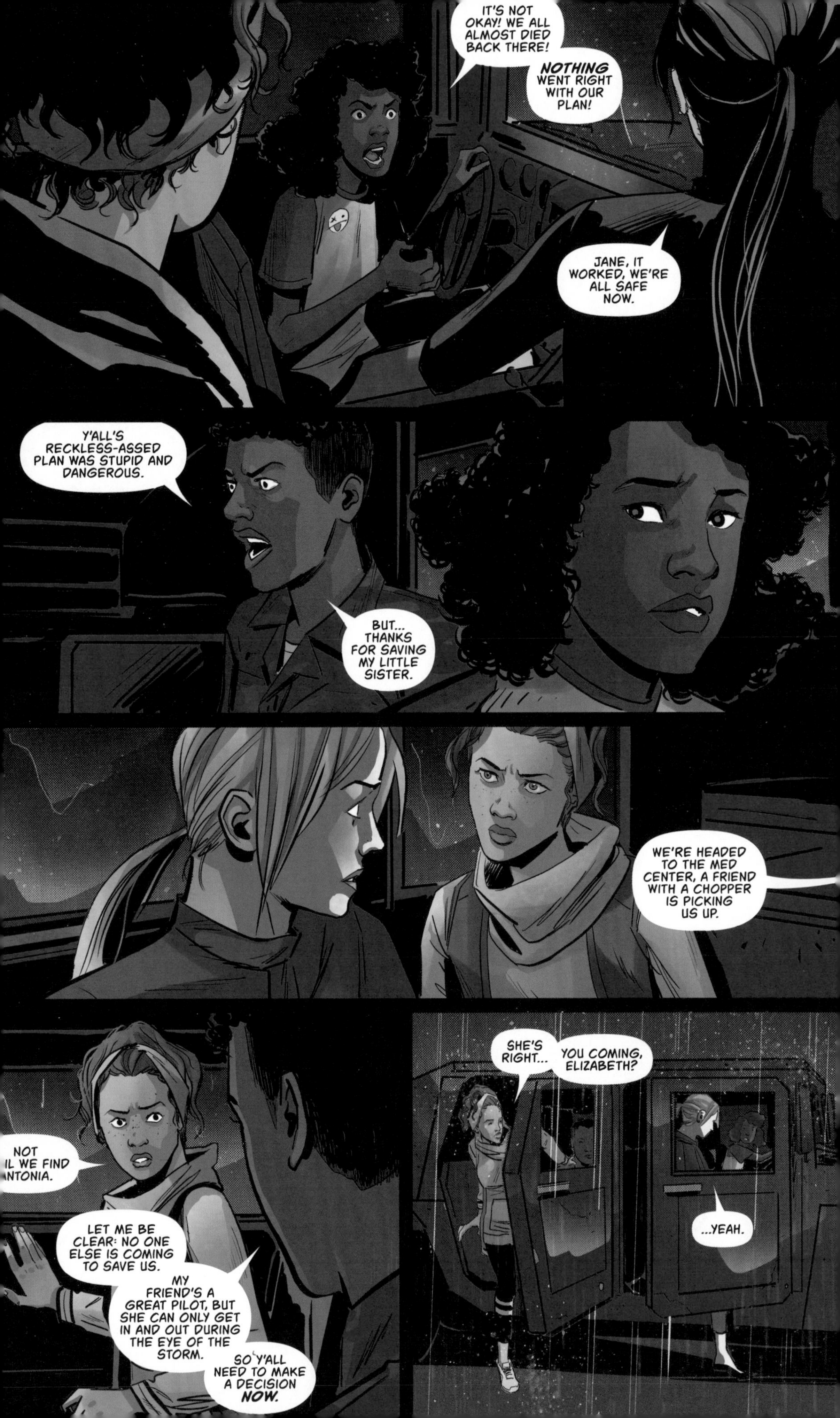
IT'S NOT OKAY! WE ALL ALMOST DIED BACK THERE!
NOTHING WENT RIGHT WITH OUR PLAN!
JANE, IT WORKED, WE'RE ALL SAFE NOW.
Y'ALL'S RECKLESS-ASSED PLAN WAS STUPID AND DANGEROUS.
BUT... THANKS FOR SAVING MY LITTLE SISTER.
WE'RE HEADED TO THE MED CENTER, A FRIEND WITH A CHOPPER IS PICKING US UP.
LET ME BE CLEAR: NO ONE ELSE IS COMING TO SAVE US.
MY FRIEND'S A GREAT PILOT, BUT SHE CAN ONLY GET IN AND OUT DURING THE EYE OF THE STORM.
SO Y'ALL NEED TO MAKE A DECISION NOW.
SHE'S RIGHT...
YOU COMING, ELIZABETH?
...YEAH.

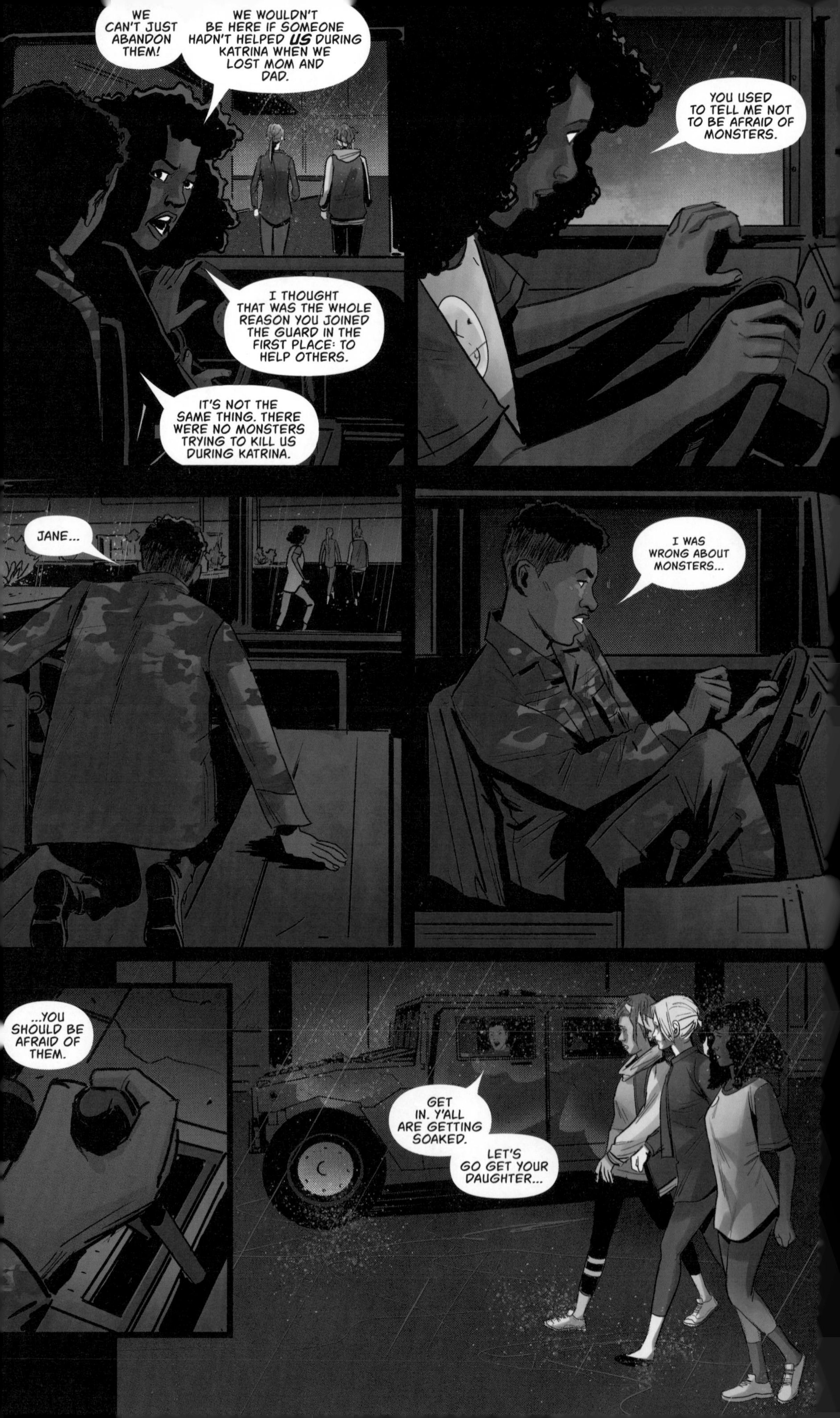
WE CAN'T JUST ABANDON THEM!
WE WOULDN'T BE HERE IF SOMEONE HADN'T HELPED US DURING KATRINA WHEN WE LOST MOM AND DAD.
I THOUGHT THAT WAS THE WHOLE REASON YOU JOINED THE GUARD IN THE FIRST PLACE: TO HELP OTHERS.
IT'S NOT THE SAME THING. THERE WERE NO MONSTERS TRYING TO KILL US DURING KATRINA.
YOU USED TO TELL ME NOT TO BE AFRAID OF MONSTERS.
JANE...
I WAS WRONG ABOUT MONSTERS...
...YOU SHOULD BE AFRAID OF THEM.
GET IN. Y'ALL ARE GETTING SOAKED.
LET'S GO GET YOUR DAUGHTER...

CHAPTER 4

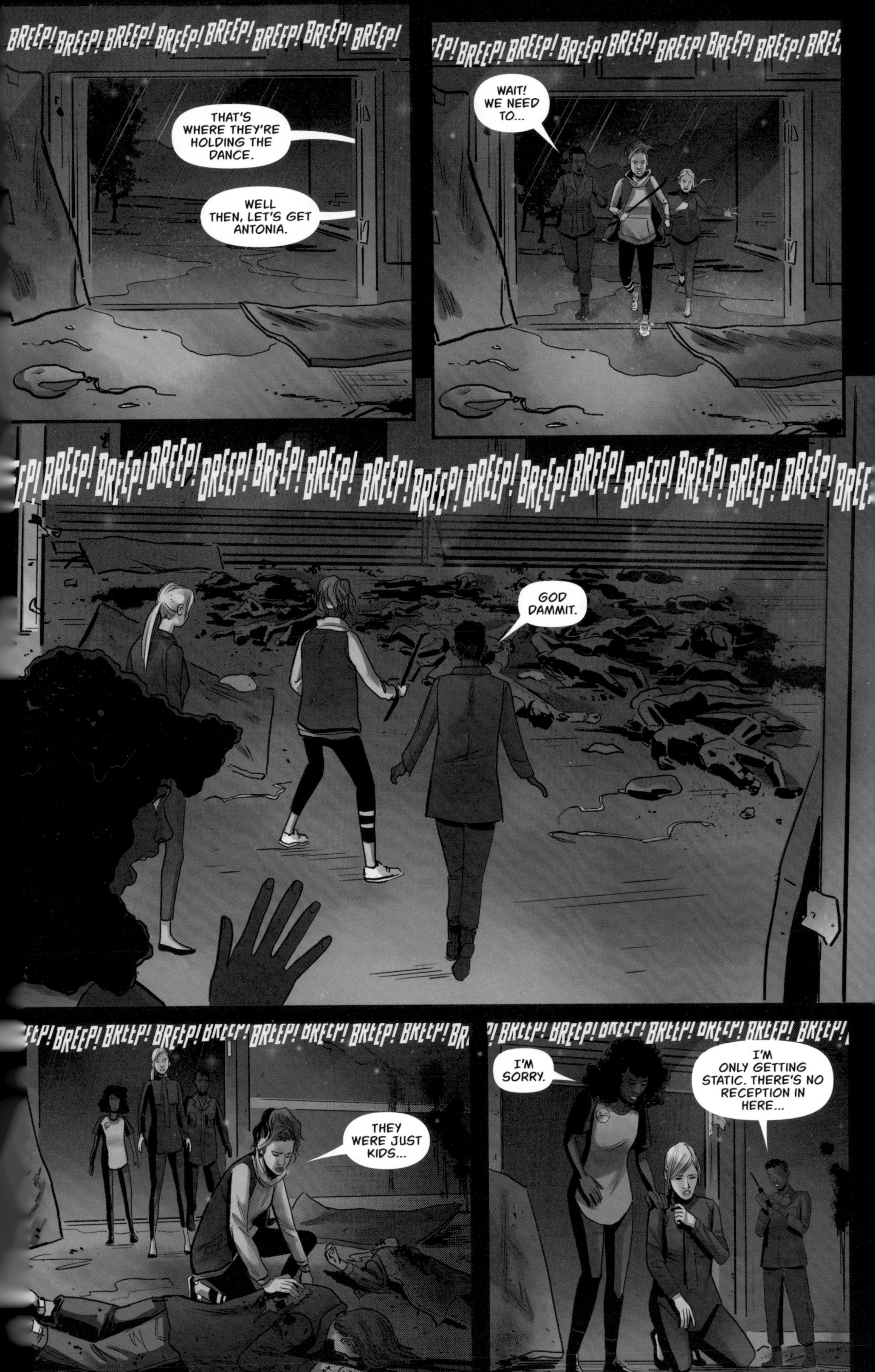
BREEP! BREEP! BREEP! BREEP! BREEP! BREEP! BREEP! BREEP!
THAT'S WHERE THEY'RE HOLDING THE DANCE.
WELL THEN, LET'S GET ANTONIA.
WAIT! WE NEED TO...
GOD DAMMIT.
THEY WERE JUST KIDS...
I'M SORRY.
I'M ONLY GETTING STATIC. THERE'S NO RECEPTION IN HERE...

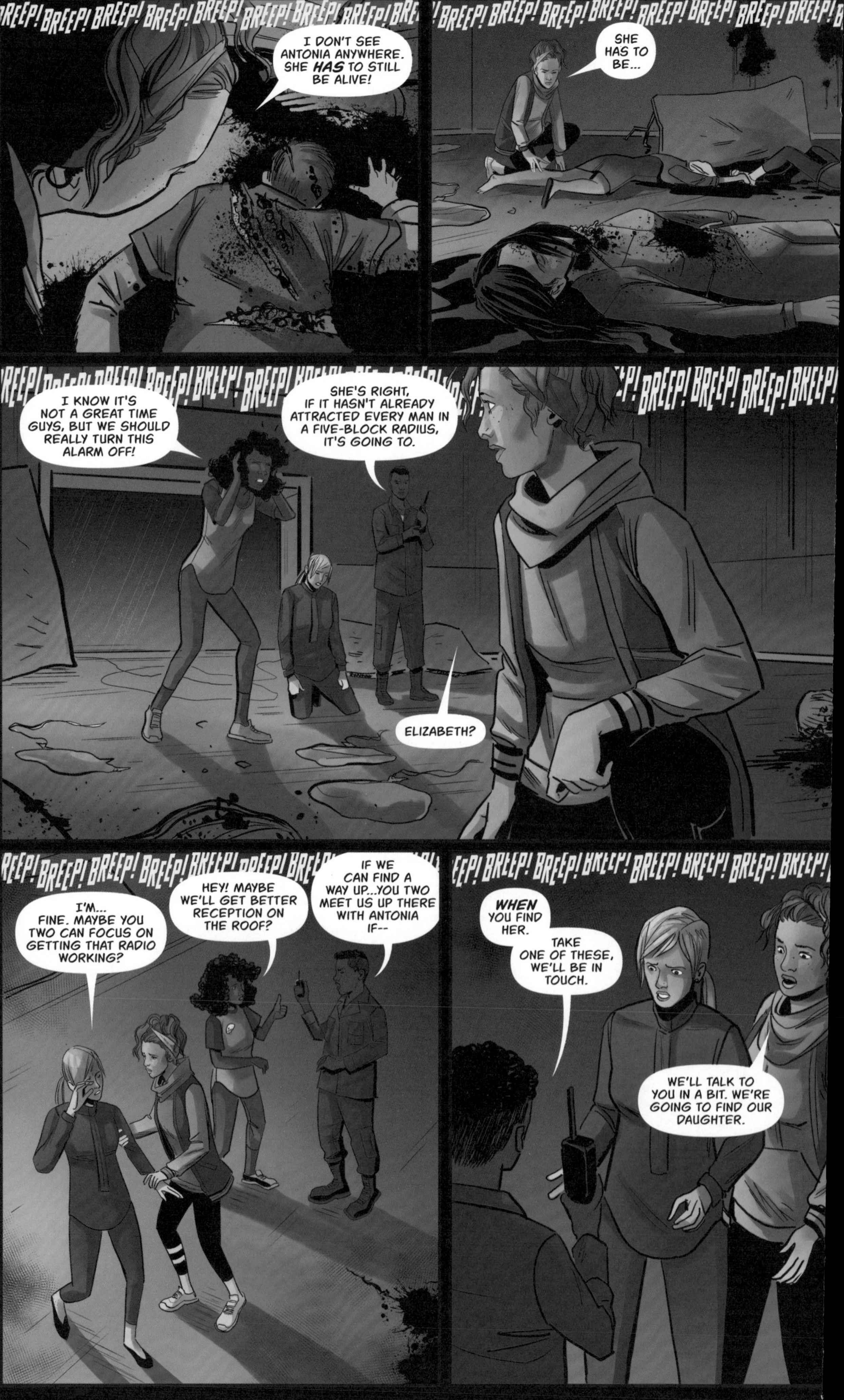
BREEP! BREEP! BREEP! BREEP!
I DON'T SEE ANTONIA ANYWHERE. SHE *HAS* TO STILL BE ALIVE!
BREEP! BREEP! BREEP! BREEP! BREEP! BREEP!
SHE HAS TO BE...
BREEP! BREEP! BREEP! BREEP! BREEP!
I KNOW IT'S NOT A GREAT TIME GUYS, BUT WE SHOULD REALLY TURN THIS ALARM OFF!
SHE'S RIGHT, IF IT HASN'T ALREADY ATTRACTED EVERY MAN IN A FIVE-BLOCK RADIUS, IT'S GOING TO.
ELIZABETH?
BREEP! BREEP! BREEP! BREEP! BREEP!
I'M... FINE. MAYBE YOU TWO CAN FOCUS ON GETTING THAT RADIO WORKING?
HEY! MAYBE WE'LL GET BETTER RECEPTION ON THE ROOF?
IF WE CAN FIND A WAY UP...YOU TWO MEET US UP THERE WITH ANTONIA IF--
BREEP! BREEP! BREEP! BREEP! BREEP! BREEP!
WHEN YOU FIND HER.
TAKE ONE OF THESE, WE'LL BE IN TOUCH.
WE'LL TALK TO YOU IN A BIT. WE'RE GOING TO FIND OUR DAUGHTER.

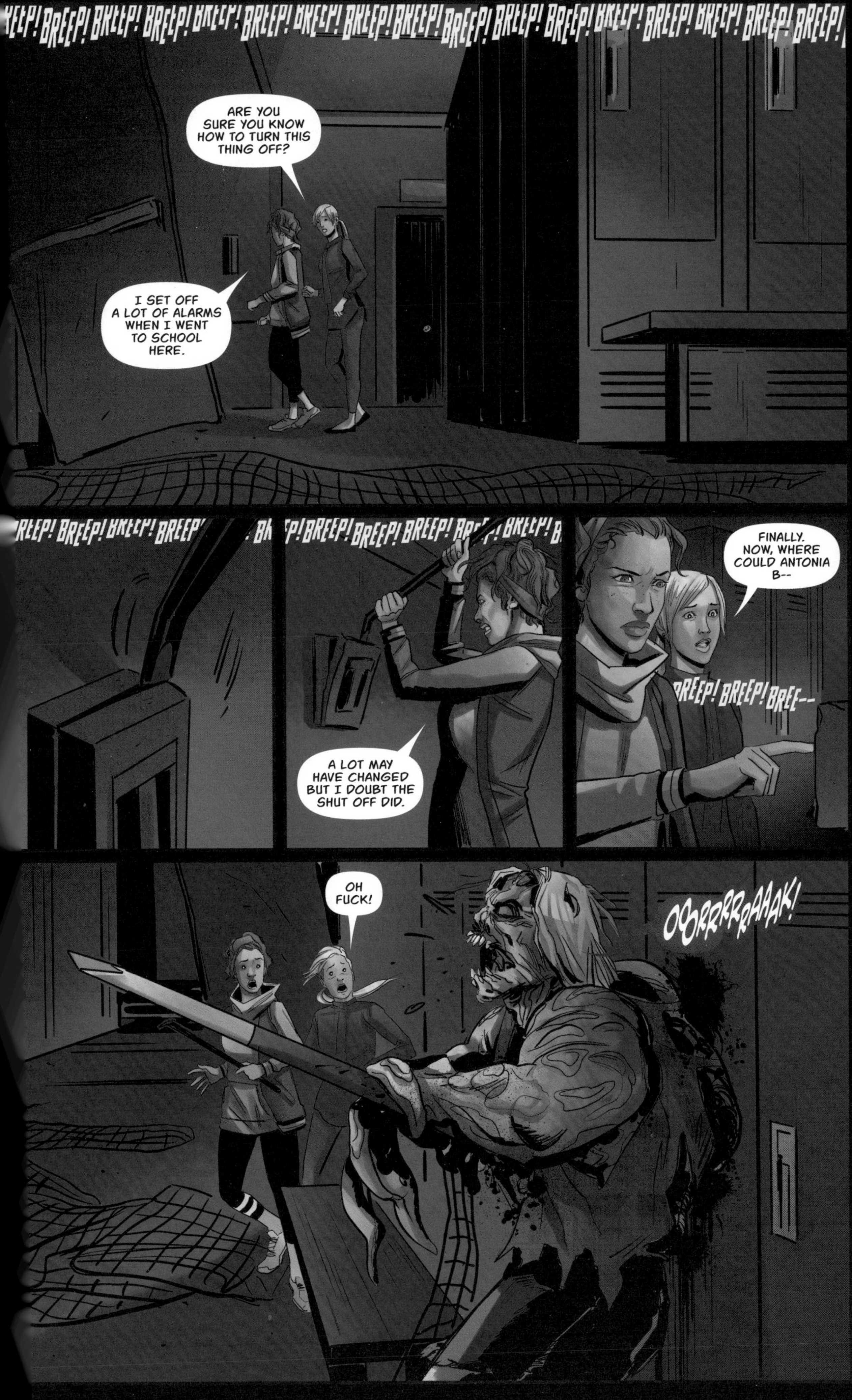
BREEP! BREEP! BREEP! BREEP! BREEP! BREEP! BREEP! BREEP! BREEP! BREEP! BREEP! BREEP! BREEP! BREEP! BREEP! BREEP! BREEP!
ARE YOU SURE YOU KNOW HOW TO TURN THIS THING OFF?
I SET OFF A LOT OF ALARMS WHEN I WENT TO SCHOOL HERE.
BREEP! BREEP! BREEP! BREEP!
BREEP! BREEP! BREEP! BREEP!
A LOT MAY HAVE CHANGED BUT I DOUBT THE SHUT OFF DID.
FINALLY. NOW, WHERE COULD ANTONIA B--
BREEP! BREEP! BREE--
OH FUCK!
OORRRRRAAAK!

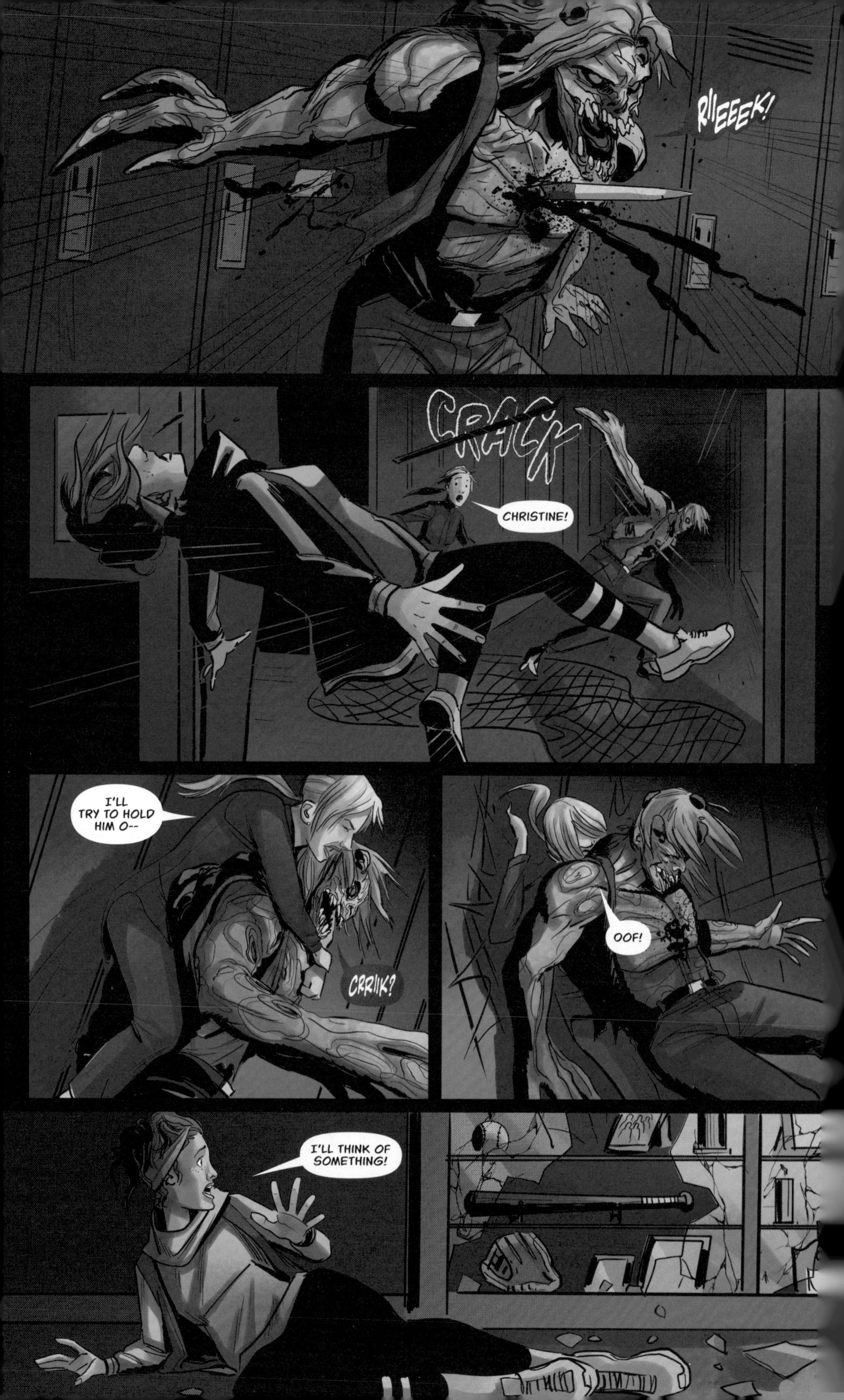
RIIEEEK!
CRACK
CHRISTINE!
I'LL TRY TO HOLD HIM O--
CRRIIK?
OOF!
I'LL THINK OF SOMETHING!

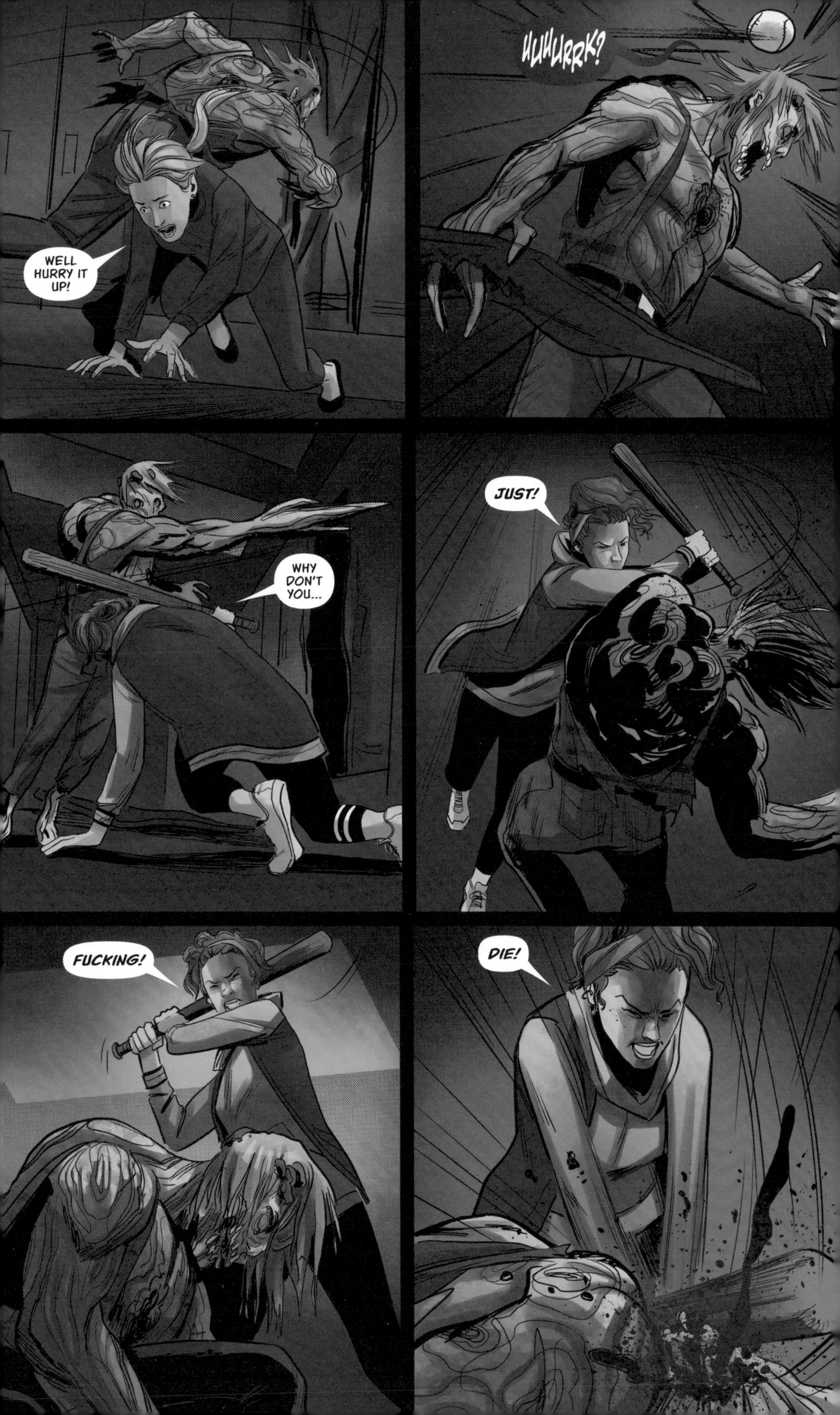
WELL HURRY IT UP!
UUUURRK?
WHY DON'T YOU...
JUST!
FUCKING!
DIE!

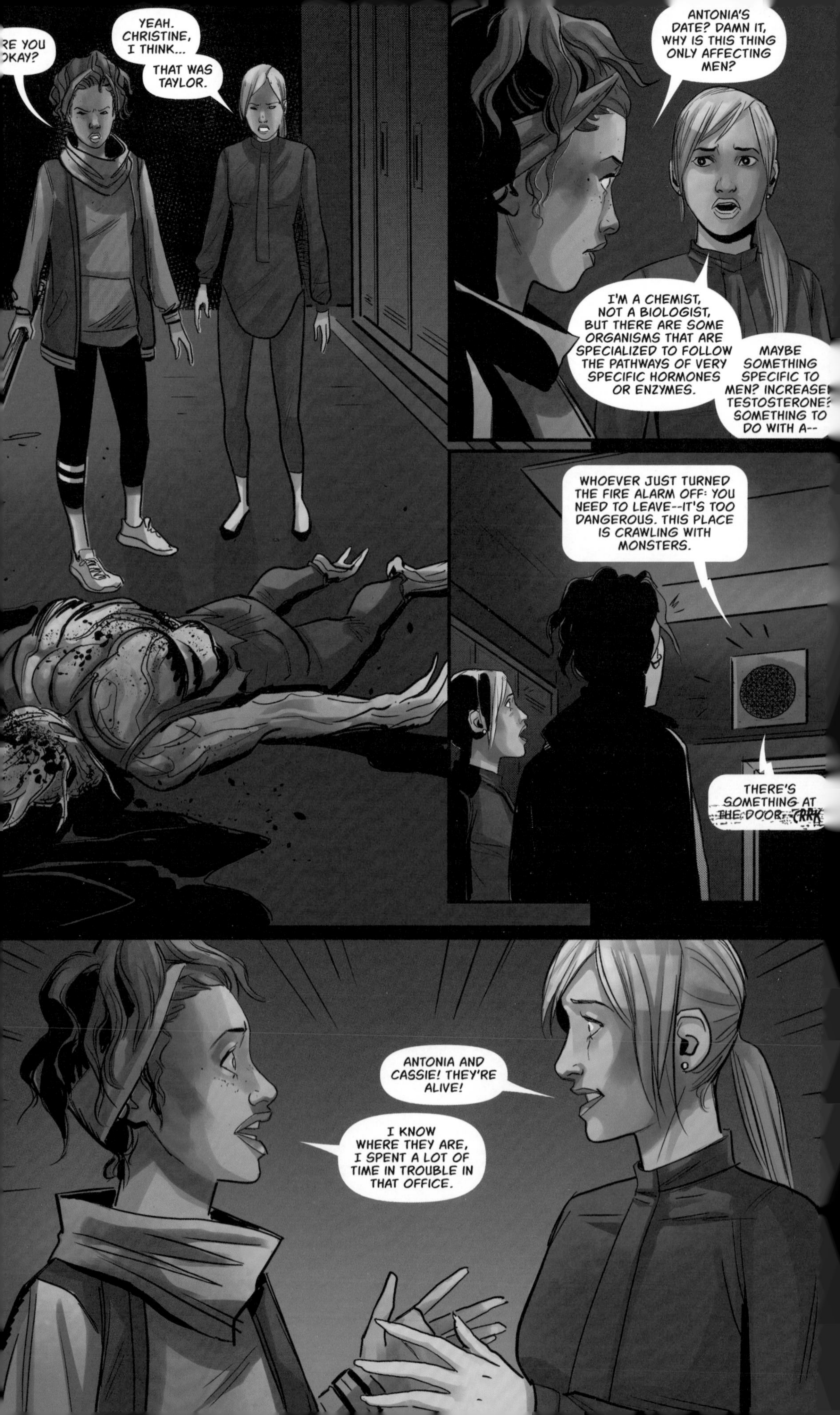
RE YOU
OKAY?
YEAH. CHRISTINE, I THINK...
THAT WAS TAYLOR.
ANTONIA'S DATE? DAMN IT, WHY IS THIS THING ONLY AFFECTING MEN?
I'M A CHEMIST, NOT A BIOLOGIST, BUT THERE ARE SOME ORGANISMS THAT ARE SPECIALIZED TO FOLLOW THE PATHWAYS OF VERY SPECIFIC HORMONES OR ENZYMES.
MAYBE SOMETHING SPECIFIC TO MEN? INCREASE TESTOSTERONE? SOMETHING TO DO WITH A--
WHOEVER JUST TURNED THE FIRE ALARM OFF: YOU NEED TO LEAVE--IT'S TOO DANGEROUS. THIS PLACE IS CRAWLING WITH MONSTERS.
THERE'S SOMETHING AT THE DOOR. CRRK
ANTONIA AND CASSIE! THEY'RE ALIVE!
I KNOW WHERE THEY ARE, I SPENT A LOT OF TIME IN TROUBLE IN THAT OFFICE.

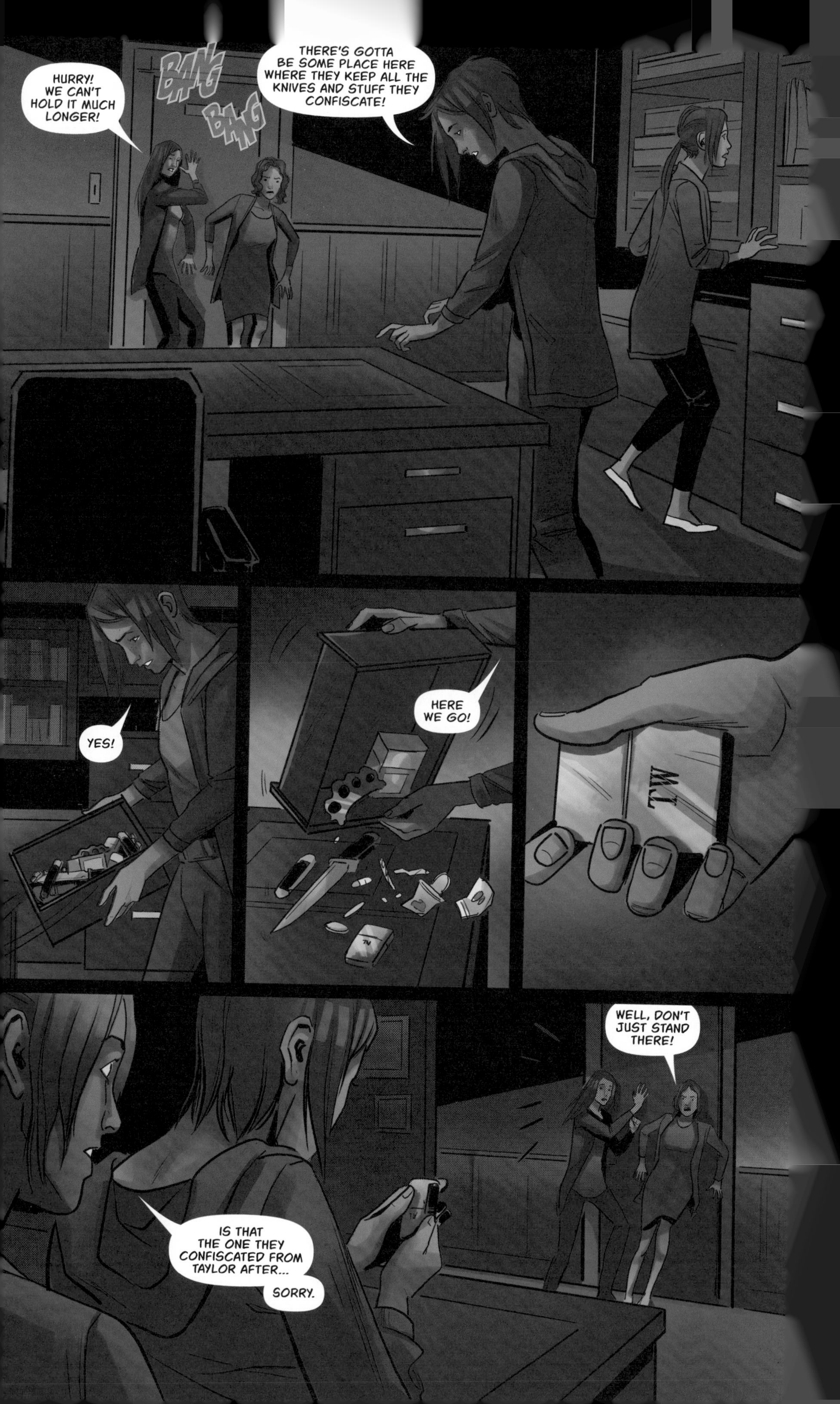
HURRY! WE CAN'T HOLD IT MUCH LONGER!
BANG
BANG
THERE'S GOTTA BE SOME PLACE HERE WHERE THEY KEEP ALL THE KNIVES AND STUFF THEY CONFISCATE!
YES!
HERE WE GO!
M.T.
WELL, DON'T JUST STAND THERE!
IS THAT THE ONE THEY CONFISCATED FROM TAYLOR AFTER...
SORRY.

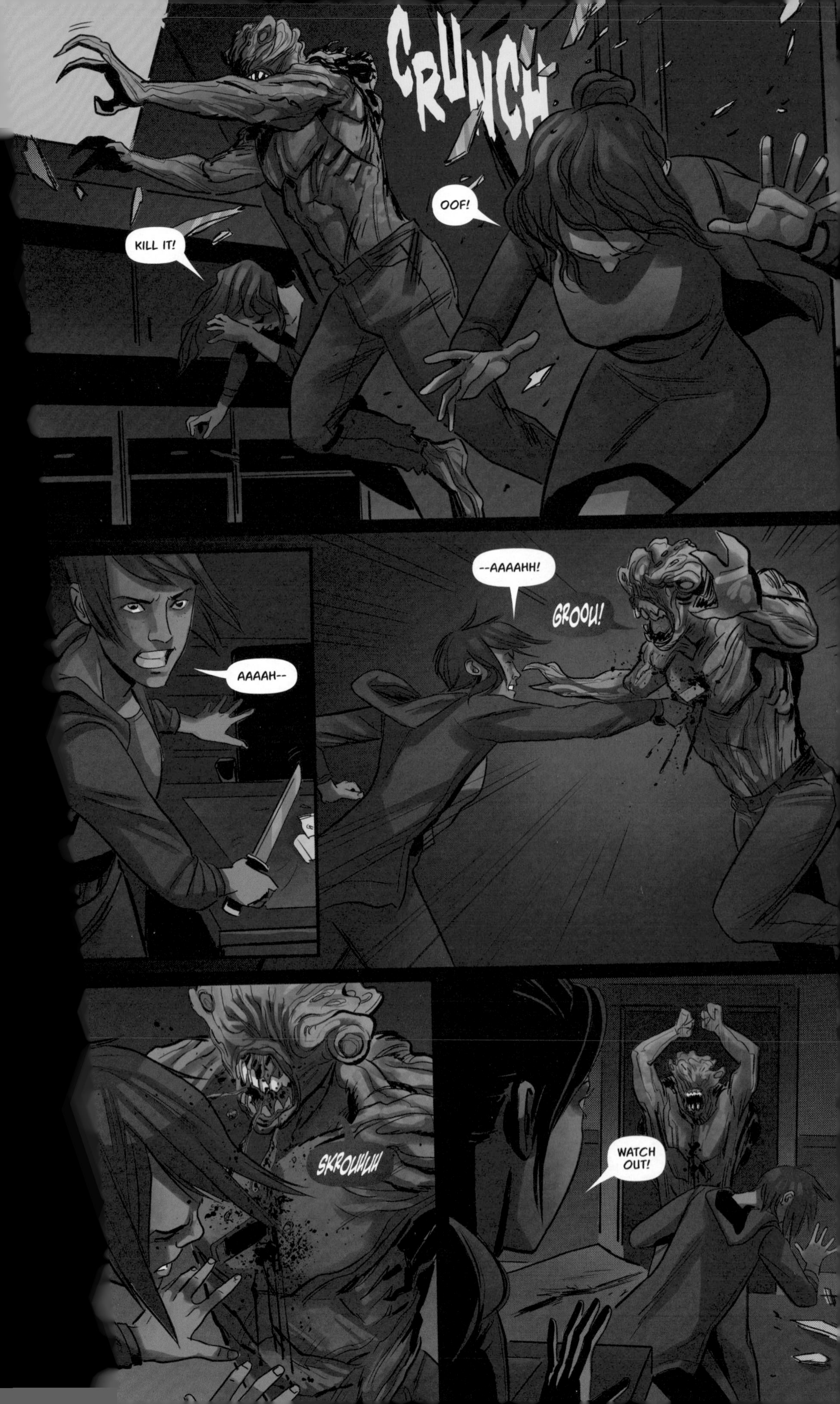
CRUNCH
OOF!
KILL IT!
AAAAH--
--AAAAHH!
GROOU!
SKROUUUU
WATCH OUT!

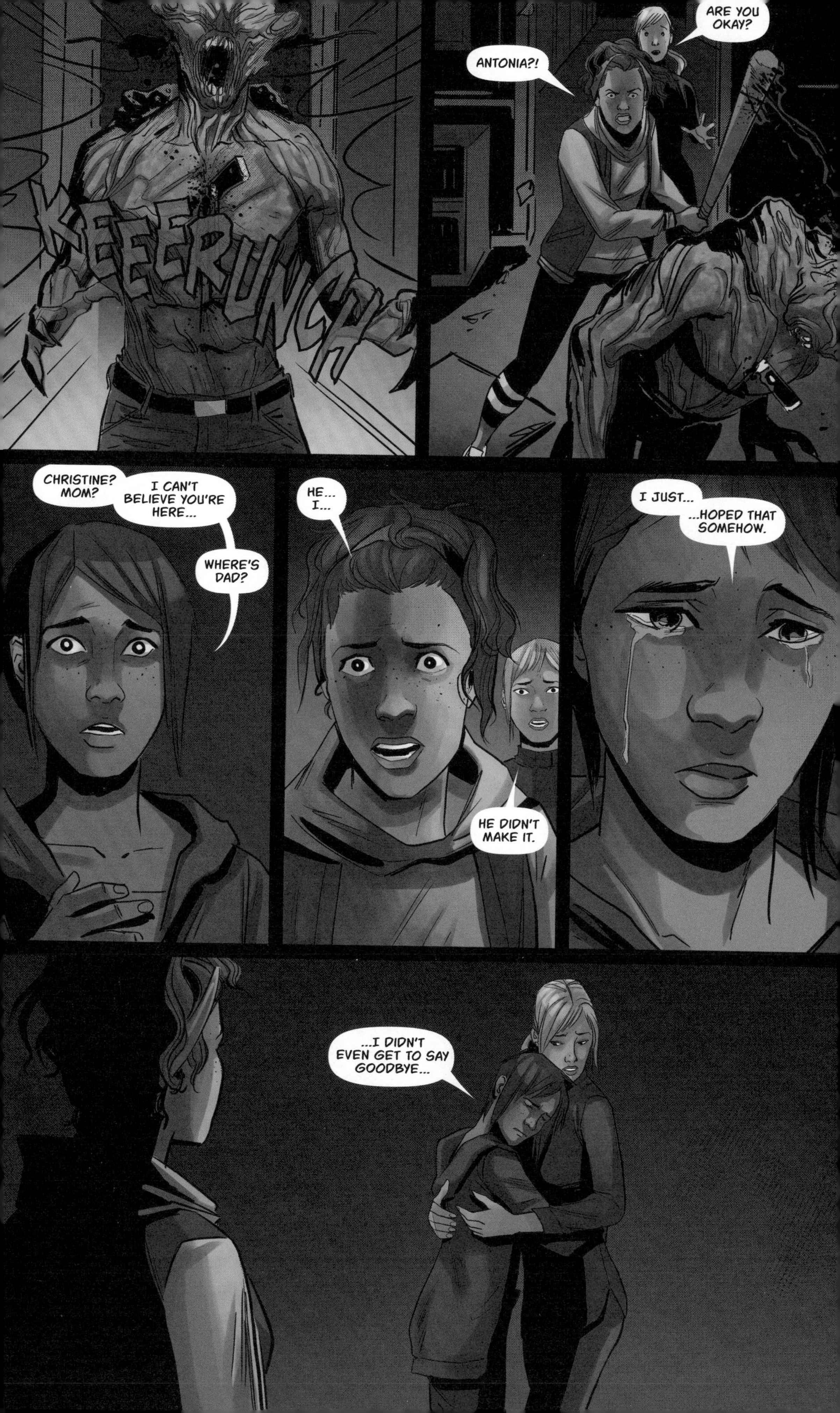
KEEERUNCH!
ANTONIA?!
ARE YOU OKAY?
CHRISTINE? MOM?
I CAN'T BELIEVE YOU'RE HERE...
WHERE'S DAD?
HE... I...
HE DIDN'T MAKE IT.
I JUST...
...HOPED THAT SOMEHOW.
...I DIDN'T EVEN GET TO SAY GOODBYE...

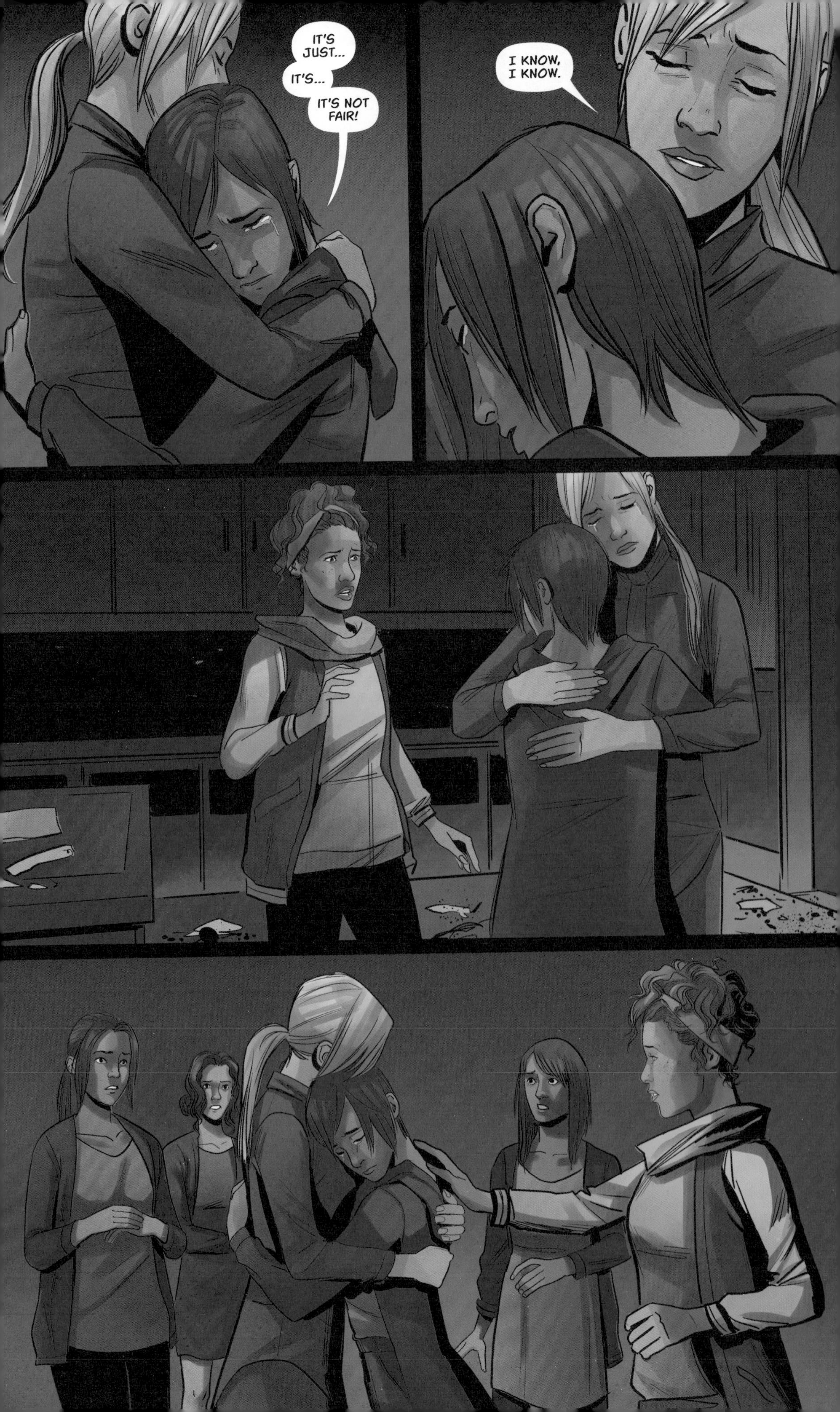
IT'S JUST...
IT'S...
IT'S NOT FAIR!
I KNOW, I KNOW.

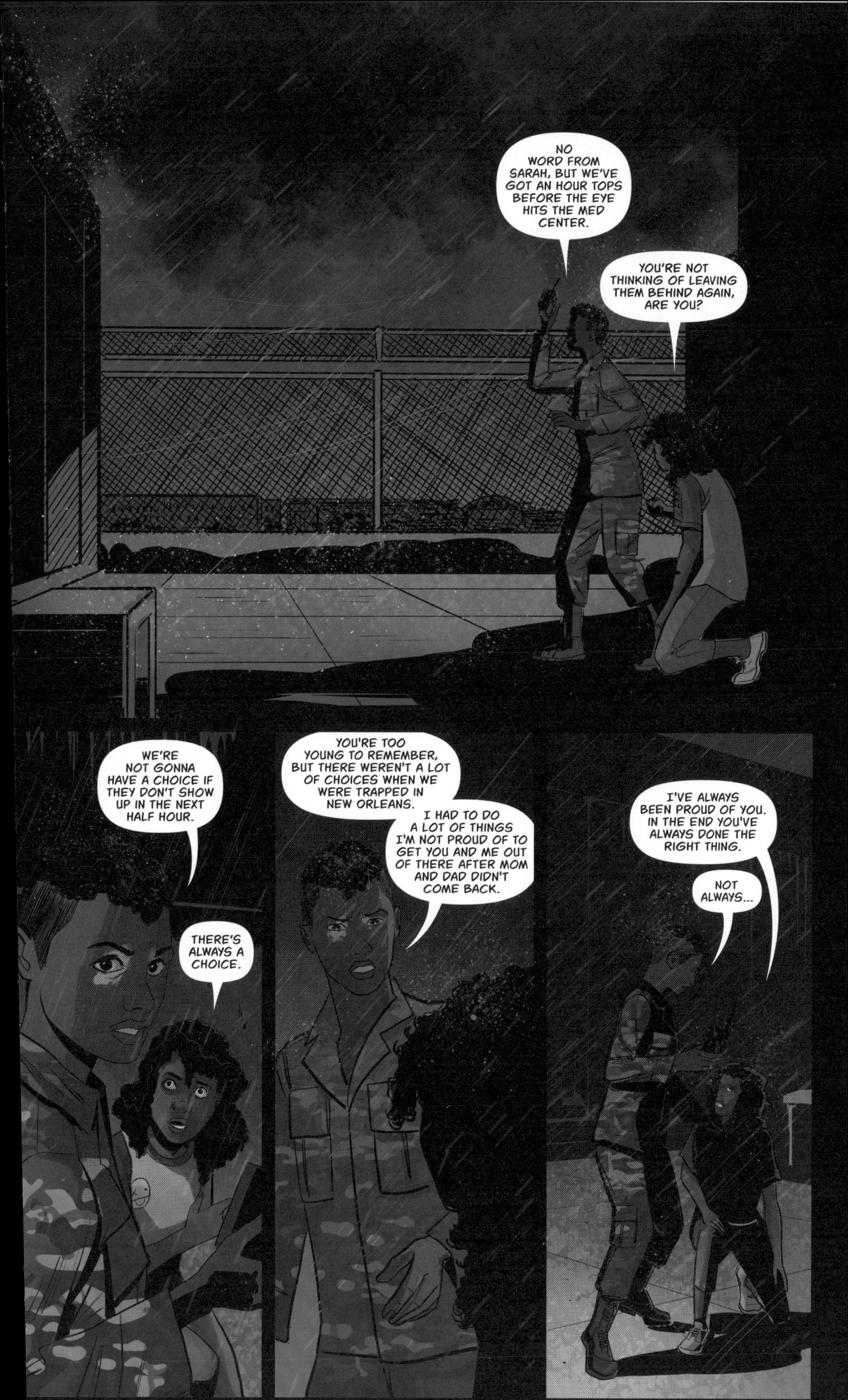
NO WORD FROM SARAH, BUT WE'VE GOT AN HOUR TOPS BEFORE THE EYE HITS THE MED CENTER.
YOU'RE NOT THINKING OF LEAVING THEM BEHIND AGAIN, ARE YOU?
WE'RE NOT GONNA HAVE A CHOICE IF THEY DON'T SHOW UP IN THE NEXT HALF HOUR.
THERE'S ALWAYS A CHOICE.
YOU'RE TOO YOUNG TO REMEMBER, BUT THERE WEREN'T A LOT OF CHOICES WHEN WE WERE TRAPPED IN NEW ORLEANS.
I HAD TO DO A LOT OF THINGS I'M NOT PROUD OF TO GET YOU AND ME OUT OF THERE AFTER MOM AND DAD DIDN'T COME BACK.
I'VE ALWAYS BEEN PROUD OF YOU. IN THE END YOU'VE ALWAYS DONE THE RIGHT THING.
NOT ALWAYS...

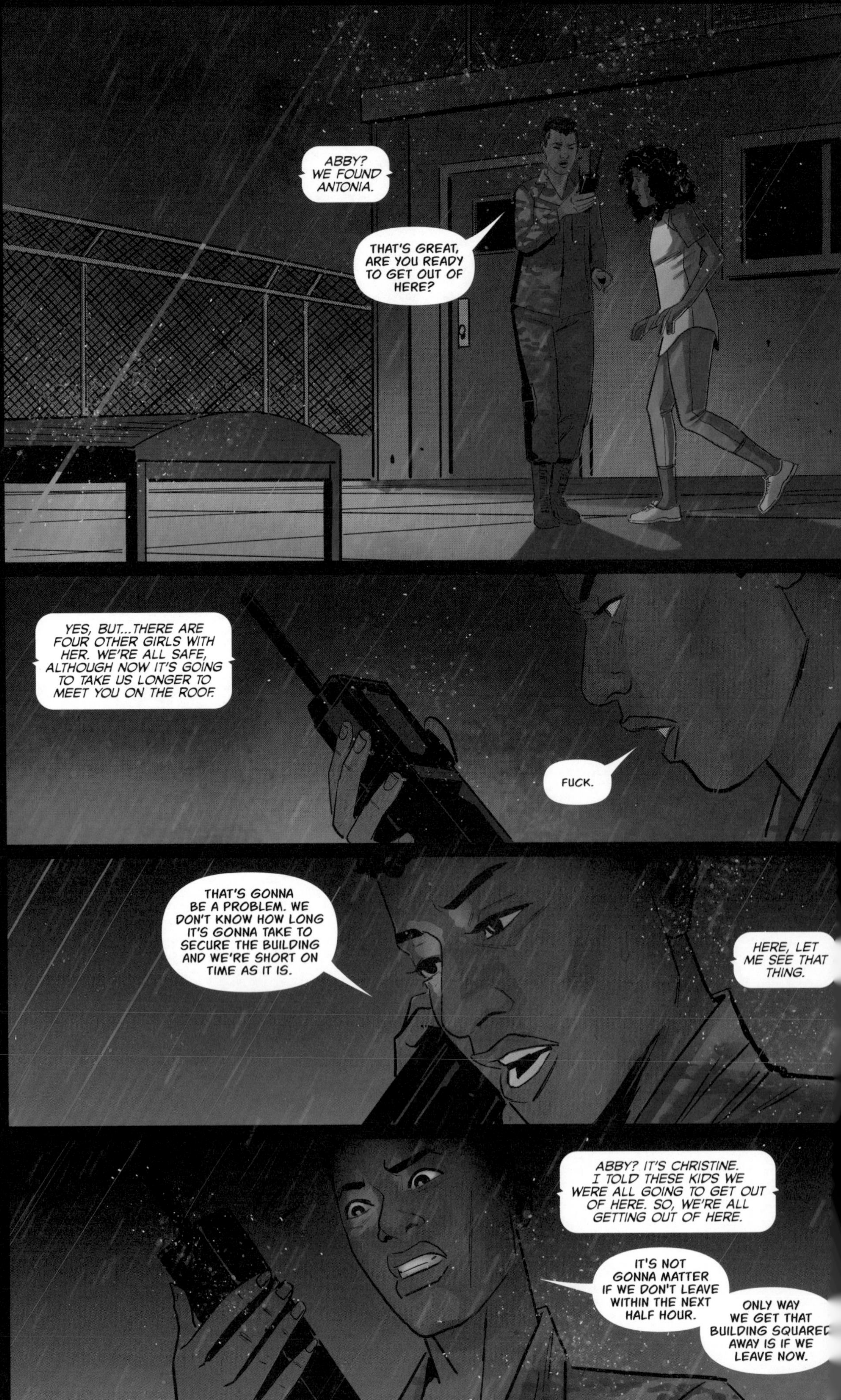
ABBY? WE FOUND ANTONIA.
THAT'S GREAT, ARE YOU READY TO GET OUT OF HERE?
YES, BUT...THERE ARE FOUR OTHER GIRLS WITH HER. WE'RE ALL SAFE, ALTHOUGH NOW IT'S GOING TO TAKE US LONGER TO MEET YOU ON THE ROOF.
FUCK.
THAT'S GONNA BE A PROBLEM. WE DON'T KNOW HOW LONG IT'S GONNA TAKE TO SECURE THE BUILDING AND WE'RE SHORT ON TIME AS IT IS.
HERE, LET ME SEE THAT THING.
ABBY? IT'S CHRISTINE. I TOLD THESE KIDS WE WERE ALL GOING TO GET OUT OF HERE. SO, WE'RE ALL GETTING OUT OF HERE.
IT'S NOT GONNA MATTER IF WE DON'T LEAVE WITHIN THE NEXT HALF HOUR.
ONLY WAY WE GET THAT BUILDING SQUARED AWAY IS IF WE LEAVE NOW.

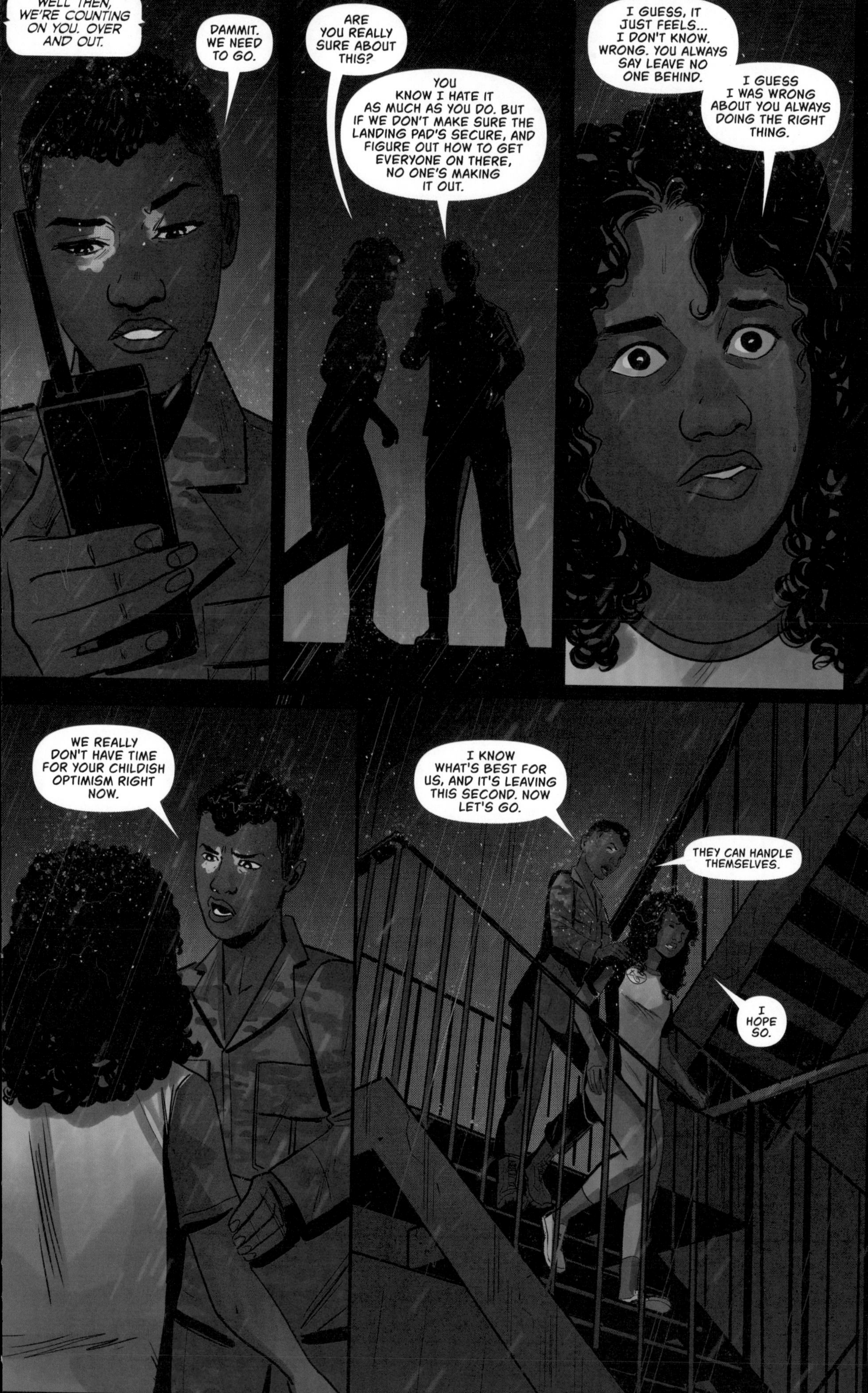
WELL THEN, WE'RE COUNTING ON YOU. OVER AND OUT.
DAMMIT. WE NEED TO GO.
ARE YOU REALLY SURE ABOUT THIS?
YOU KNOW I HATE IT AS MUCH AS YOU DO. BUT IF WE DON'T MAKE SURE THE LANDING PAD'S SECURE, AND FIGURE OUT HOW TO GET EVERYONE ON THERE, NO ONE'S MAKING IT OUT.
I GUESS, IT JUST FEELS... I DON'T KNOW. WRONG. YOU ALWAYS SAY LEAVE NO ONE BEHIND.
I GUESS I WAS WRONG ABOUT YOU ALWAYS DOING THE RIGHT THING.
WE REALLY DON'T HAVE TIME FOR YOUR CHILDISH OPTIMISM RIGHT NOW.
I KNOW WHAT'S BEST FOR US, AND IT'S LEAVING THIS SECOND. NOW LET'S GO.
THEY CAN HANDLE THEMSELVES.
I HOPE SO.

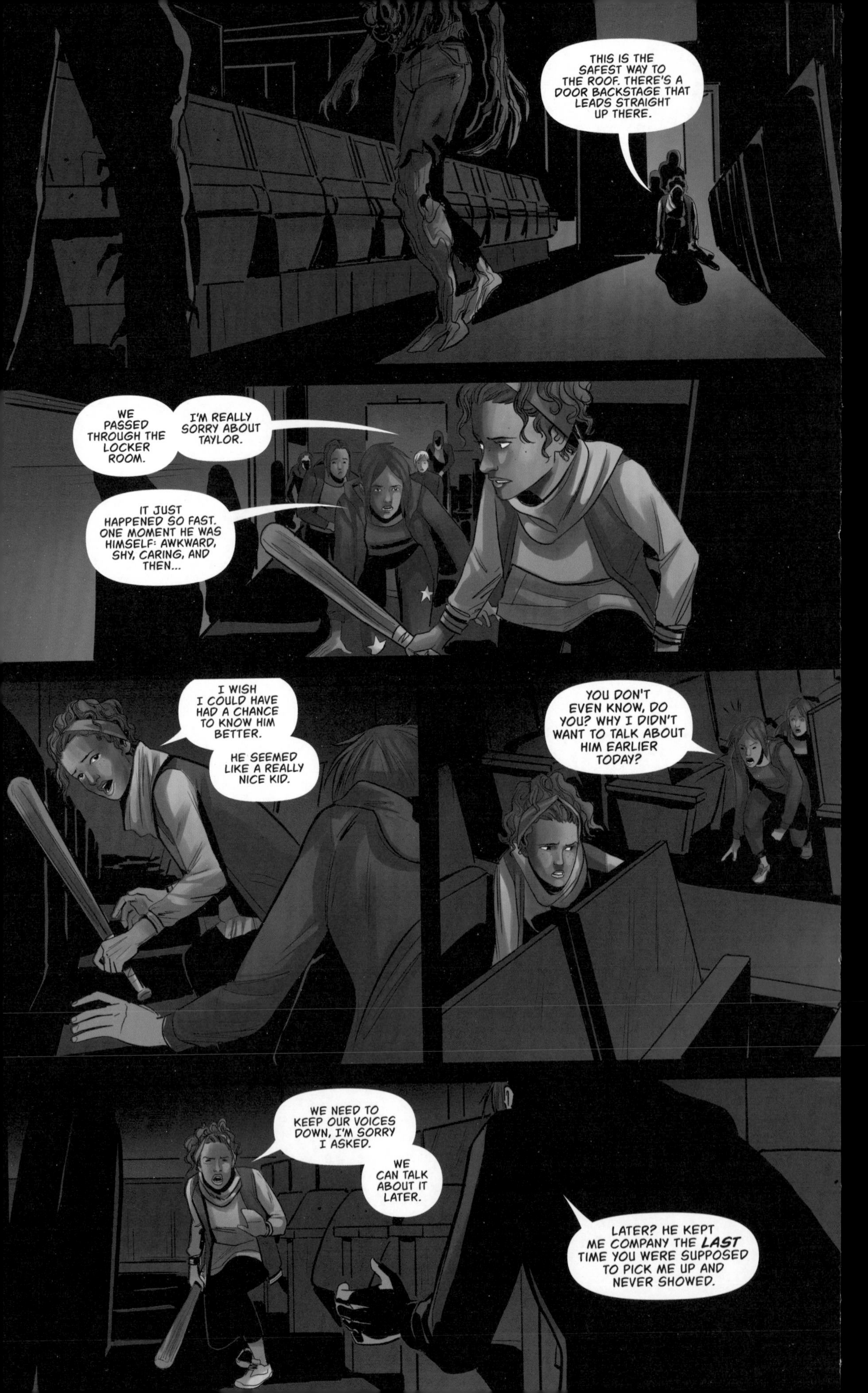
THIS IS THE SAFEST WAY TO THE ROOF. THERE'S A DOOR BACKSTAGE THAT LEADS STRAIGHT UP THERE.
WE PASSED THROUGH THE LOCKER ROOM.
I'M REALLY SORRY ABOUT TAYLOR.
IT JUST HAPPENED SO FAST. ONE MOMENT HE WAS HIMSELF: AWKWARD, SHY, CARING, AND THEN...
I WISH I COULD HAVE HAD A CHANCE TO KNOW HIM BETTER.
HE SEEMED LIKE A REALLY NICE KID.
YOU DON'T EVEN KNOW, DO YOU? WHY I DIDN'T WANT TO TALK ABOUT HIM EARLIER TODAY?
WE NEED TO KEEP OUR VOICES DOWN, I'M SORRY I ASKED.
WE CAN TALK ABOUT IT LATER.
LATER? HE KEPT ME COMPANY THE LAST TIME YOU WERE SUPPOSED TO PICK ME UP AND NEVER SHOWED.

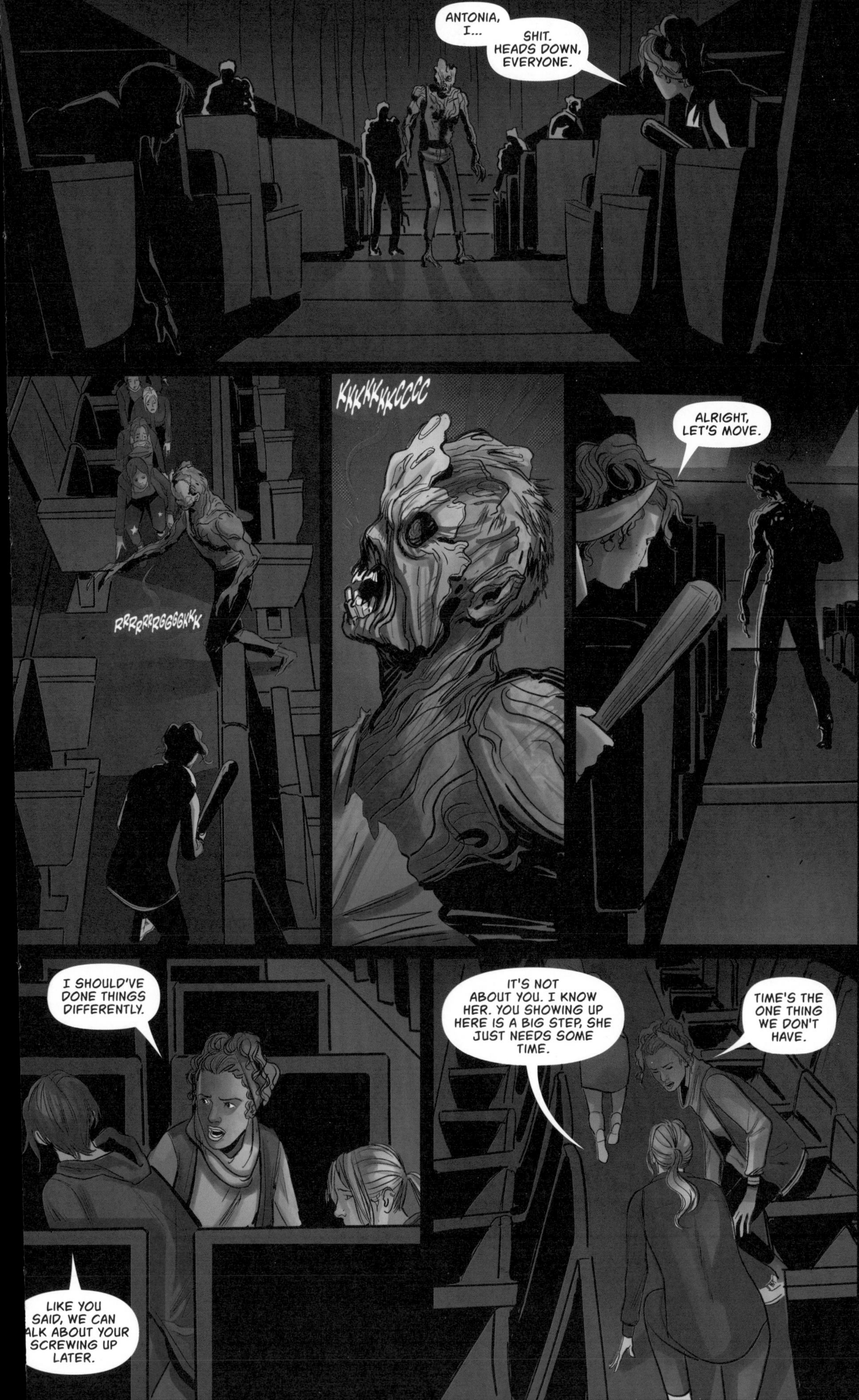
ANTONIA, I...
SHIT. HEADS DOWN, EVERYONE.
RRRRRRGGGGKKK
KKKKKKKCCCC
ALRIGHT, LET'S MOVE.
I SHOULD'VE DONE THINGS DIFFERENTLY.
LIKE YOU SAID, WE CAN ALK ABOUT YOUR SCREWING UP LATER.
IT'S NOT ABOUT YOU. I KNOW HER. YOU SHOWING UP HERE IS A BIG STEP, SHE JUST NEEDS SOME TIME.
TIME'S THE ONE THING WE DON'T HAVE.

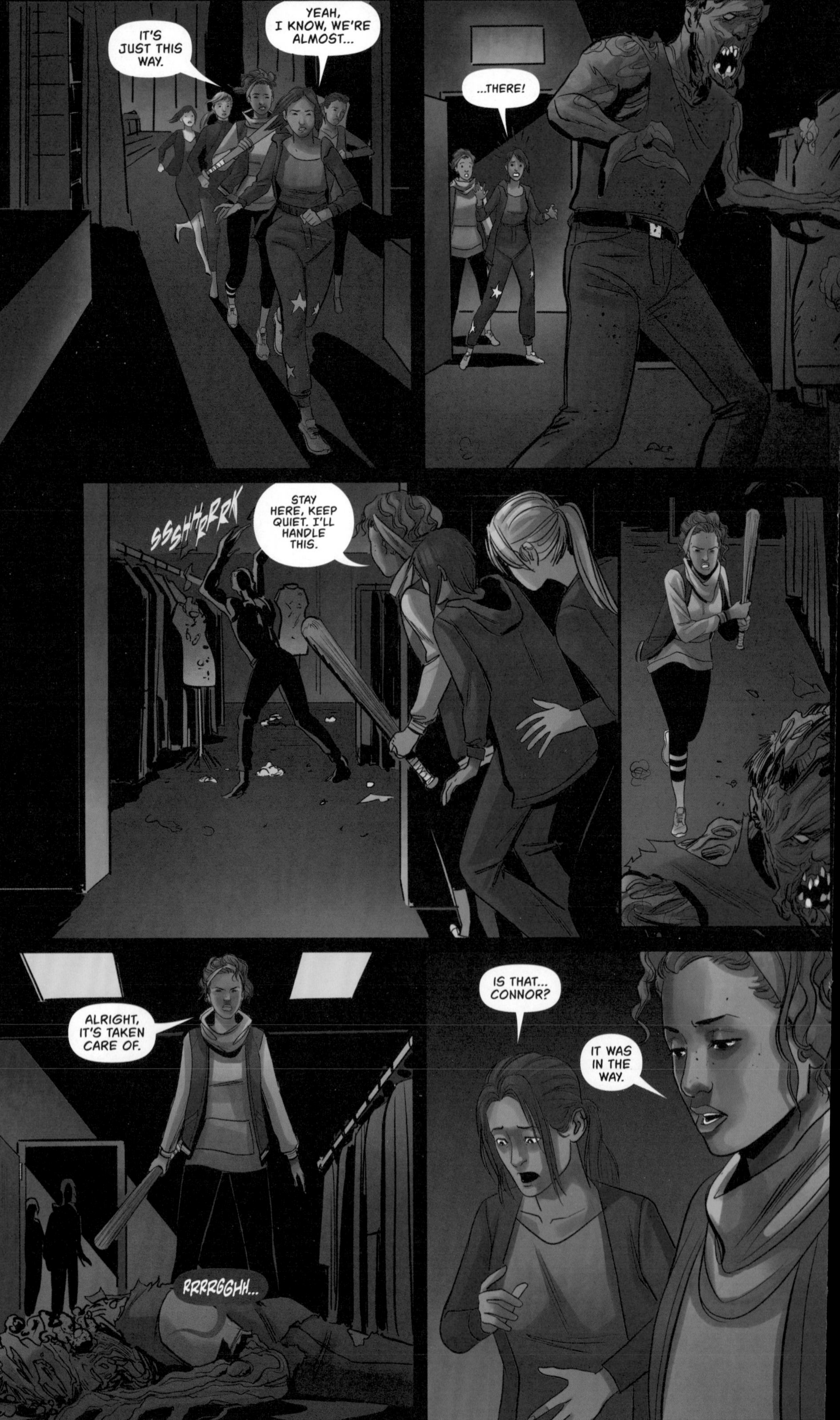
IT'S JUST THIS WAY.
YEAH, I KNOW, WE'RE ALMOST...
...THERE!
SSSHHRRRK
STAY HERE, KEEP QUIET. I'LL HANDLE THIS.
ALRIGHT, IT'S TAKEN CARE OF.
RRRRGGHH...
IS THAT... CONNOR?
IT WAS IN THE WAY.

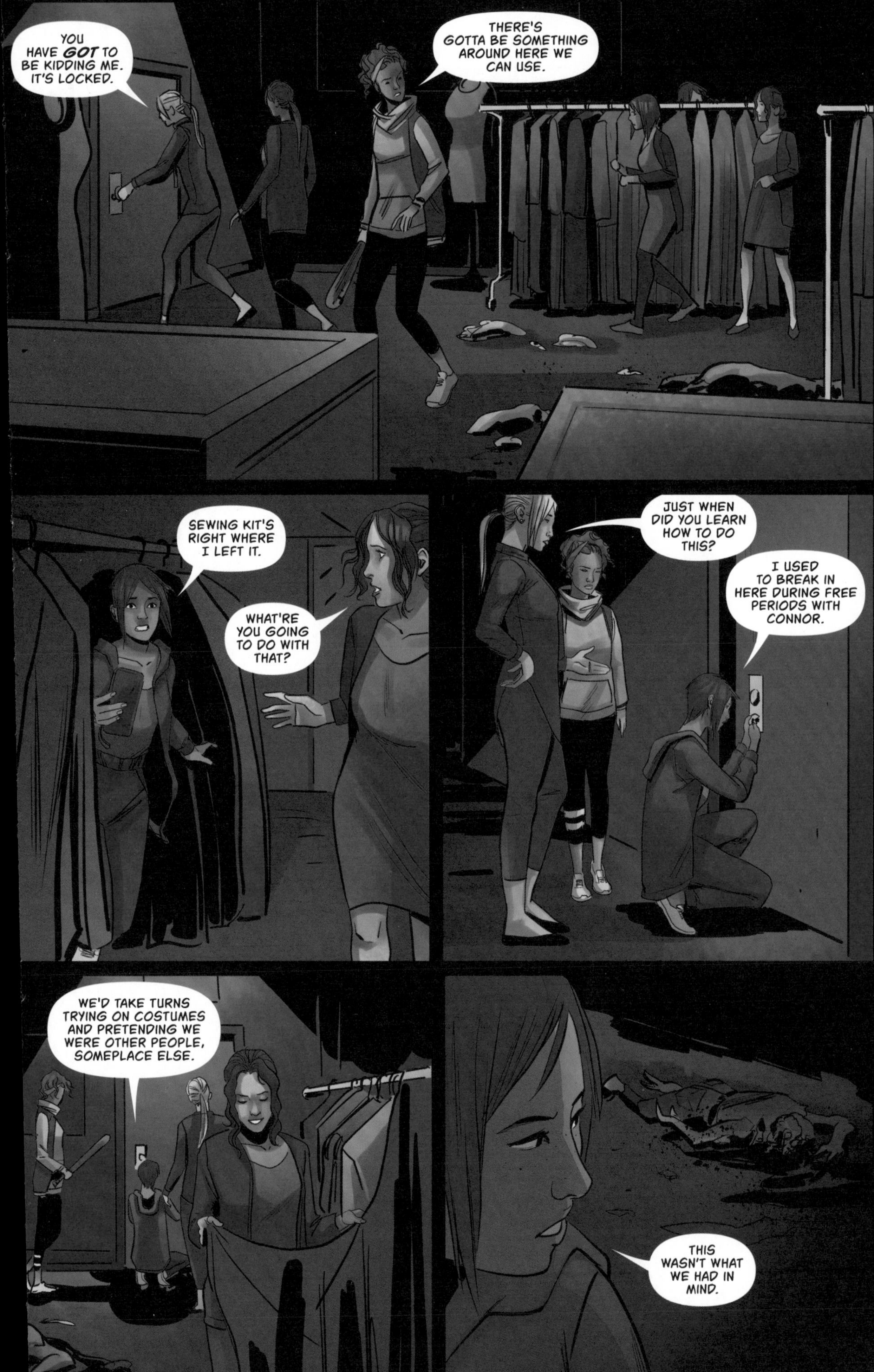
YOU HAVE GOT TO BE KIDDING ME. IT'S LOCKED.
THERE'S GOTTA BE SOMETHING AROUND HERE WE CAN USE.
SEWING KIT'S RIGHT WHERE I LEFT IT.
WHAT'RE YOU GOING TO DO WITH THAT?
JUST WHEN DID YOU LEARN HOW TO DO THIS?
I USED TO BREAK IN HERE DURING FREE PERIODS WITH CONNOR.
WE'D TAKE TURNS TRYING ON COSTUMES AND PRETENDING WE WERE OTHER PEOPLE, SOMEPLACE ELSE.
THIS WASN'T WHAT WE HAD IN MIND.

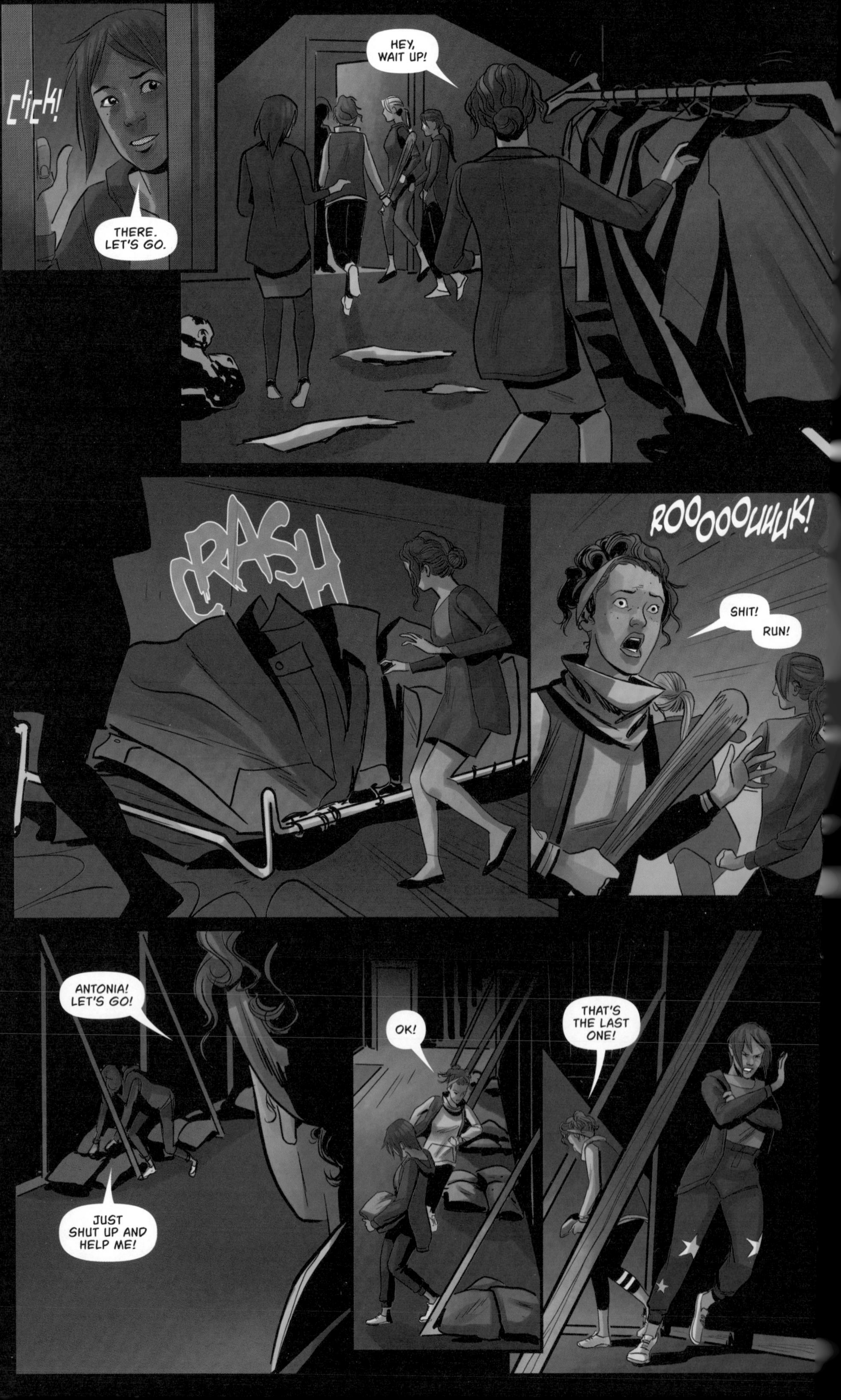

CLICK!
THERE. LET'S GO.
HEY, WAIT UP!
CRASH
ROOOOOUUUK!
SHIT!
RUN!
ANTONIA! LET'S GO!
JUST SHUT UP AND HELP ME!
OK!
THAT'S THE LAST ONE!

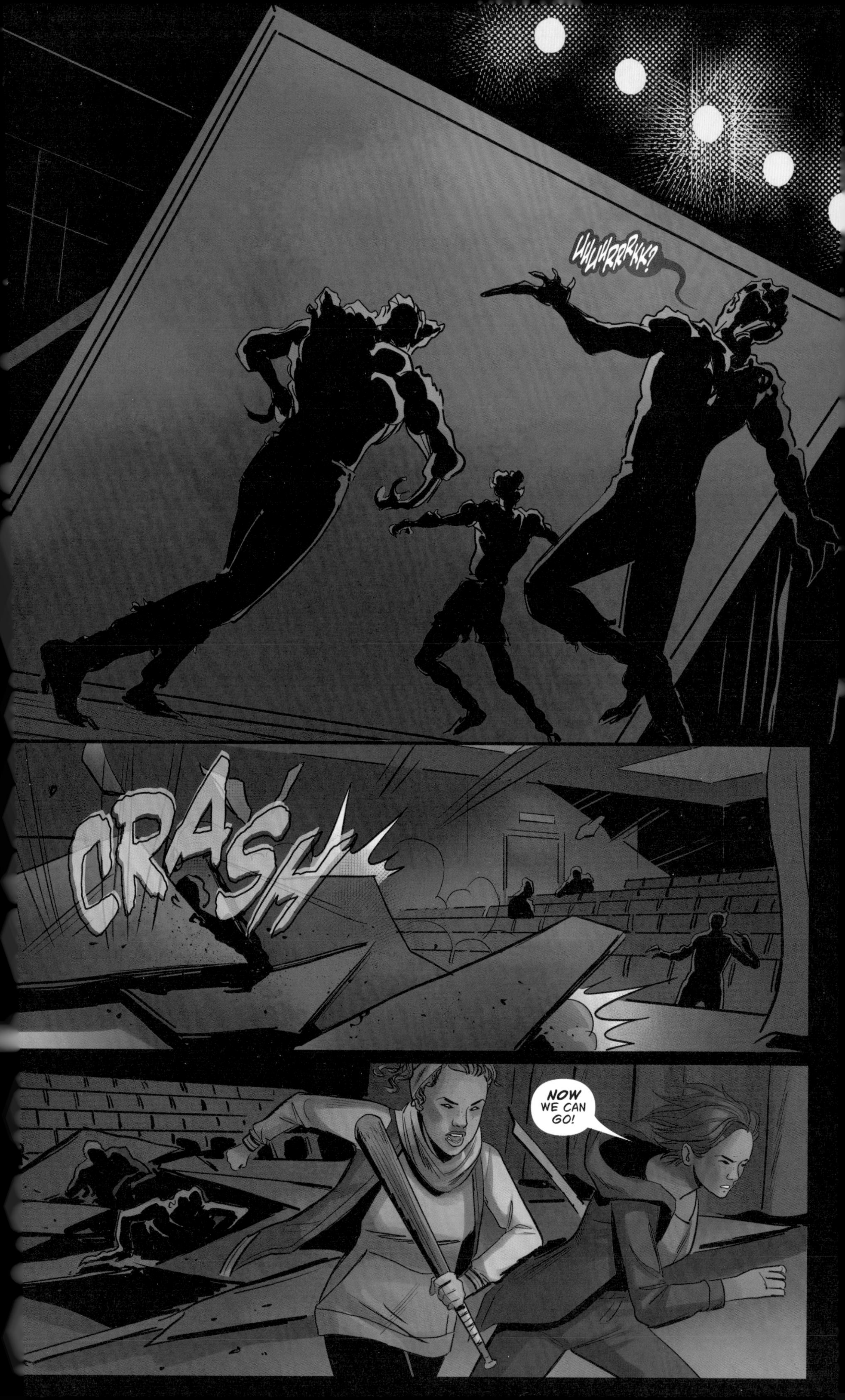
UUUHRRRKK?
CRASH
NOW WE CAN GO!

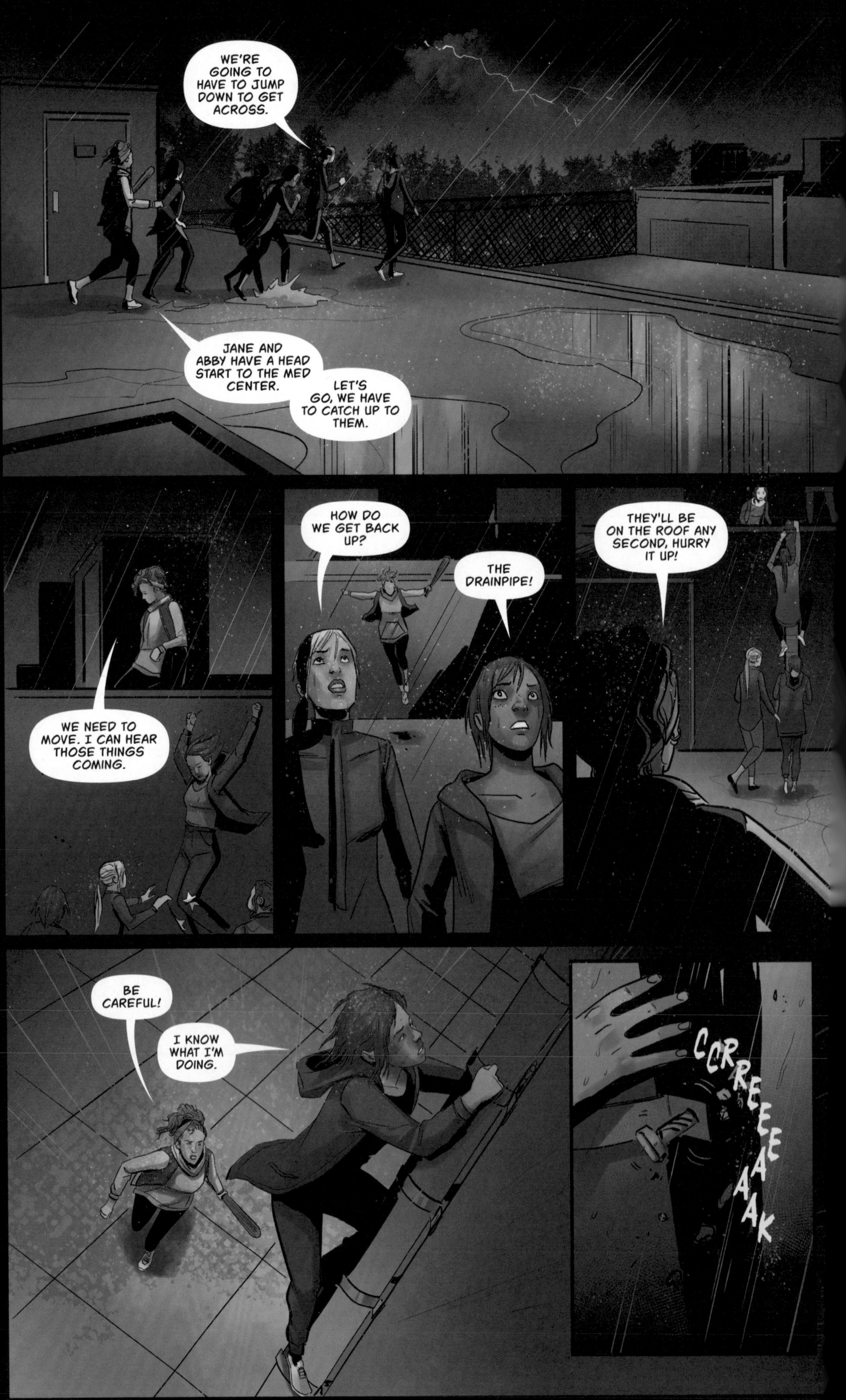
WE'RE GOING TO HAVE TO JUMP DOWN TO GET ACROSS.
JANE AND ABBY HAVE A HEAD START TO THE MED CENTER.
LET'S GO, WE HAVE TO CATCH UP TO THEM.
WE NEED TO MOVE. I CAN HEAR THOSE THINGS COMING.
HOW DO WE GET BACK UP?
THE DRAINPIPE!
THEY'LL BE ON THE ROOF ANY SECOND, HURRY IT UP!
BE CAREFUL!
I KNOW WHAT I'M DOING.
CCRREEEEAAAK

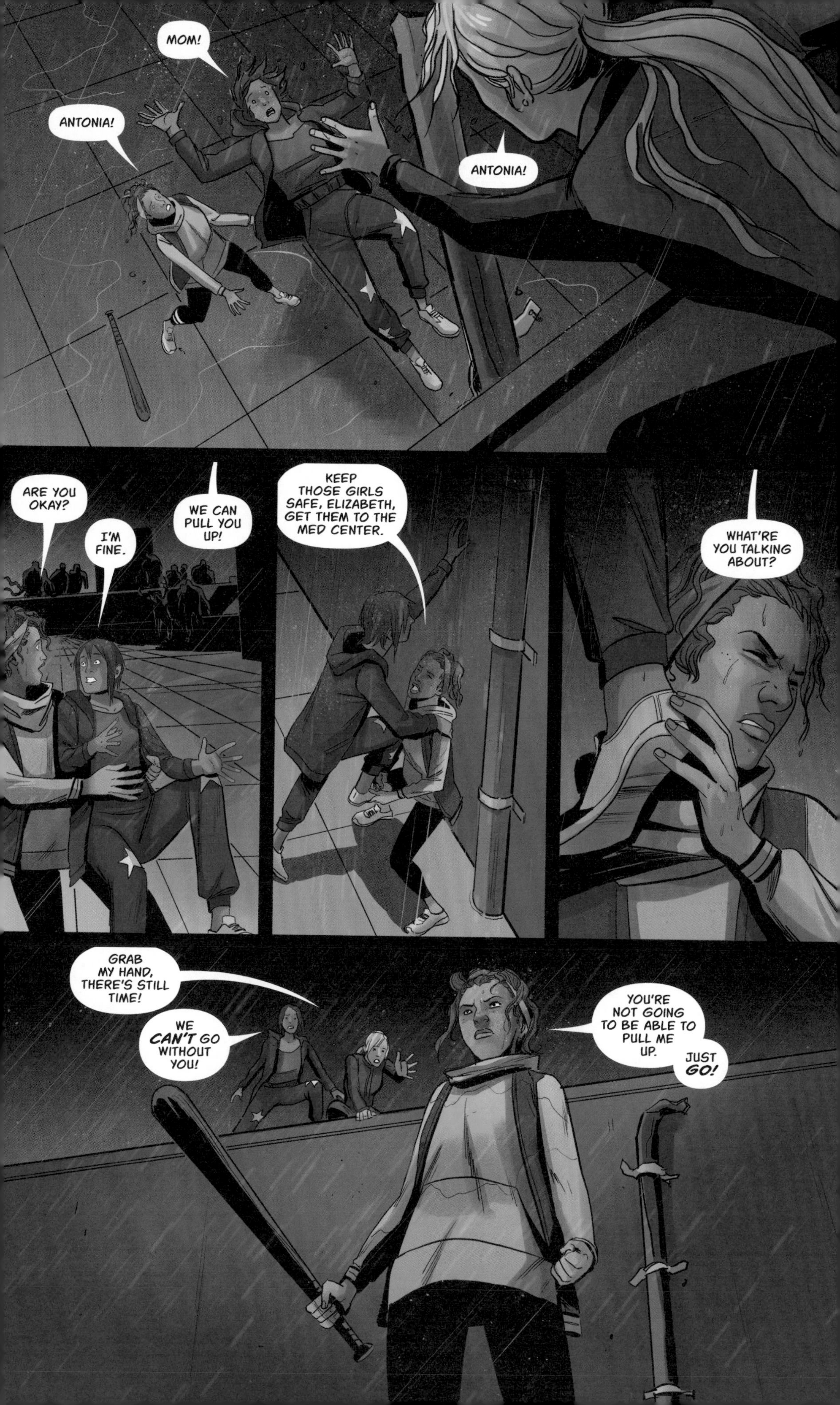
MOM!
ANTONIA!
ANTONIA!
ARE YOU OKAY?
I'M FINE.
WE CAN PULL YOU UP!
KEEP THOSE GIRLS SAFE, ELIZABETH, GET THEM TO THE MED CENTER.
WHAT'RE YOU TALKING ABOUT?
GRAB MY HAND, THERE'S STILL TIME!
WE CAN'T GO WITHOUT YOU!
YOU'RE NOT GOING TO BE ABLE TO PULL ME UP.
JUST GO!

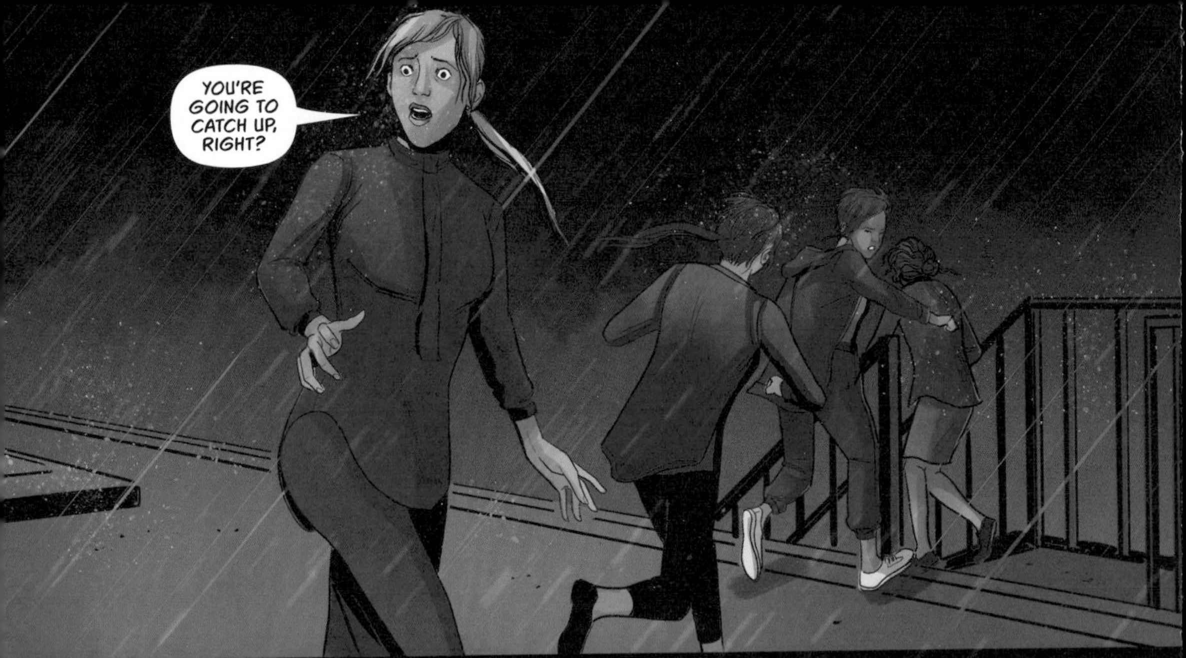
YOU'RE GOING TO CATCH UP, RIGHT?

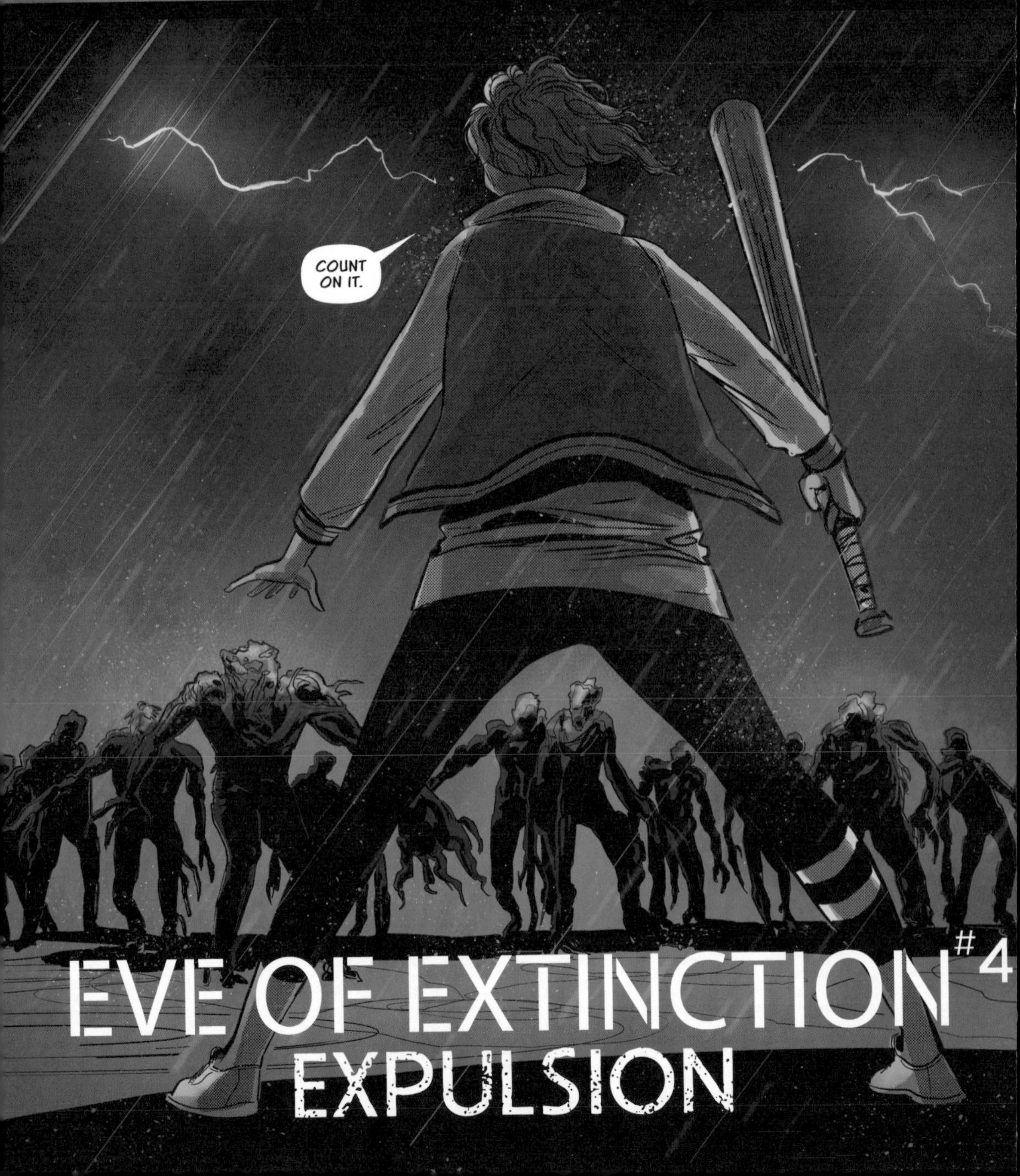
COUNT ON IT.
EVE OF EXTINCTION #4
EXPULSION

CHAPTER 5

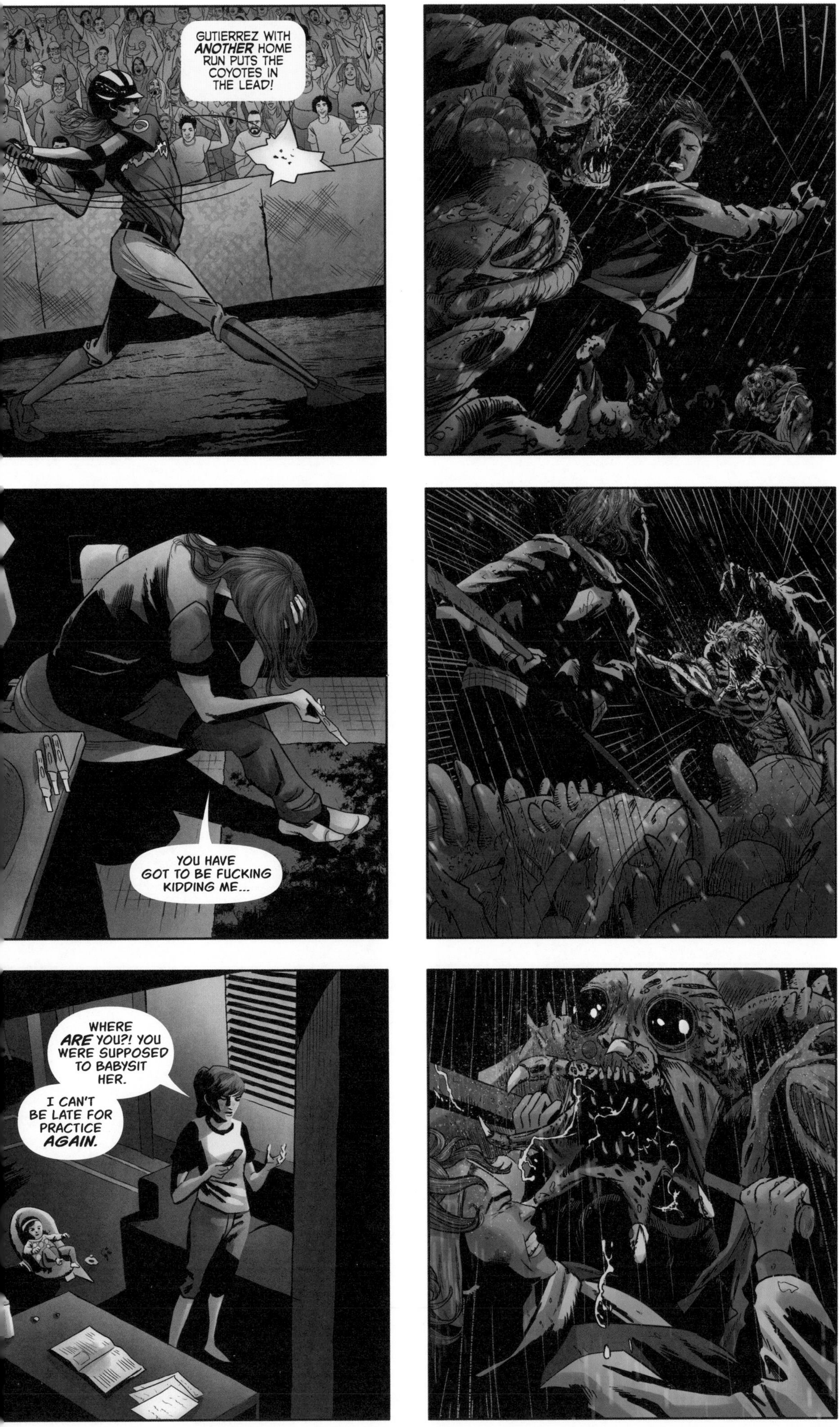
GUTIERREZ WITH ANOTHER HOME RUN PUTS THE COYOTES IN THE LEAD!
YOU HAVE GOT TO BE FUCKING KIDDING ME...
WHERE ARE YOU?! YOU WERE SUPPOSED TO BABYSIT HER.
I CAN'T BE LATE FOR PRACTICE AGAIN.

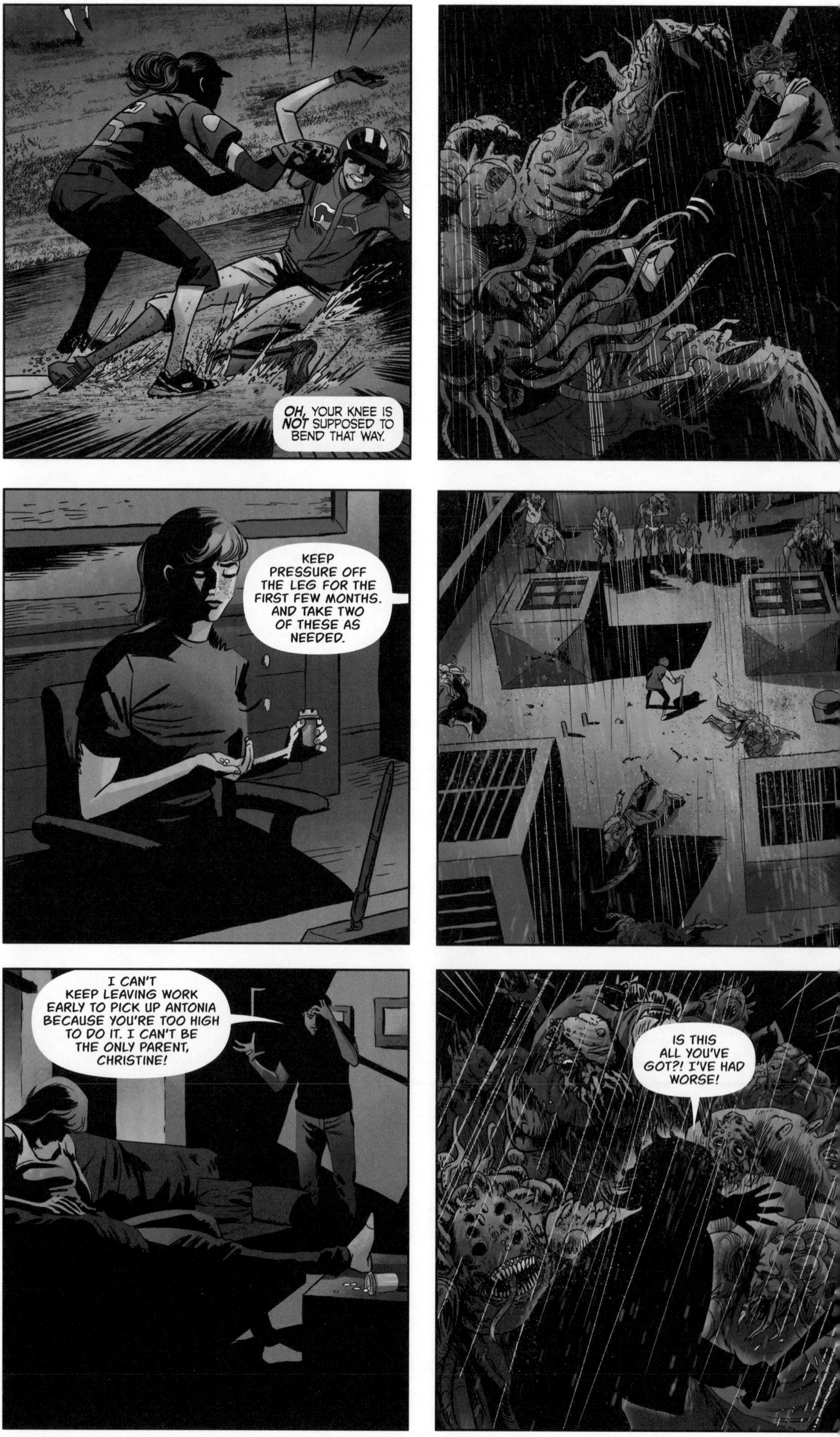
OH, YOUR KNEE IS NOT SUPPOSED TO BEND THAT WAY.
KEEP PRESSURE OFF THE LEG FOR THE FIRST FEW MONTHS. AND TAKE TWO OF THESE AS NEEDED.
I CAN'T KEEP LEAVING WORK EARLY TO PICK UP ANTONIA BECAUSE YOU'RE TOO HIGH TO DO IT. I CAN'T BE THE ONLY PARENT, CHRISTINE!
IS THIS ALL YOU'VE GOT?! I'VE HAD WORSE!

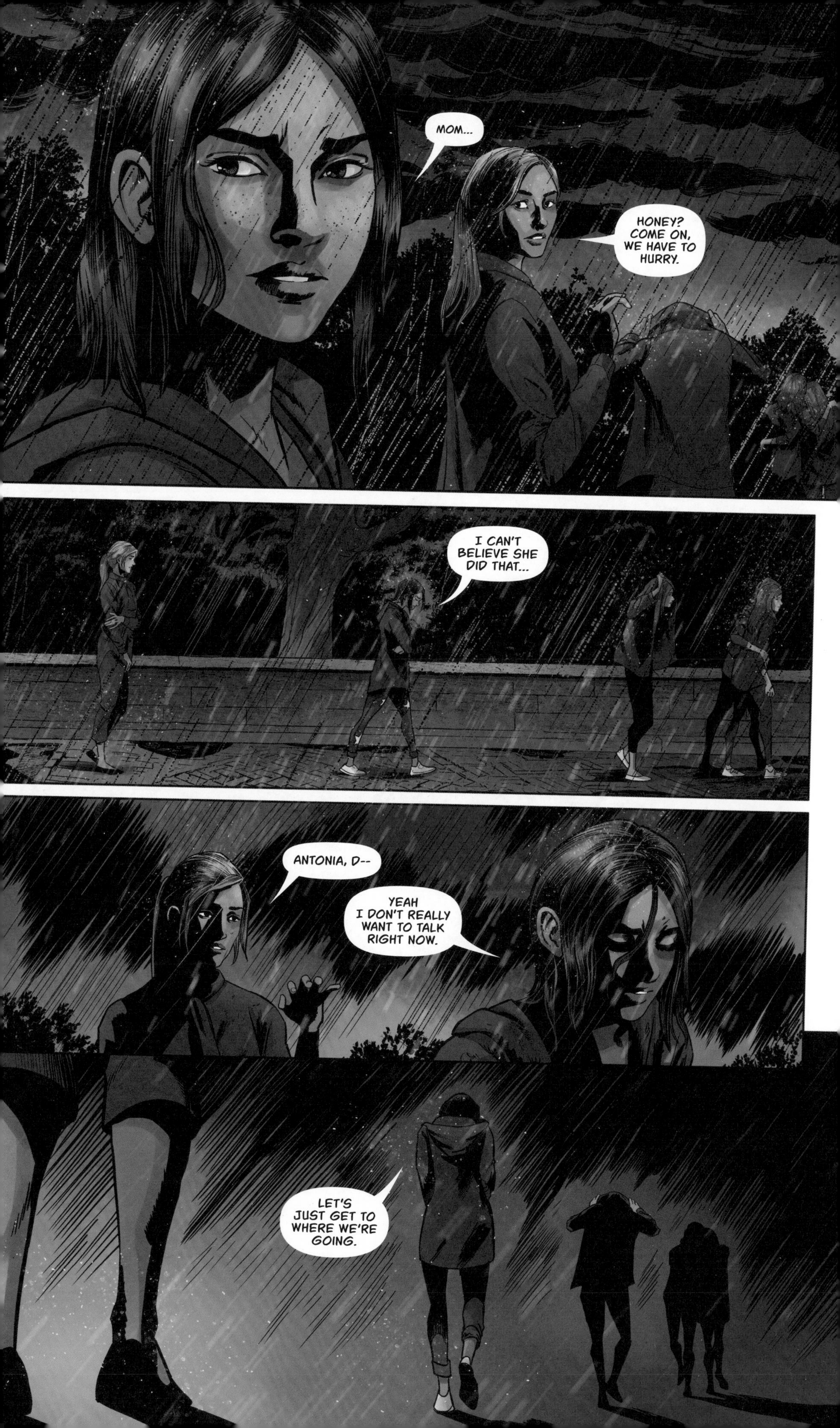
MOM...
HONEY? COME ON, WE HAVE TO HURRY.
I CAN'T BELIEVE SHE DID THAT...
ANTONIA, D--
YEAH I DON'T REALLY WANT TO TALK RIGHT NOW.
LET'S JUST GET TO WHERE WE'RE GOING.

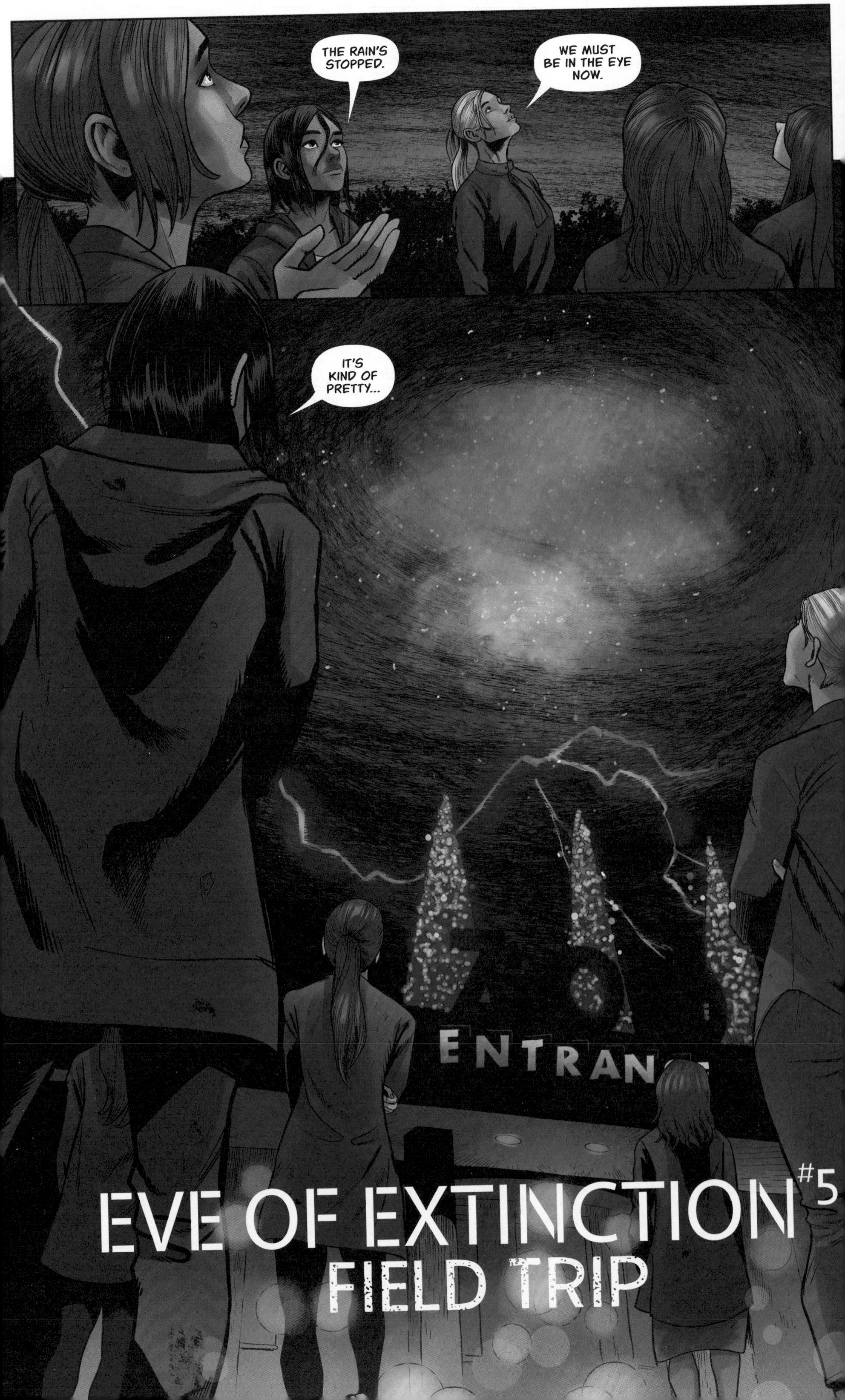

THE RAIN'S STOPPED.
WE MUST BE IN THE EYE NOW.
IT'S KIND OF PRETTY...
ENTRANC
EVE OF EXTINCTION #5
FIELD TRIP

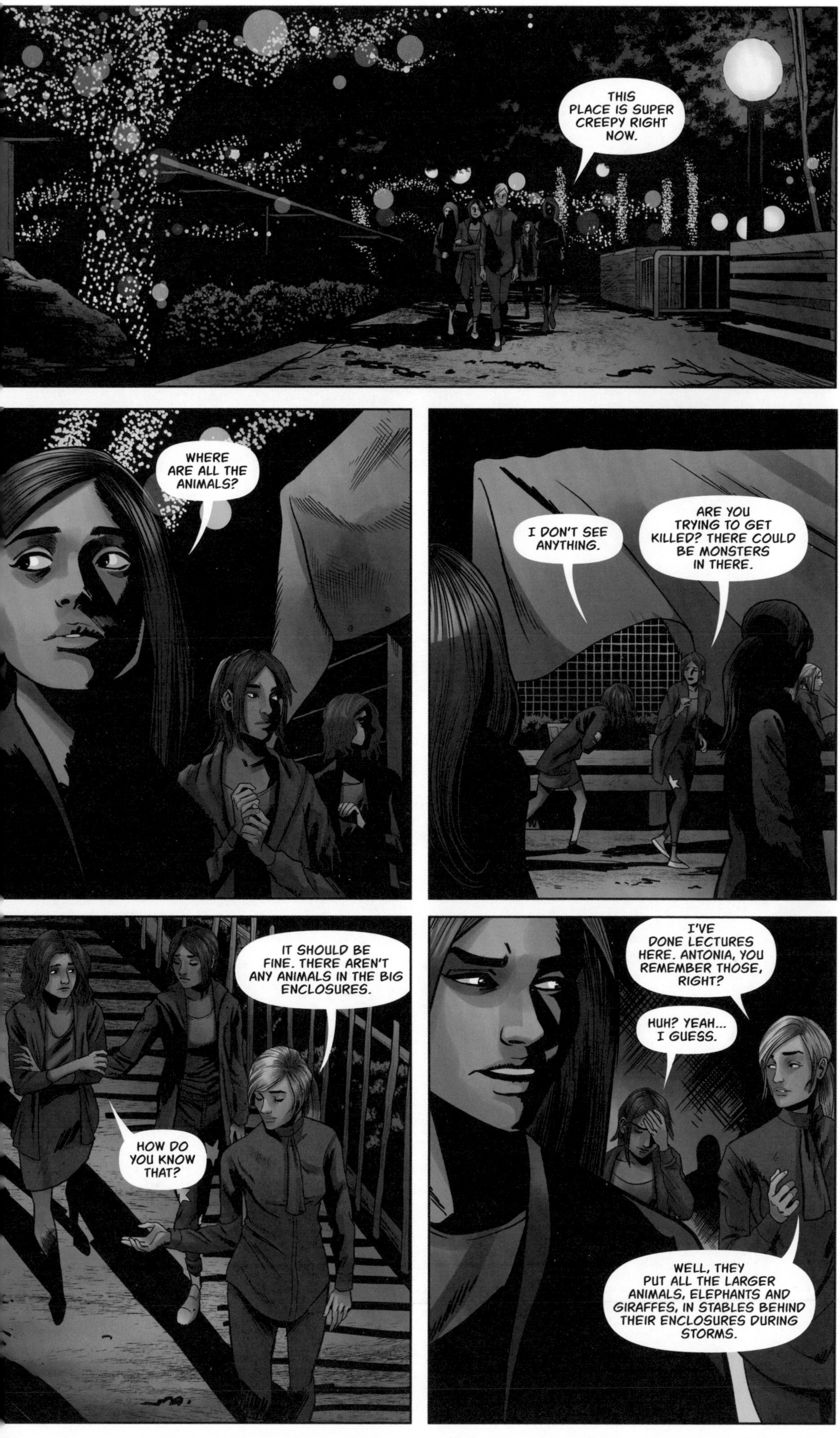
THIS PLACE IS SUPER CREEPY RIGHT NOW.
WHERE ARE ALL THE ANIMALS?
I DON'T SEE ANYTHING.
ARE YOU TRYING TO GET KILLED? THERE COULD BE MONSTERS IN THERE.
IT SHOULD BE FINE. THERE AREN'T ANY ANIMALS IN THE BIG ENCLOSURES.
HOW DO YOU KNOW THAT?
I'VE DONE LECTURES HERE. ANTONIA, YOU REMEMBER THOSE, RIGHT?
HUH? YEAH... I GUESS.
WELL, THEY PUT ALL THE LARGER ANIMALS, ELEPHANTS AND GIRAFFES, IN STABLES BEHIND THEIR ENCLOSURES DURING STORMS.

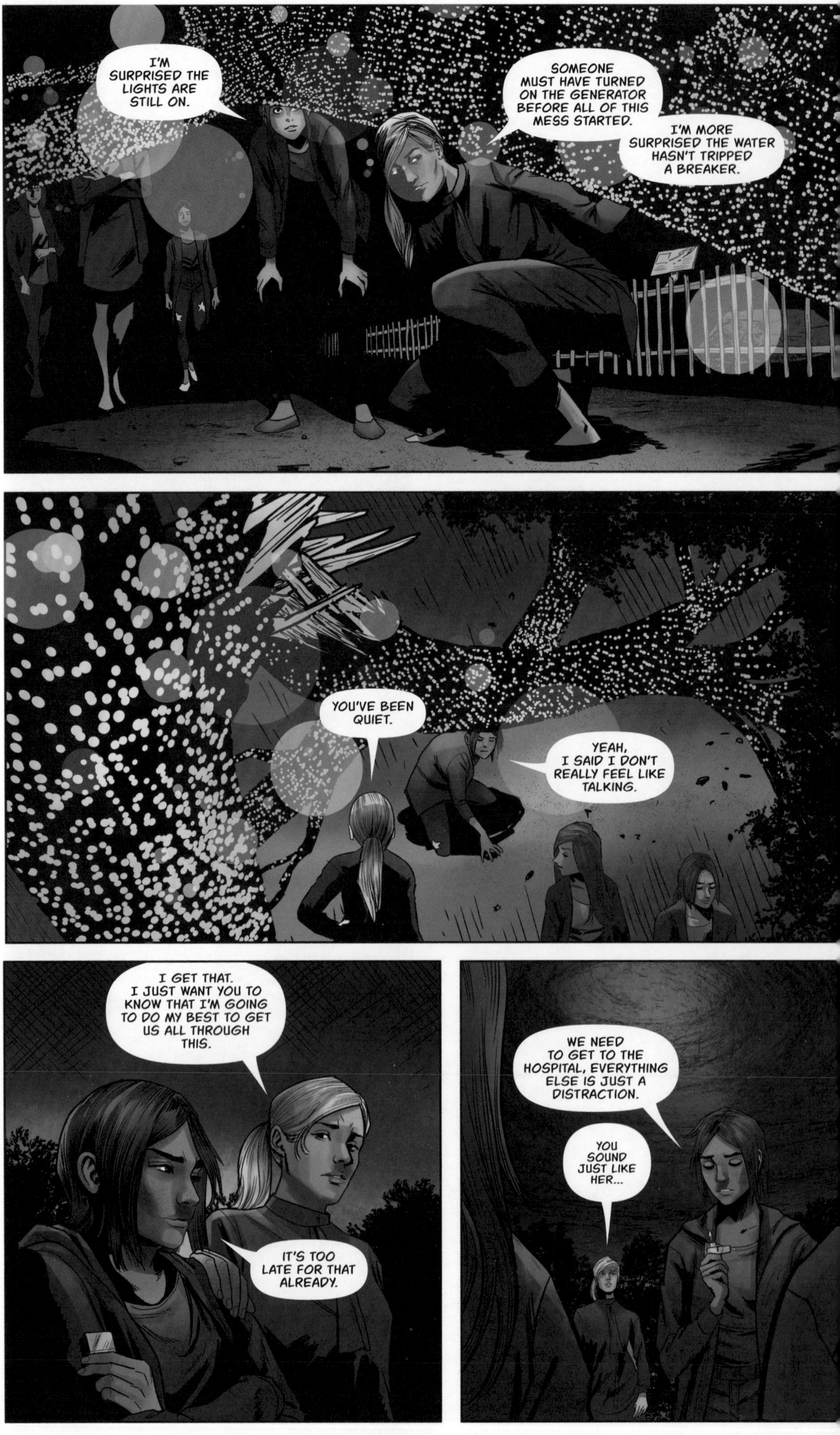
I'M SURPRISED THE LIGHTS ARE STILL ON.
SOMEONE MUST HAVE TURNED ON THE GENERATOR BEFORE ALL OF THIS MESS STARTED.
I'M MORE SURPRISED THE WATER HASN'T TRIPPED A BREAKER.
YOU'VE BEEN QUIET.
YEAH, I SAID I DON'T REALLY FEEL LIKE TALKING.
I GET THAT. I JUST WANT YOU TO KNOW THAT I'M GOING TO DO MY BEST TO GET US ALL THROUGH THIS.
IT'S TOO LATE FOR THAT ALREADY.
WE NEED TO GET TO THE HOSPITAL, EVERYTHING ELSE IS JUST A DISTRACTION.
YOU SOUND JUST LIKE HER...

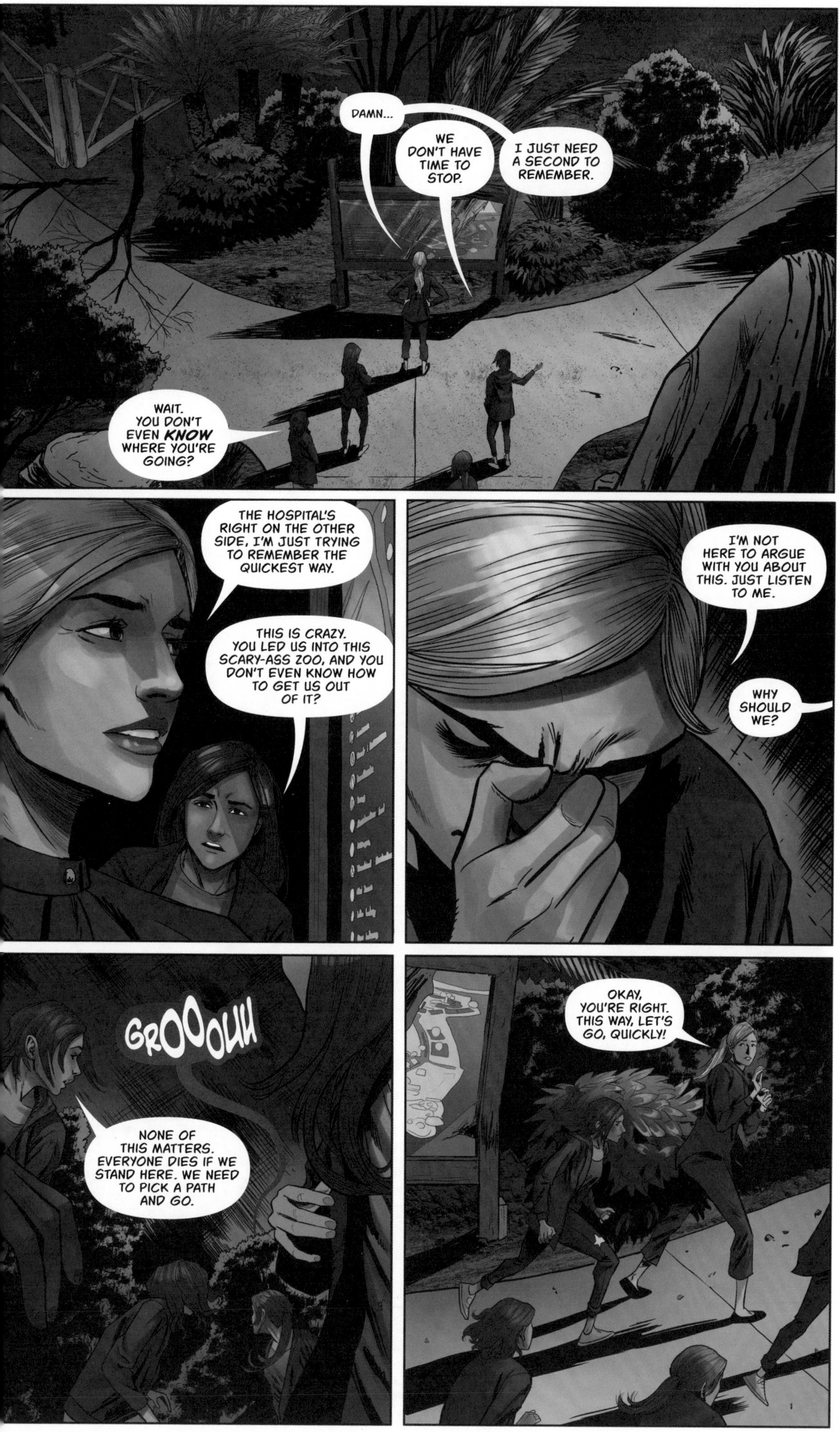
DAMN...
WE DON'T HAVE TIME TO STOP.
I JUST NEED A SECOND TO REMEMBER.
WAIT. YOU DON'T EVEN **KNOW** WHERE YOU'RE GOING?
THE HOSPITAL'S RIGHT ON THE OTHER SIDE, I'M JUST TRYING TO REMEMBER THE QUICKEST WAY.
THIS IS CRAZY. YOU LED US INTO THIS SCARY-ASS ZOO, AND YOU DON'T EVEN KNOW HOW TO GET US OUT OF IT?
I'M NOT HERE TO ARGUE WITH YOU ABOUT THIS. JUST LISTEN TO ME.
WHY SHOULD WE?
GROOOUH
NONE OF THIS MATTERS. EVERYONE DIES IF WE STAND HERE. WE NEED TO PICK A PATH AND GO.
OKAY, YOU'RE RIGHT. THIS WAY, LET'S GO, QUICKLY!

AAAA*AAAAHH*HH!

WAIT!

NO! I'M NOT GOING TO DIE HERE!

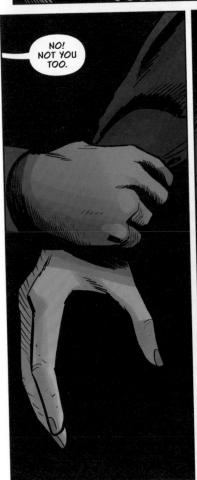

NO! NOT YOU TOO.

DON'T GO! IT'S NOT SAFE!

WE *HAVE* TO GO AFTER HER.

I KNOW. IT'S JUST...

I KNOW...

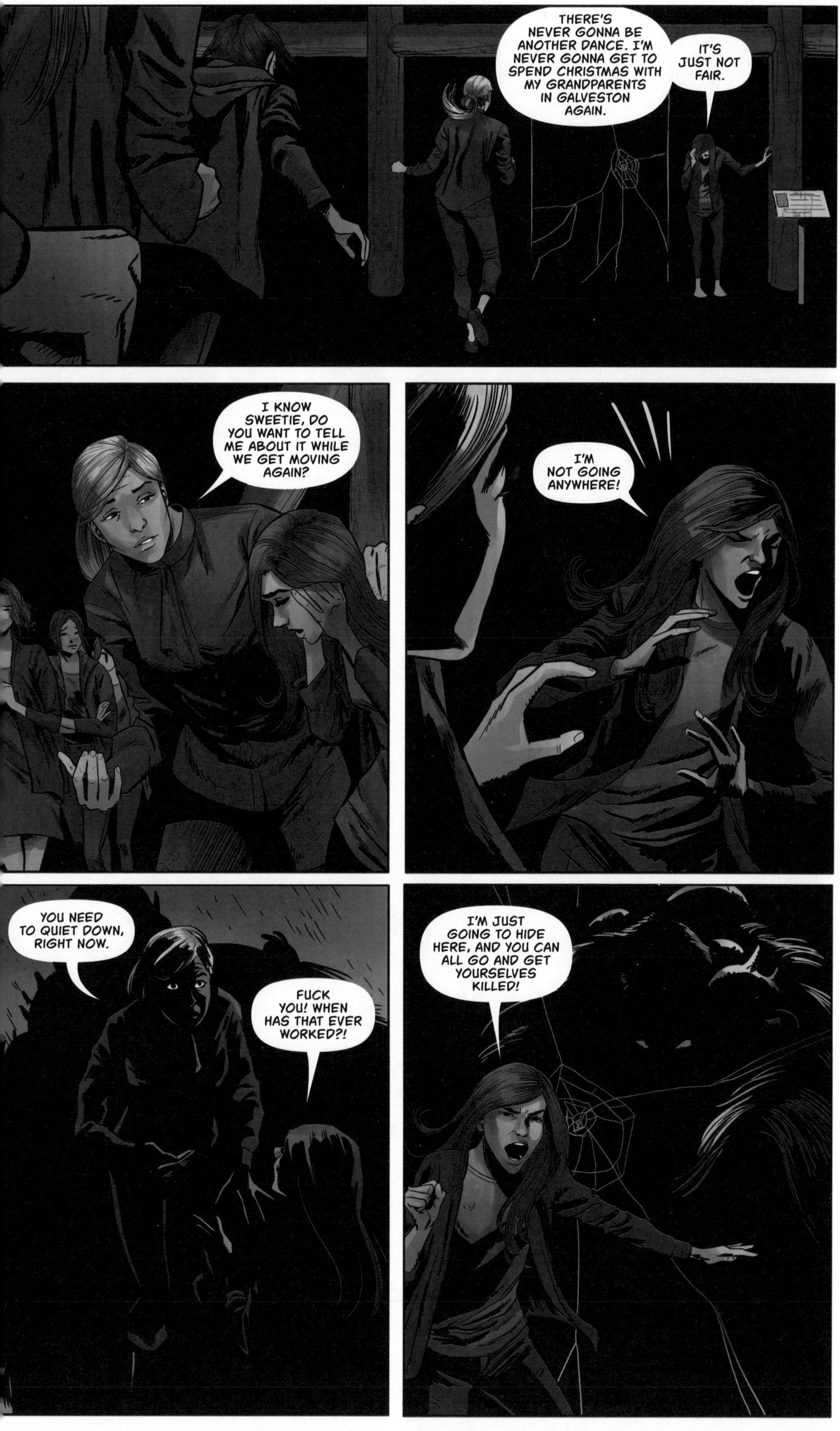
THERE'S NEVER GONNA BE ANOTHER DANCE. I'M NEVER GONNA GET TO SPEND CHRISTMAS WITH MY GRANDPARENTS IN GALVESTON AGAIN.
IT'S JUST NOT FAIR.
I KNOW SWEETIE, DO YOU WANT TO TELL ME ABOUT IT WHILE WE GET MOVING AGAIN?
I'M NOT GOING ANYWHERE!
YOU NEED TO QUIET DOWN, RIGHT NOW.
FUCK YOU! WHEN HAS THAT EVER WORKED?!
I'M JUST GOING TO HIDE HERE, AND YOU CAN ALL GO AND GET YOURSELVES KILLED!

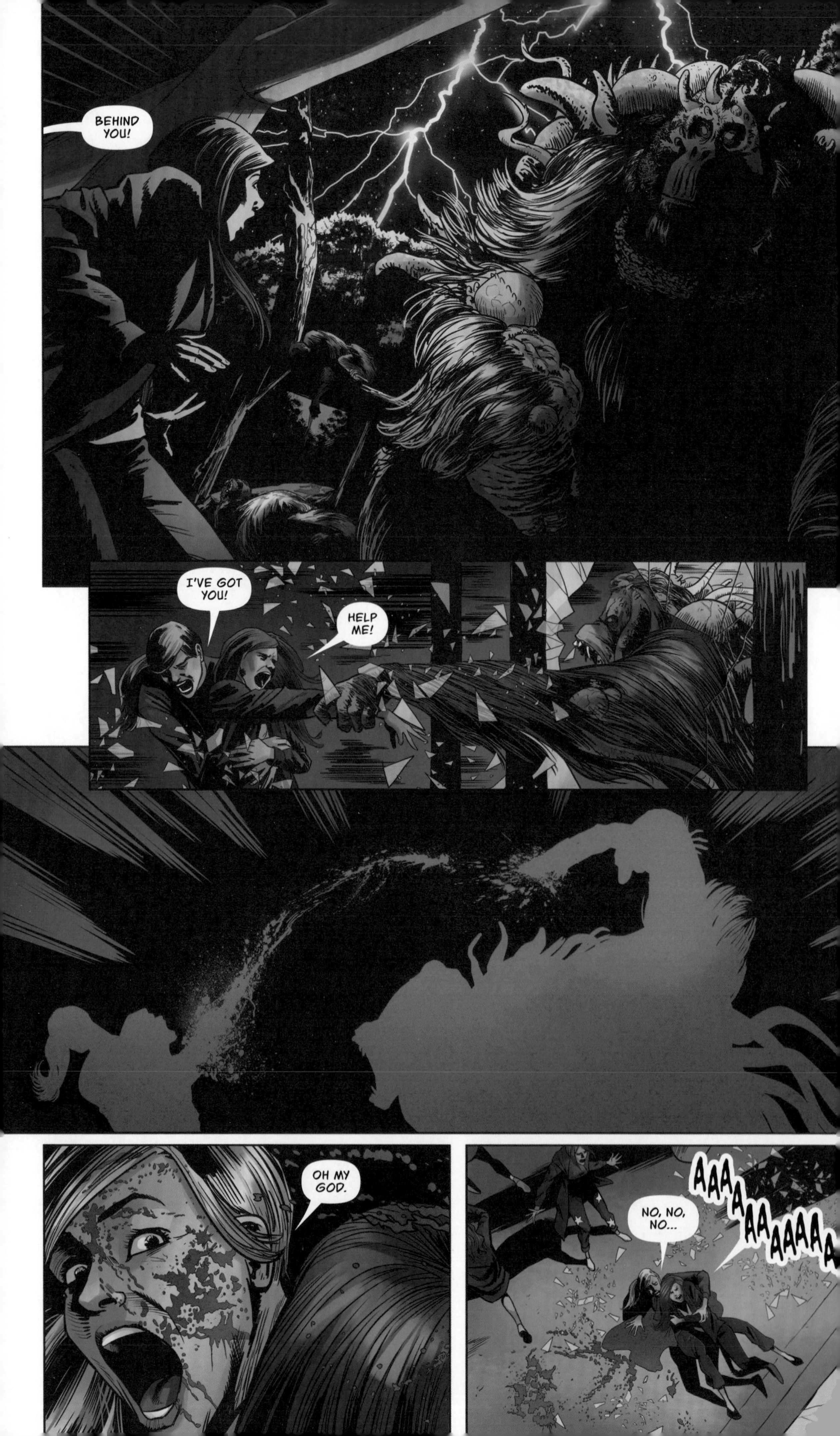
BEHIND YOU!
I'VE GOT YOU!
HELP ME!
OH MY GOD.
NO, NO, NO...
AAAAAAAAAAA

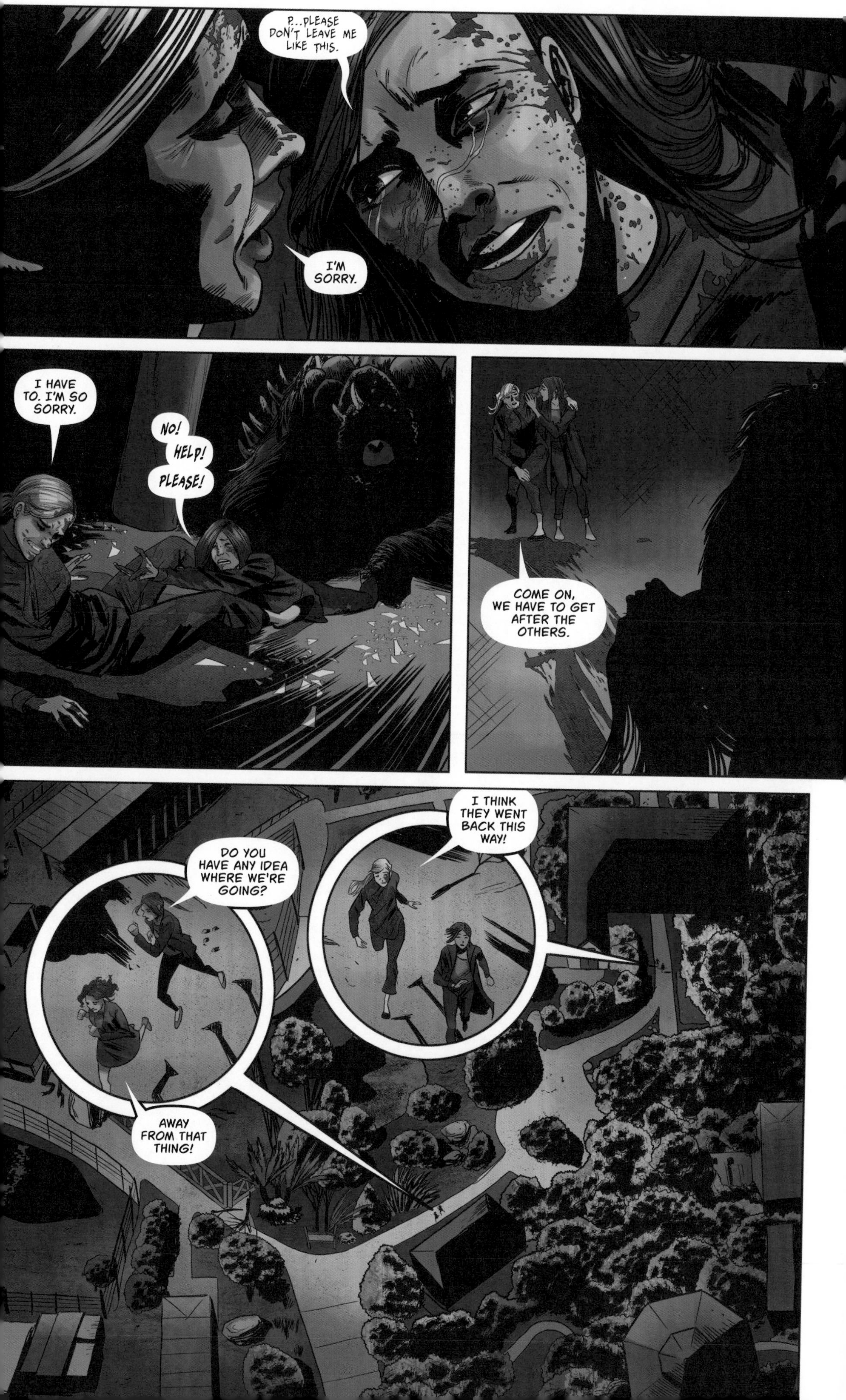
P...PLEASE DON'T LEAVE ME LIKE THIS.
I'M SORRY.
I HAVE TO. I'M SO SORRY.
NO!
HELP!
PLEASE!
COME ON, WE HAVE TO GET AFTER THE OTHERS.
DO YOU HAVE ANY IDEA WHERE WE'RE GOING?
AWAY FROM THAT THING!
I THINK THEY WENT BACK THIS WAY!

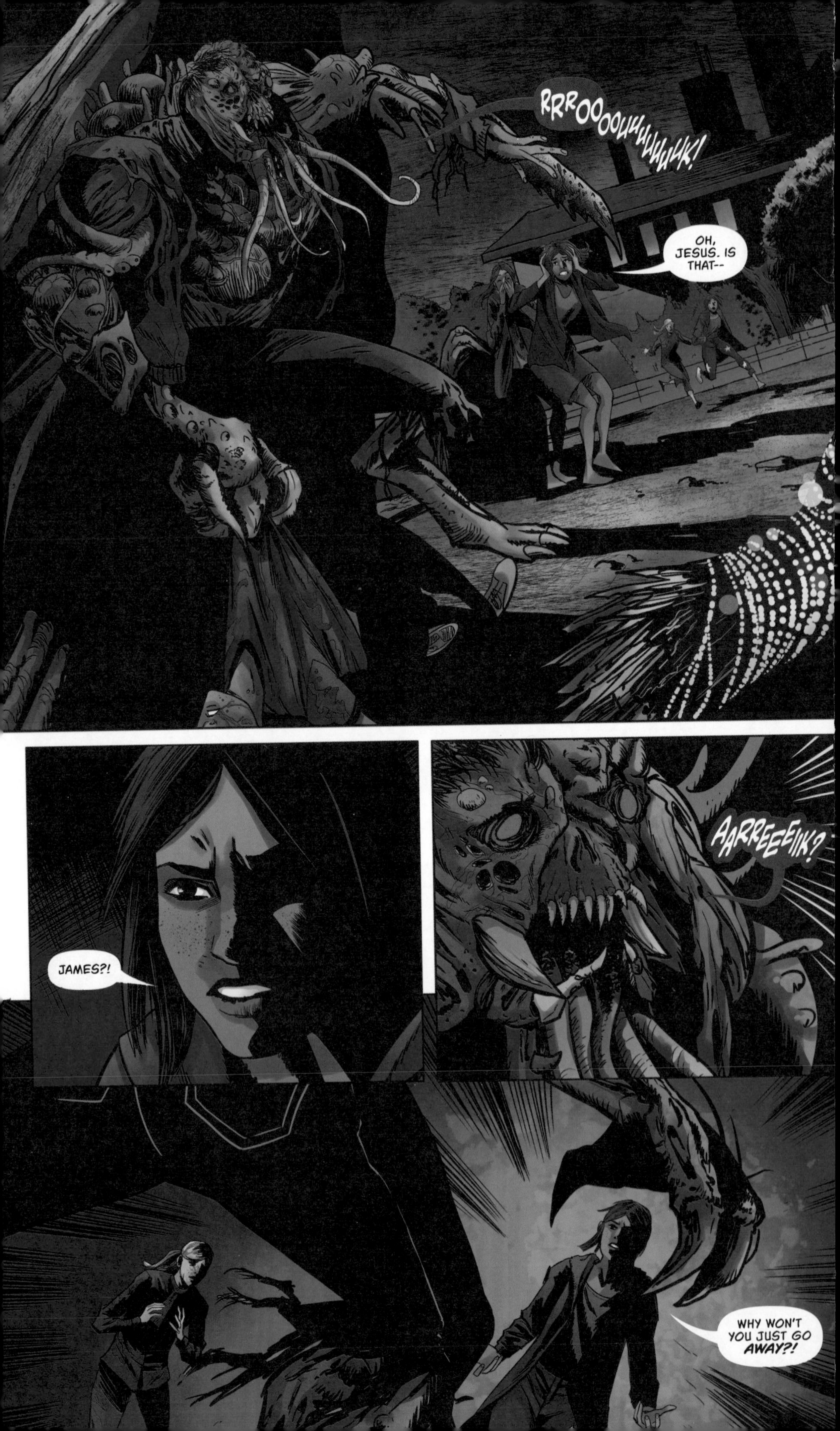
RRROOOUUUUUUUK!
OH, JESUS. IS THAT--
JAMES?!
AARREEEIIK?
WHY WON'T YOU JUST GO AWAY?!

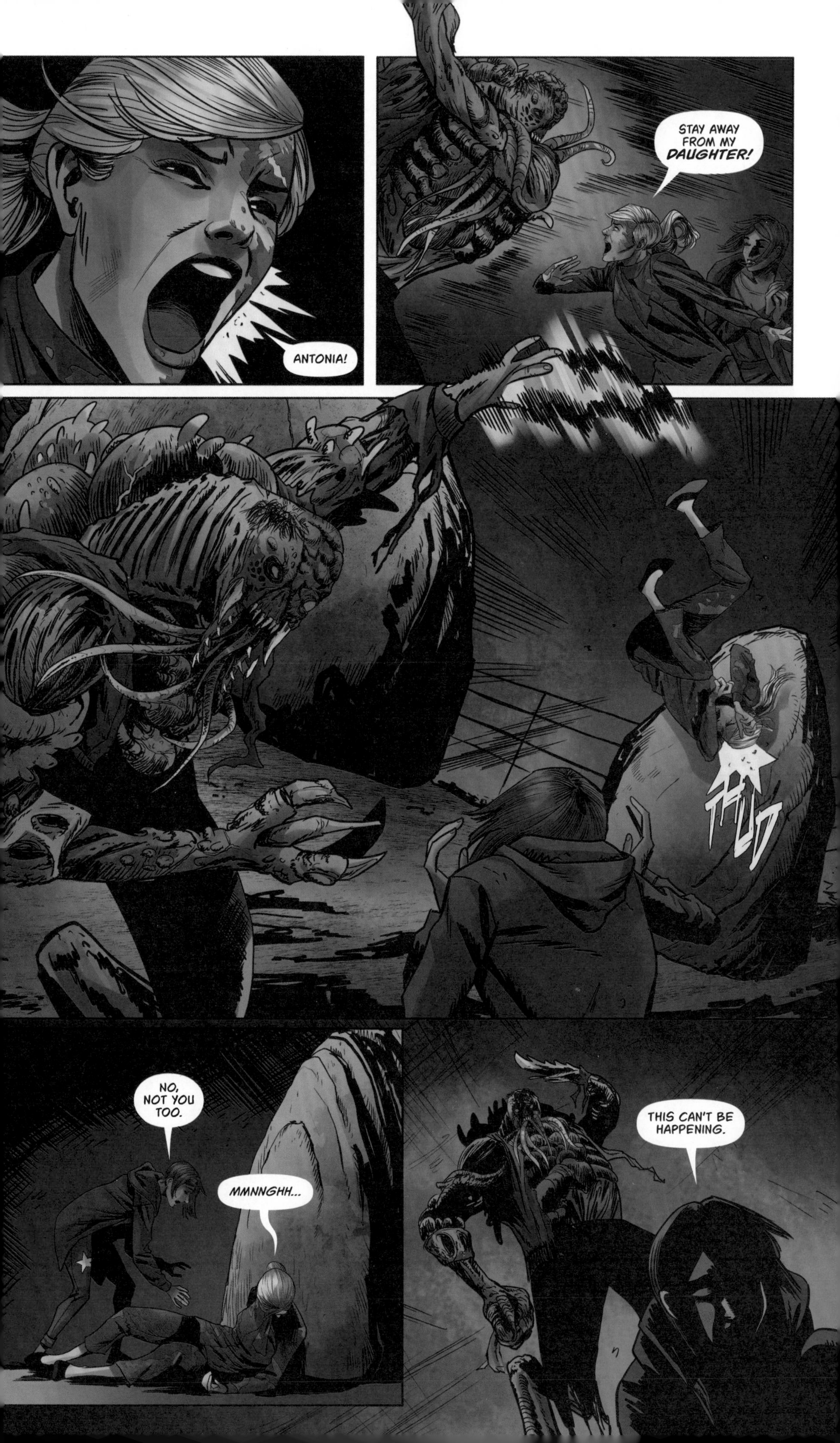
ANTONIA!
STAY AWAY FROM MY DAUGHTER!
THUD
NO, NOT YOU TOO.
MMNNGHH...
THIS CAN'T BE HAPPENING.

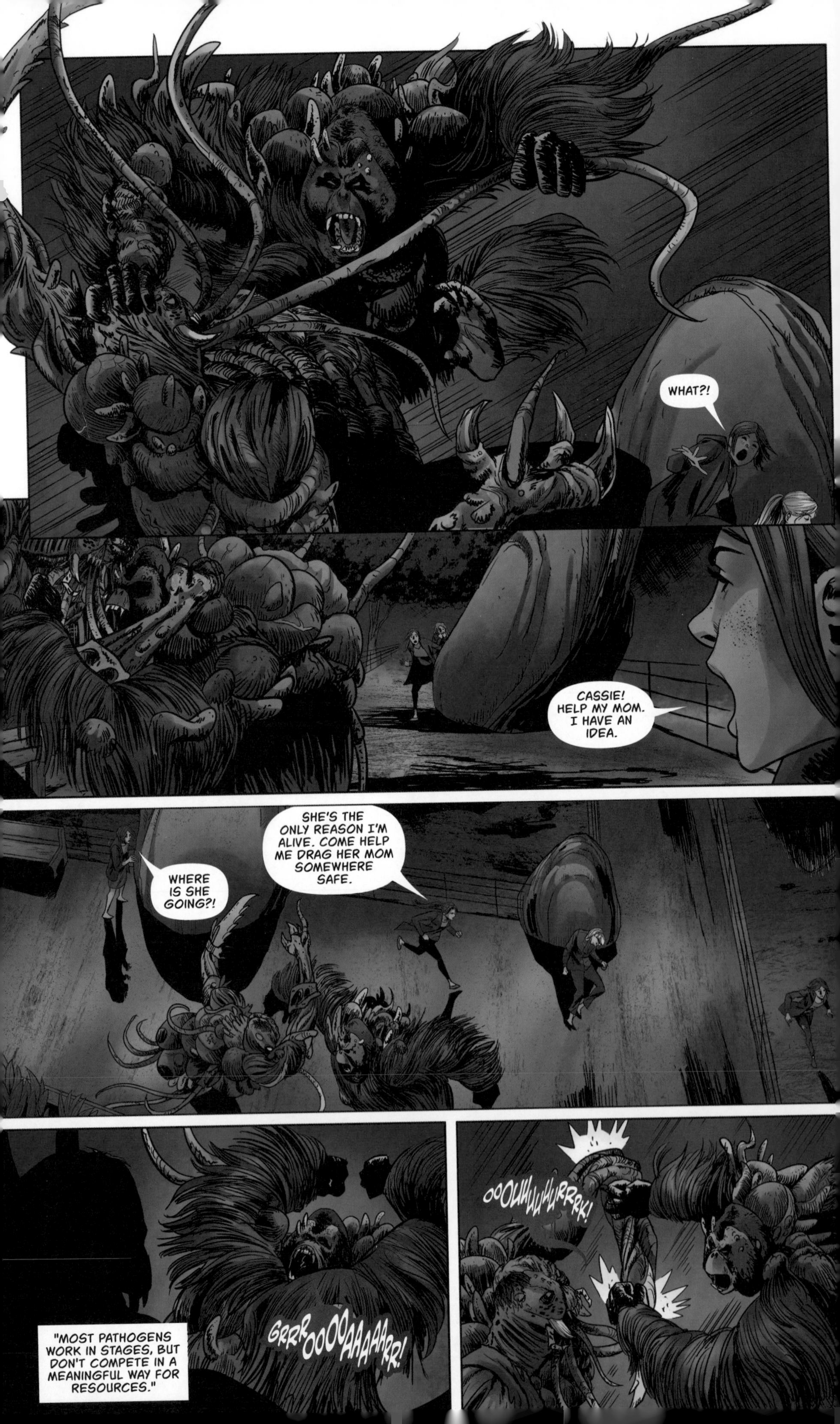
WHAT?!
CASSIE! HELP MY MOM. I HAVE AN IDEA.
WHERE IS SHE GOING?!
SHE'S THE ONLY REASON I'M ALIVE. COME HELP ME DRAG HER MOM SOMEWHERE SAFE.
"MOST PATHOGENS WORK IN STAGES, BUT DON'T COMPETE IN A MEANINGFUL WAY FOR RESOURCES."
GRRROOOOAAAAARR!
OOOUUUUUURRRK!

RROOOUUUK!

"BUT THEY SEE EACH OTHER AS COMPETITION.

"A THREAT TO EACH OTHER'S SURVIVAL."

CCC RRIIIK

VRIP

THUNK

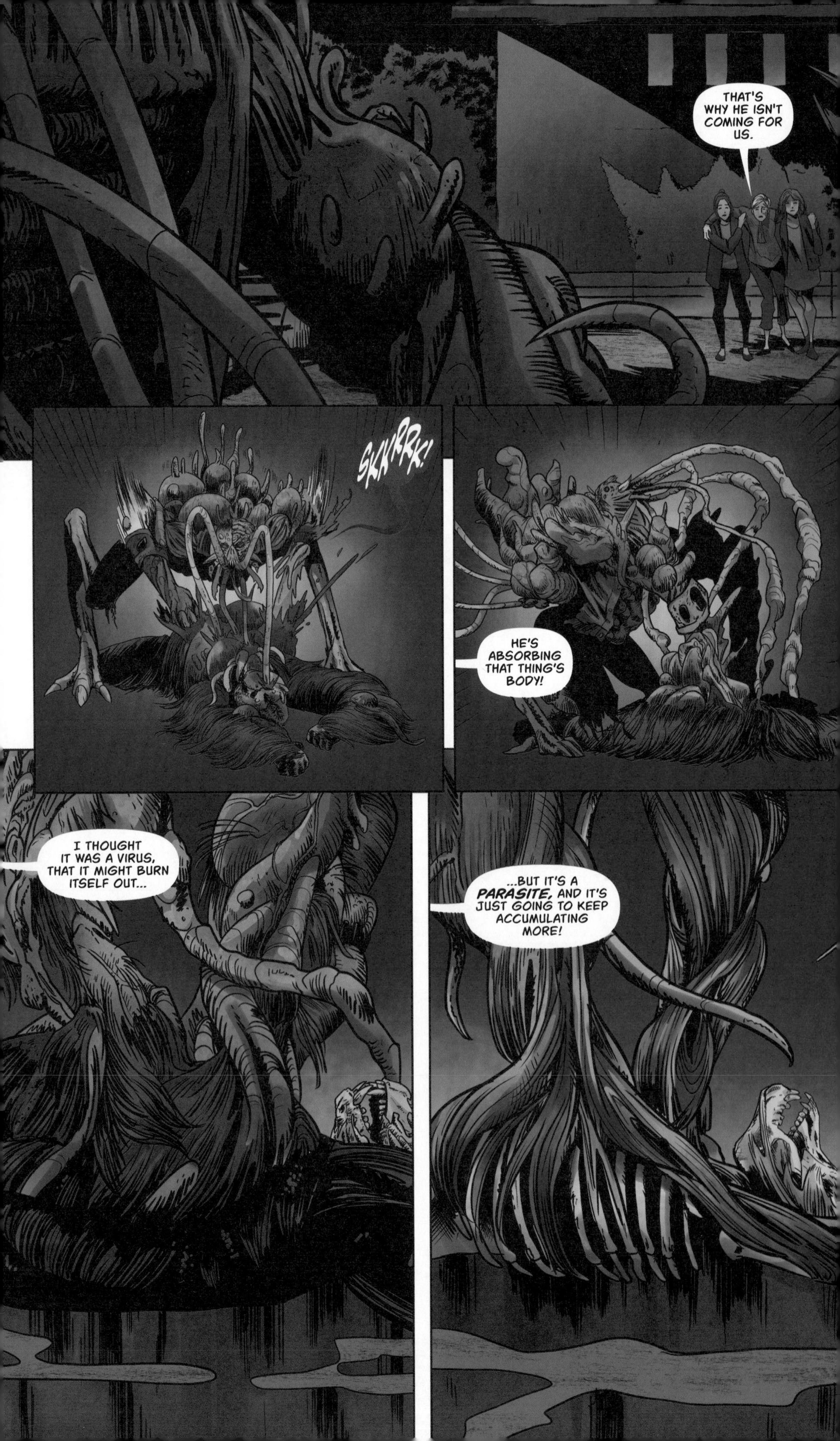
THAT'S WHY HE ISN'T COMING FOR US.
SKKRRK!
HE'S ABSORBING THAT THING'S BODY!
I THOUGHT IT WAS A VIRUS, THAT IT MIGHT BURN ITSELF OUT...
...BUT IT'S A PARASITE, AND IT'S JUST GOING TO KEEP ACCUMULATING MORE!

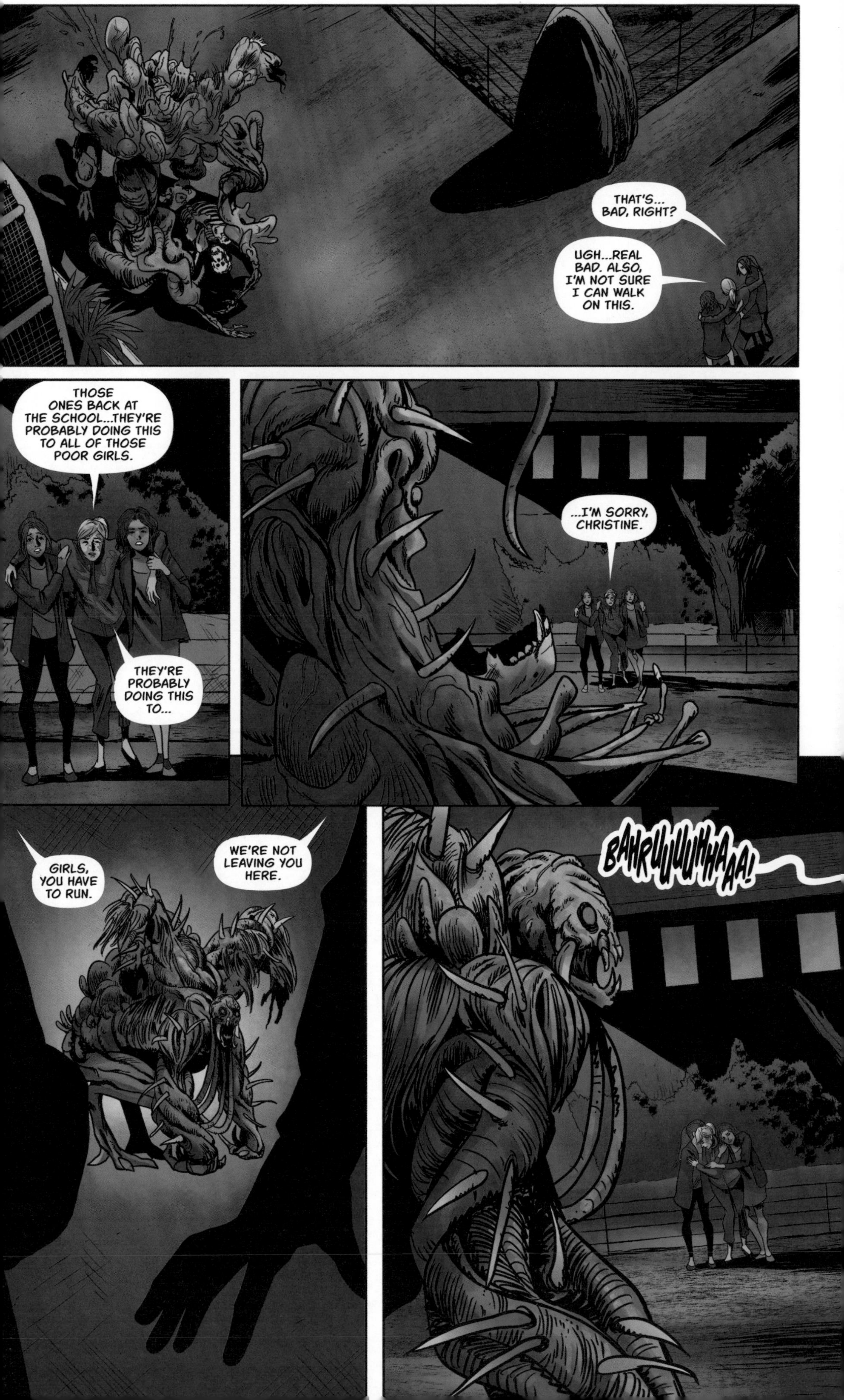
THAT'S... BAD, RIGHT?
UGH...REAL BAD. ALSO, I'M NOT SURE I CAN WALK ON THIS.
THOSE ONES BACK AT THE SCHOOL...THEY'RE PROBABLY DOING THIS TO ALL OF THOSE POOR GIRLS.
THEY'RE PROBABLY DOING THIS TO...
...I'M SORRY, CHRISTINE.
GIRLS, YOU HAVE TO RUN.
WE'RE NOT LEAVING YOU HERE.
BAHRUUUUHHAAA!

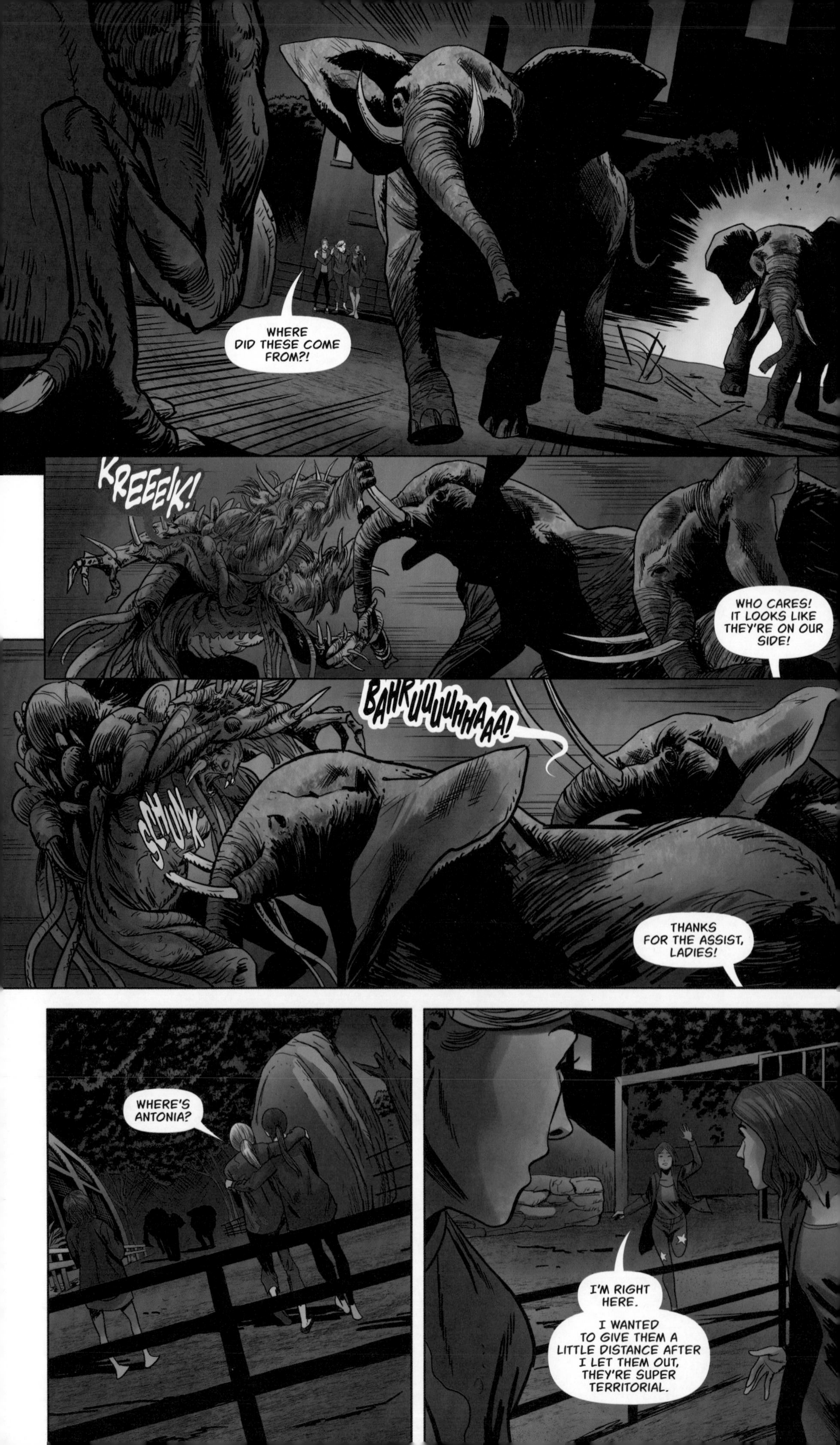
WHERE DID THESE COME FROM?!
KREEEIK!
WHO CARES! IT LOOKS LIKE THEY'RE ON OUR SIDE!
BAHRUUUUHHAAA!
SCHUNK
THANKS FOR THE ASSIST, LADIES!
WHERE'S ANTONIA?
I'M RIGHT HERE.
I WANTED TO GIVE THEM A LITTLE DISTANCE AFTER I LET THEM OUT, THEY'RE SUPER TERRITORIAL.

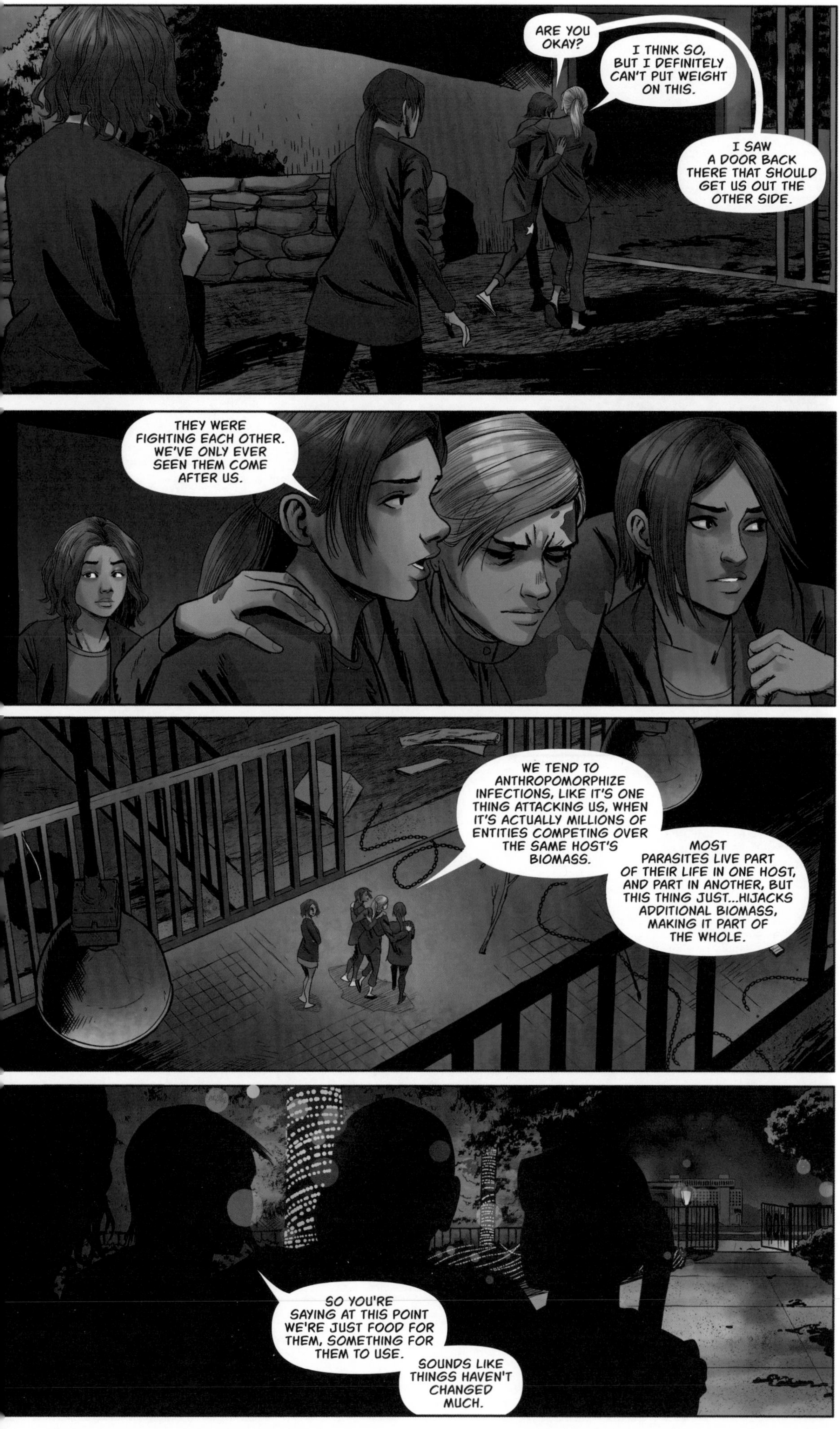
ARE YOU OKAY?
I THINK SO, BUT I DEFINITELY CAN'T PUT WEIGHT ON THIS.
I SAW A DOOR BACK THERE THAT SHOULD GET US OUT THE OTHER SIDE.
THEY WERE FIGHTING EACH OTHER. WE'VE ONLY EVER SEEN THEM COME AFTER US.
WE TEND TO ANTHROPOMORPHIZE INFECTIONS, LIKE IT'S ONE THING ATTACKING US, WHEN IT'S ACTUALLY MILLIONS OF ENTITIES COMPETING OVER THE SAME HOST'S BIOMASS.
MOST PARASITES LIVE PART OF THEIR LIFE IN ONE HOST, AND PART IN ANOTHER, BUT THIS THING JUST...HIJACKS ADDITIONAL BIOMASS, MAKING IT PART OF THE WHOLE.
SO YOU'RE SAYING AT THIS POINT WE'RE JUST FOOD FOR THEM, SOMETHING FOR THEM TO USE.
SOUNDS LIKE THINGS HAVEN'T CHANGED MUCH.

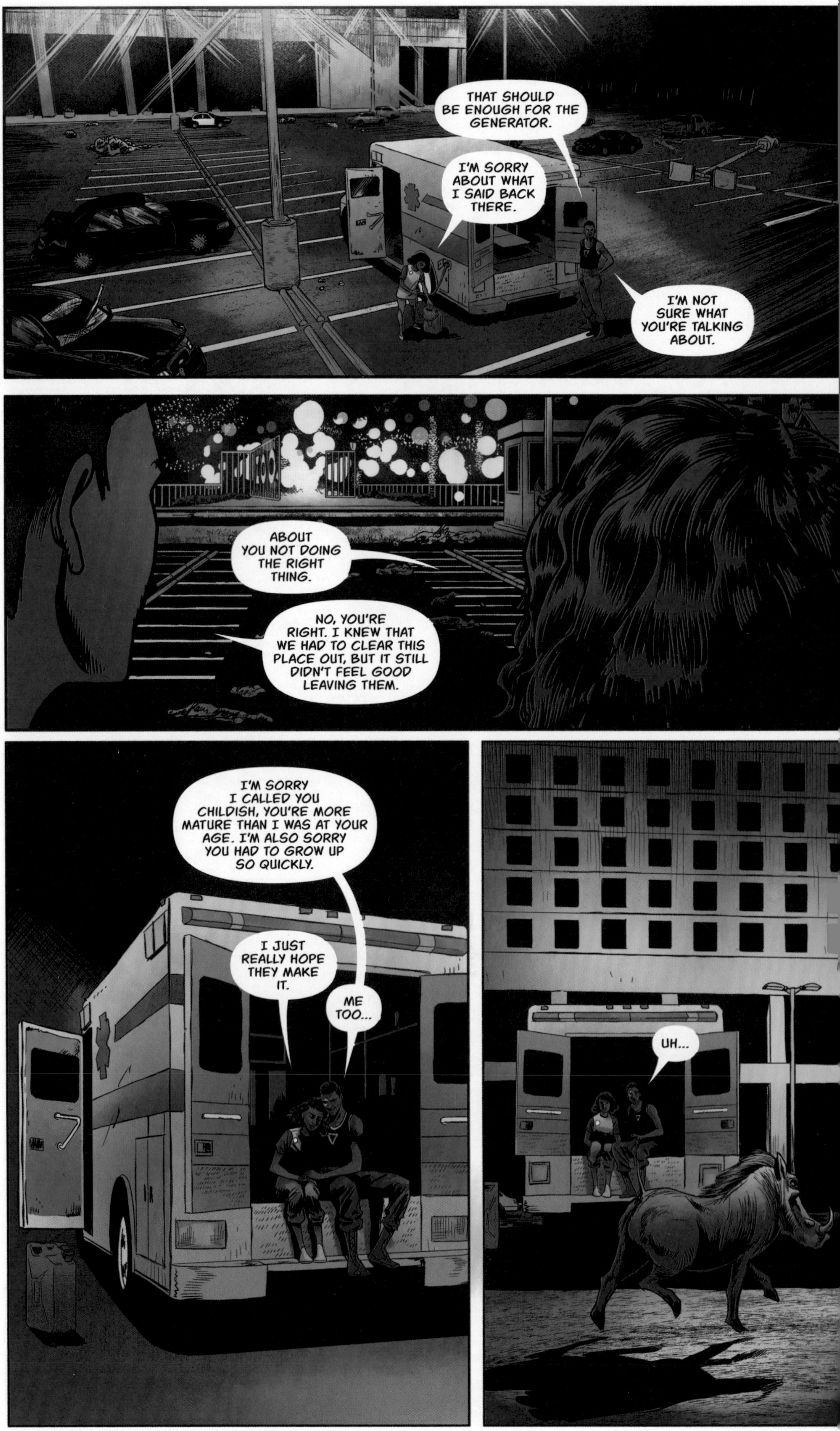
THAT SHOULD BE ENOUGH FOR THE GENERATOR.
I'M SORRY ABOUT WHAT I SAID BACK THERE.
I'M NOT SURE WHAT YOU'RE TALKING ABOUT.
ABOUT YOU NOT DOING THE RIGHT THING.
NO, YOU'RE RIGHT. I KNEW THAT WE HAD TO CLEAR THIS PLACE OUT, BUT IT STILL DIDN'T FEEL GOOD LEAVING THEM.
I'M SORRY I CALLED YOU CHILDISH, YOU'RE MORE MATURE THAN I WAS AT YOUR AGE. I'M ALSO SORRY YOU HAD TO GROW UP SO QUICKLY.
I JUST REALLY HOPE THEY MAKE IT.
ME TOO...
UH...

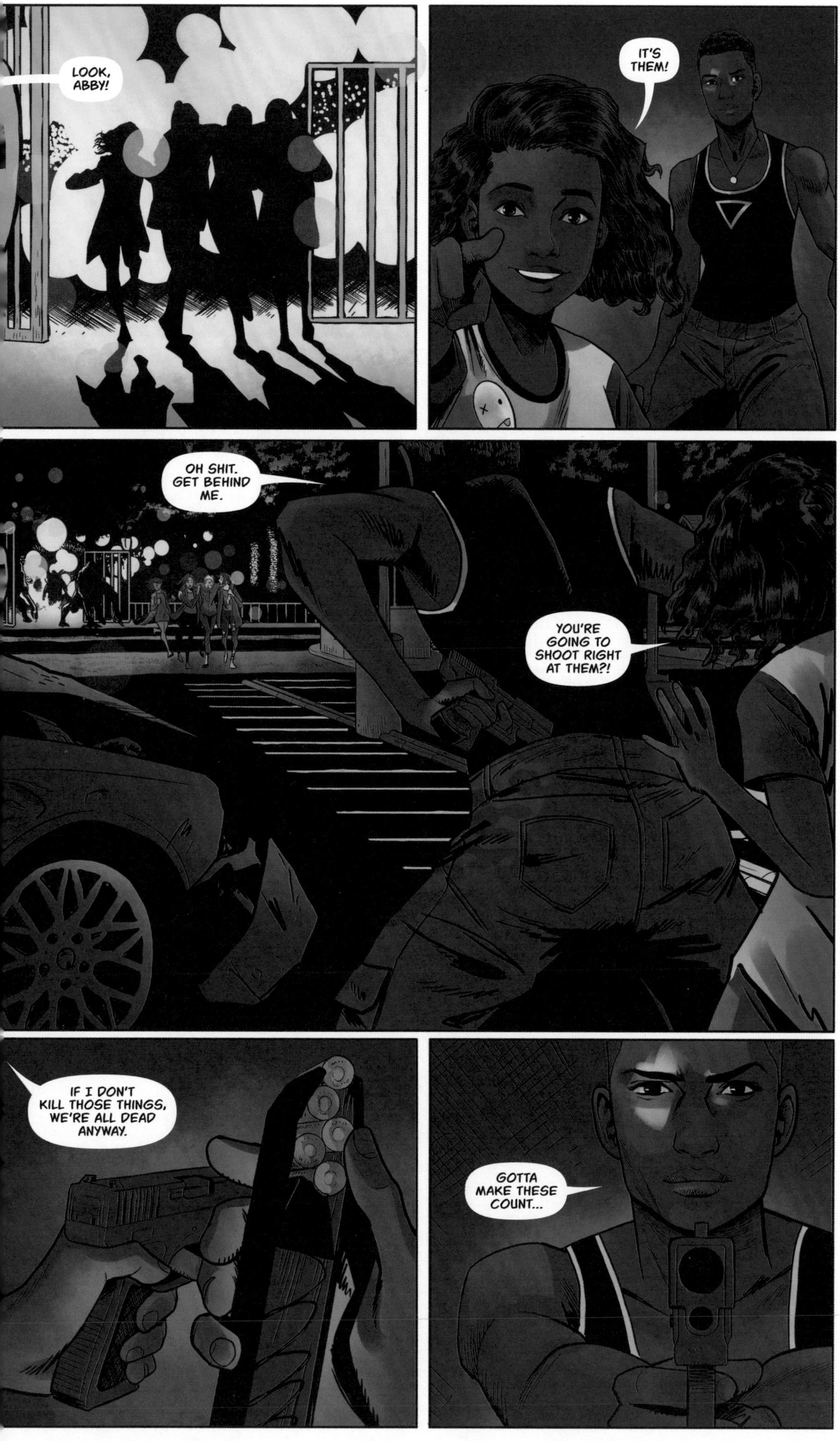
LOOK, ABBY!
IT'S THEM!
OH SHIT. GET BEHIND ME.
YOU'RE GOING TO SHOOT RIGHT AT THEM?!
IF I DON'T KILL THOSE THINGS, WE'RE ALL DEAD ANYWAY.
GOTTA MAKE THESE COUNT...

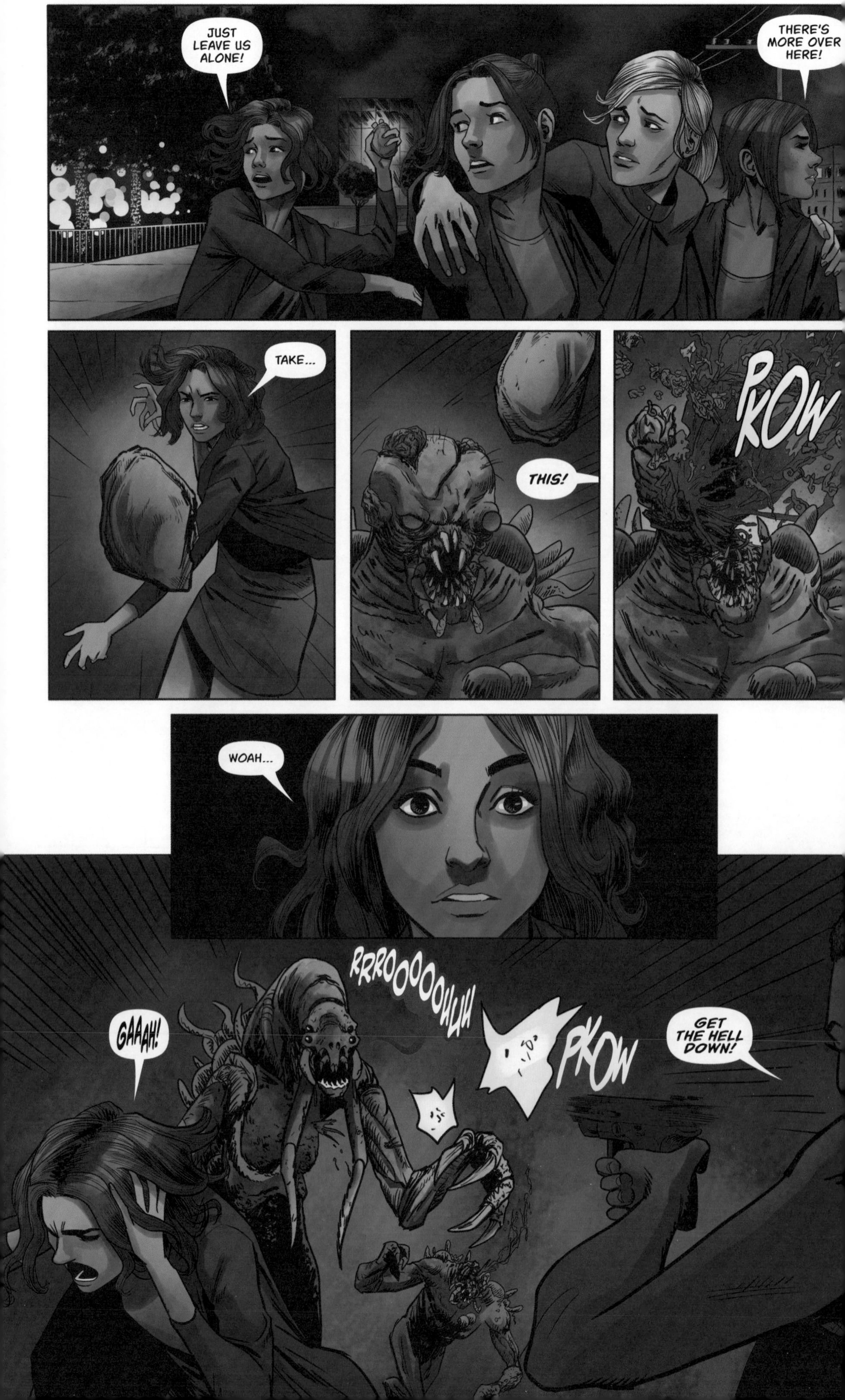
JUST LEAVE US ALONE!
THERE'S MORE OVER HERE!
TAKE...
THIS!
PKOW
WOAH...
GAAAH!
RRROOOOOUUU
PKOW
GET THE HELL DOWN!

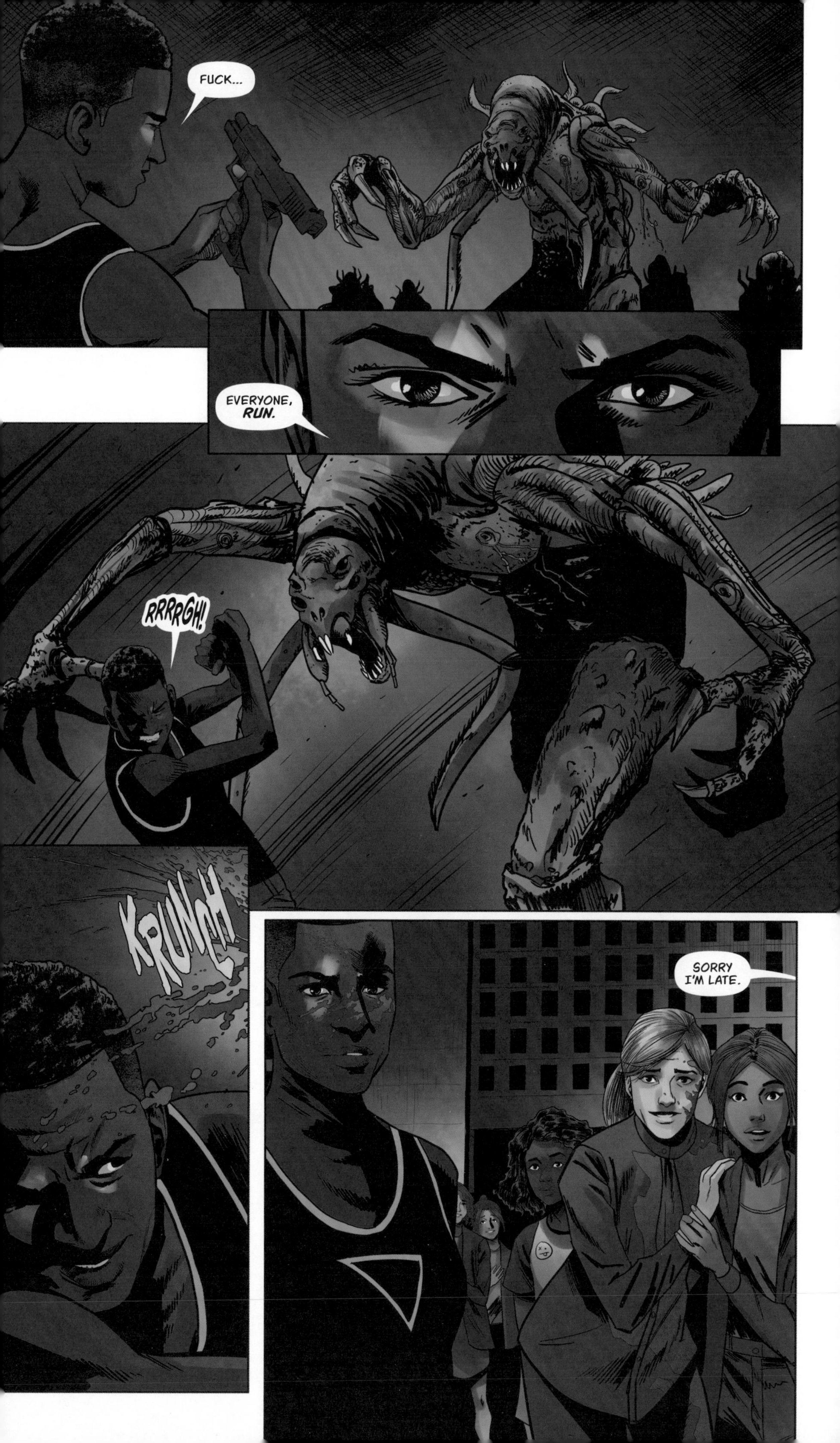
FUCK...
EVERYONE, *RUN.*
RRRRGH!
KRUNCH
SORRY I'M LATE.

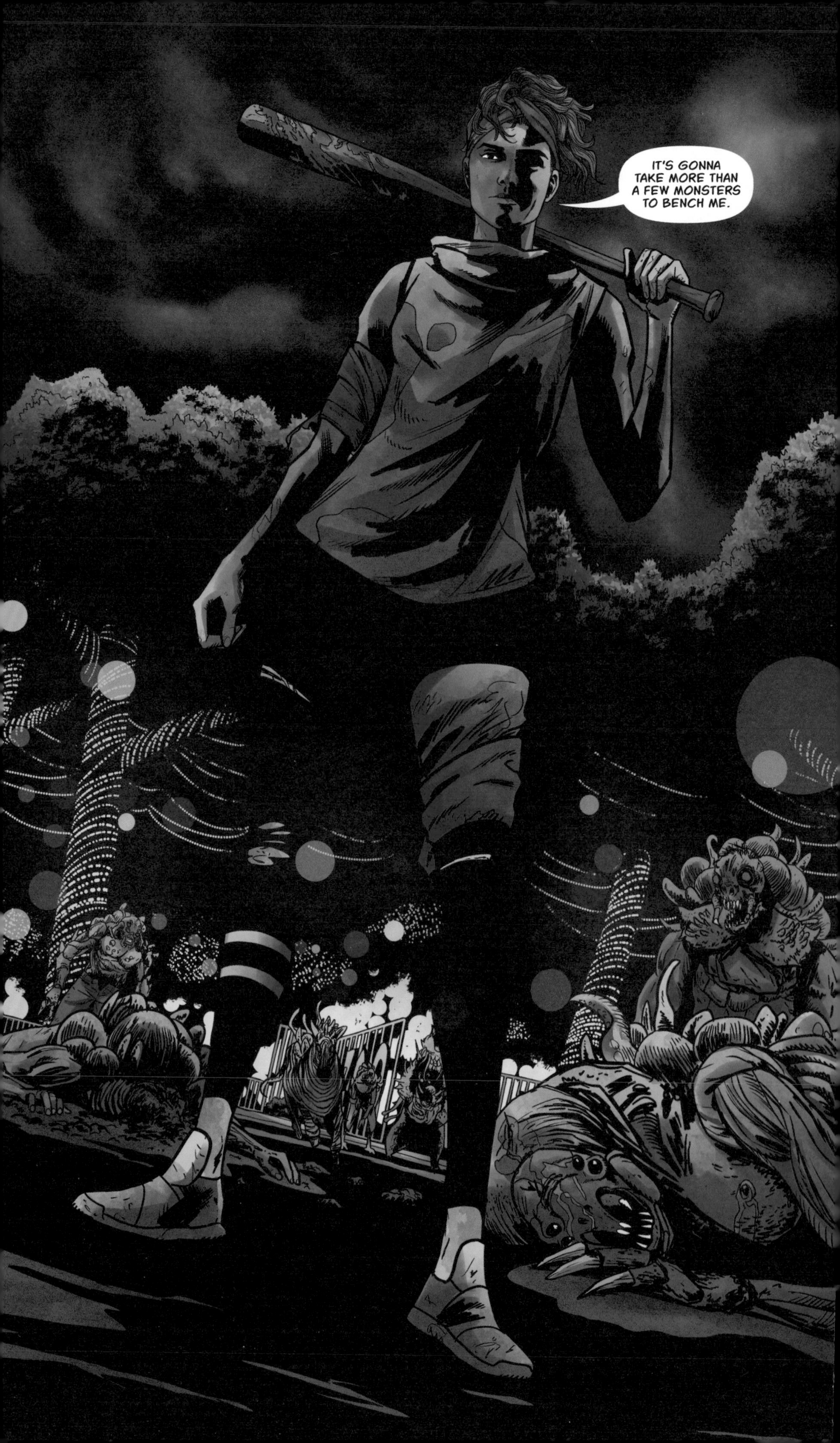
IT'S GONNA TAKE MORE THAN A FEW MONSTERS TO BENCH ME.

CHAPTER 6

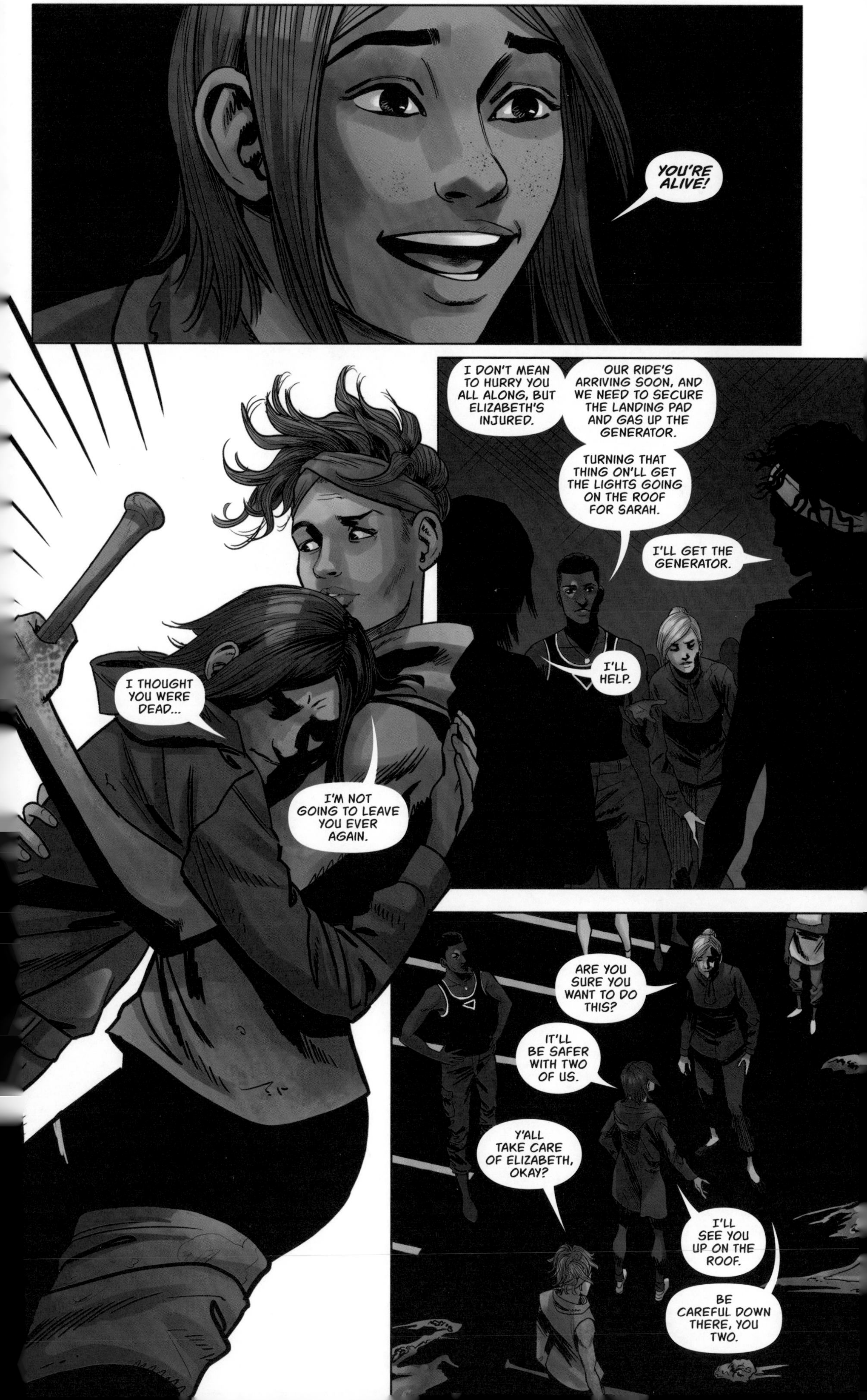
YOU'RE ALIVE!
I THOUGHT YOU WERE DEAD...
I'M NOT GOING TO LEAVE YOU EVER AGAIN.
I DON'T MEAN TO HURRY YOU ALL ALONG, BUT ELIZABETH'S INJURED.
OUR RIDE'S ARRIVING SOON, AND WE NEED TO SECURE THE LANDING PAD AND GAS UP THE GENERATOR.
TURNING THAT THING ON'LL GET THE LIGHTS GOING ON THE ROOF FOR SARAH.
I'LL GET THE GENERATOR.
I'LL HELP.
ARE YOU SURE YOU WANT TO DO THIS?
IT'LL BE SAFER WITH TWO OF US.
Y'ALL TAKE CARE OF ELIZABETH, OKAY?
I'LL SEE YOU UP ON THE ROOF.
BE CAREFUL DOWN THERE, YOU TWO.

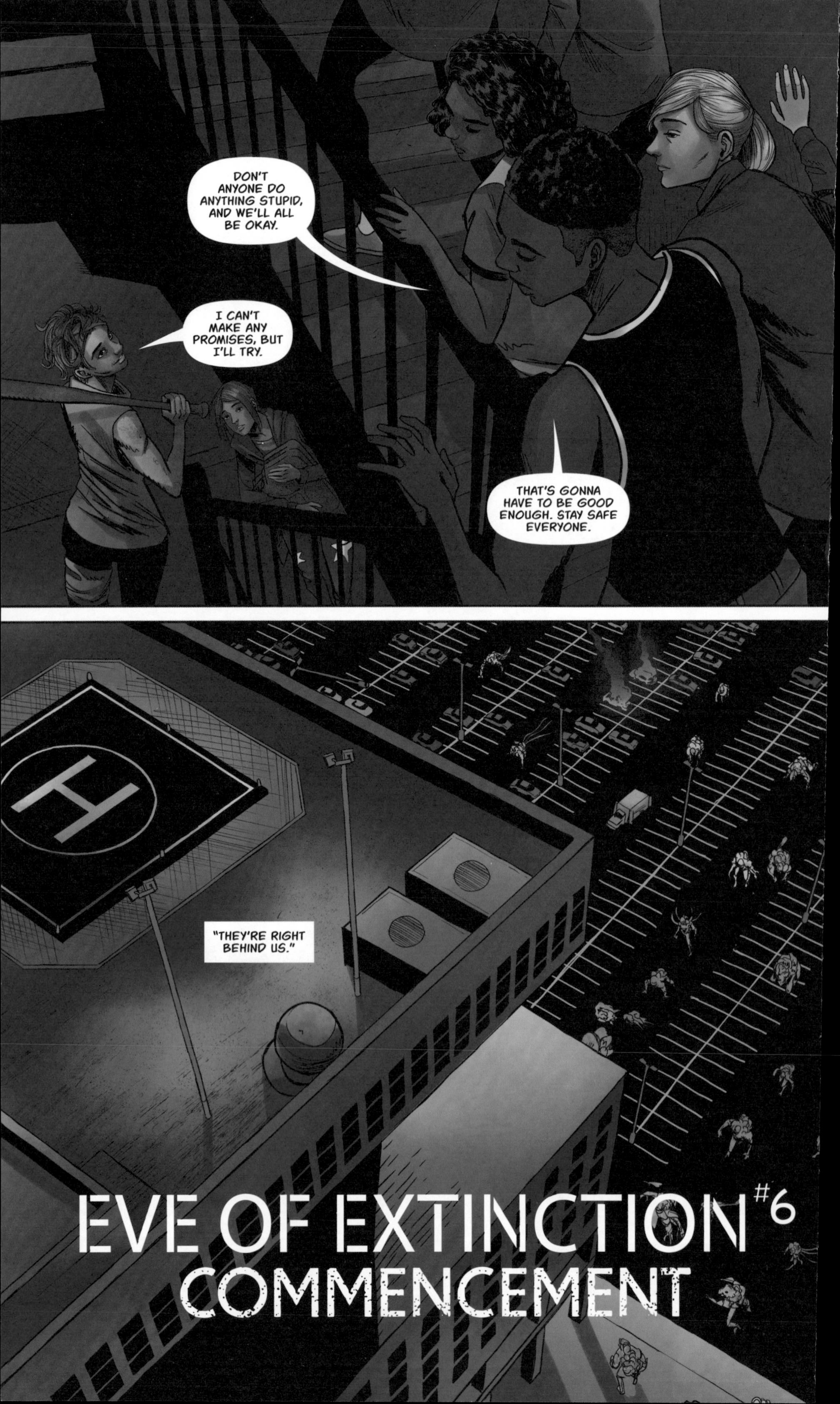
DON'T ANYONE DO ANYTHING STUPID, AND WE'LL ALL BE OKAY.
I CAN'T MAKE ANY PROMISES, BUT I'LL TRY.
THAT'S GONNA HAVE TO BE GOOD ENOUGH. STAY SAFE EVERYONE.
"THEY'RE RIGHT BEHIND US."
EVE OF EXTINCTION #6
COMMENCEMENT

THIS...IS UNEXPECTED. I DIDN'T REALIZE THE FLOODING WAS THIS BAD.

I HOPE IT DOESN'T GET DEEPER, I CAN BARELY SWIM.

SORRY, THAT WAS SUPPOSED TO BE MY JOB.

I APPRECIATE THAT, BUT I DIDN'T MEAN ANYTHING BY IT.

REEEEEINNKK!

SHIT. WE'D BETTER HURRY.

HEY LOOK!

8-wing →
Generator Room →
Mortuary →
Laboratories ←
A-wing/Elevators ←

Mortuary

I THINK THEY'RE GETTING CLOSER.

Mortuary

FINALLY!

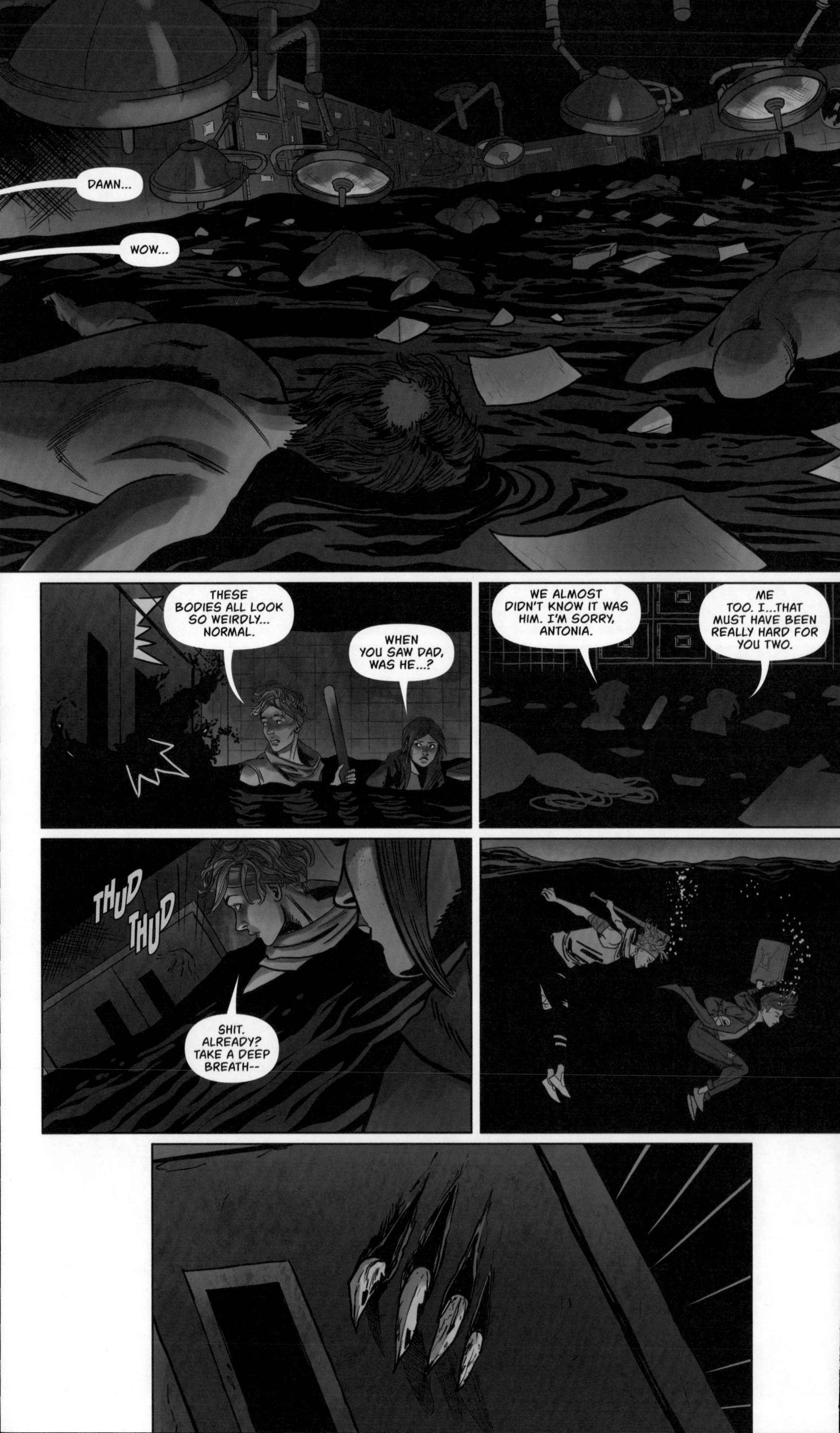
DAMN...
WOW...
THESE BODIES ALL LOOK SO WEIRDLY... NORMAL.
WHEN YOU SAW DAD, WAS HE...?
WE ALMOST DIDN'T KNOW IT WAS HIM. I'M SORRY, ANTONIA.
ME TOO. I...THAT MUST HAVE BEEN REALLY HARD FOR YOU TWO.
THUD
THUD
SHIT. ALREADY? TAKE A DEEP BREATH--

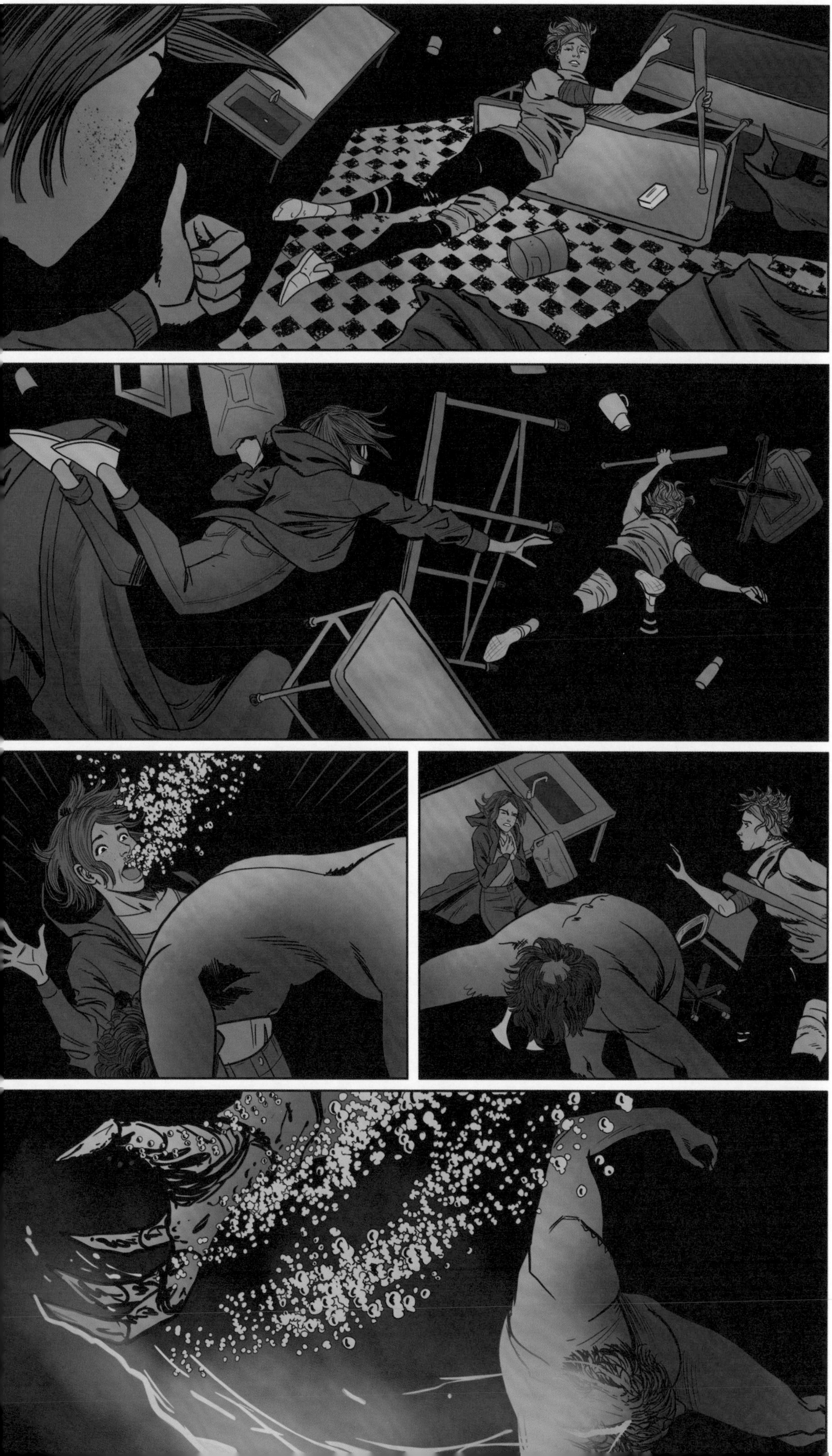

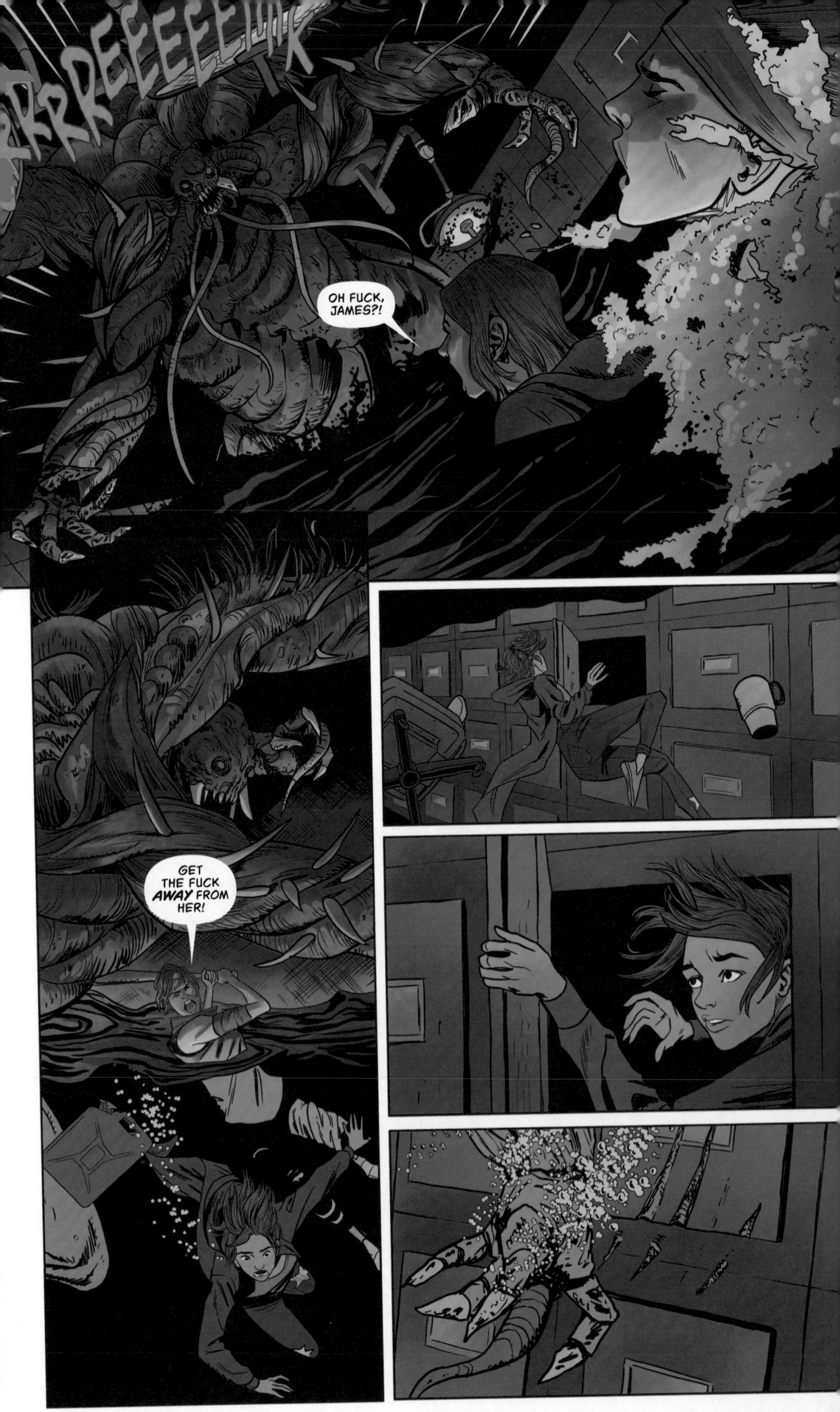
KRREEEEEUNK
OH FUCK, JAMES?!
GET THE FUCK AWAY FROM HER!

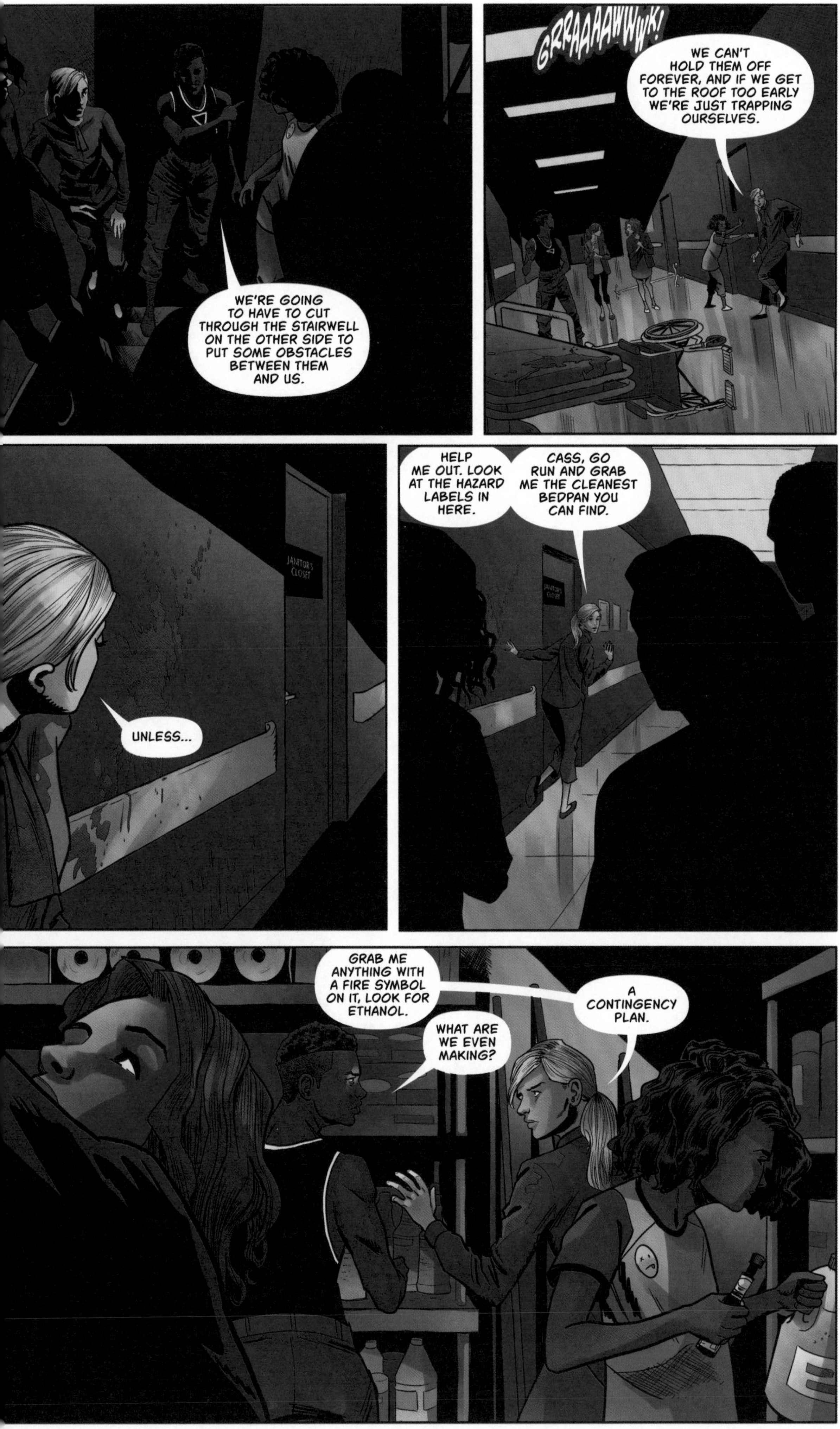
WE'RE GOING TO HAVE TO CUT THROUGH THE STAIRWELL ON THE OTHER SIDE TO PUT SOME OBSTACLES BETWEEN THEM AND US.
GRRAAAAWWWK!
WE CAN'T HOLD THEM OFF FOREVER, AND IF WE GET TO THE ROOF TOO EARLY WE'RE JUST TRAPPING OURSELVES.
JANITOR'S CLOSET
UNLESS...
HELP ME OUT. LOOK AT THE HAZARD LABELS IN HERE.
CASS, GO RUN AND GRAB ME THE CLEANEST BEDPAN YOU CAN FIND.
GRAB ME ANYTHING WITH A FIRE SYMBOL ON IT, LOOK FOR ETHANOL.
A CONTINGENCY PLAN.
WHAT ARE WE EVEN MAKING?

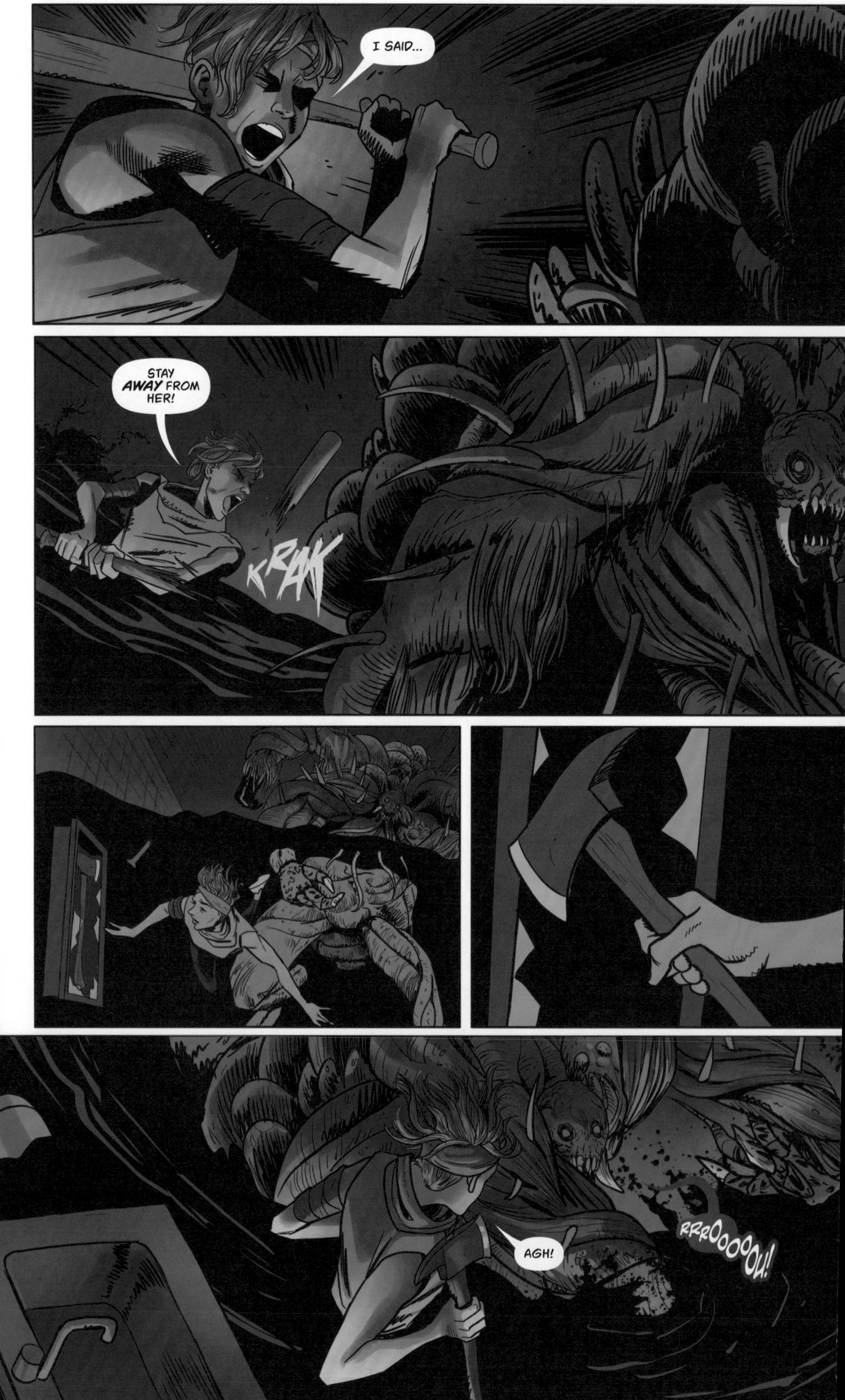
I SAID...
STAY AWAY FROM HER!
K-RAK
AGH!
RRROOOOOU!

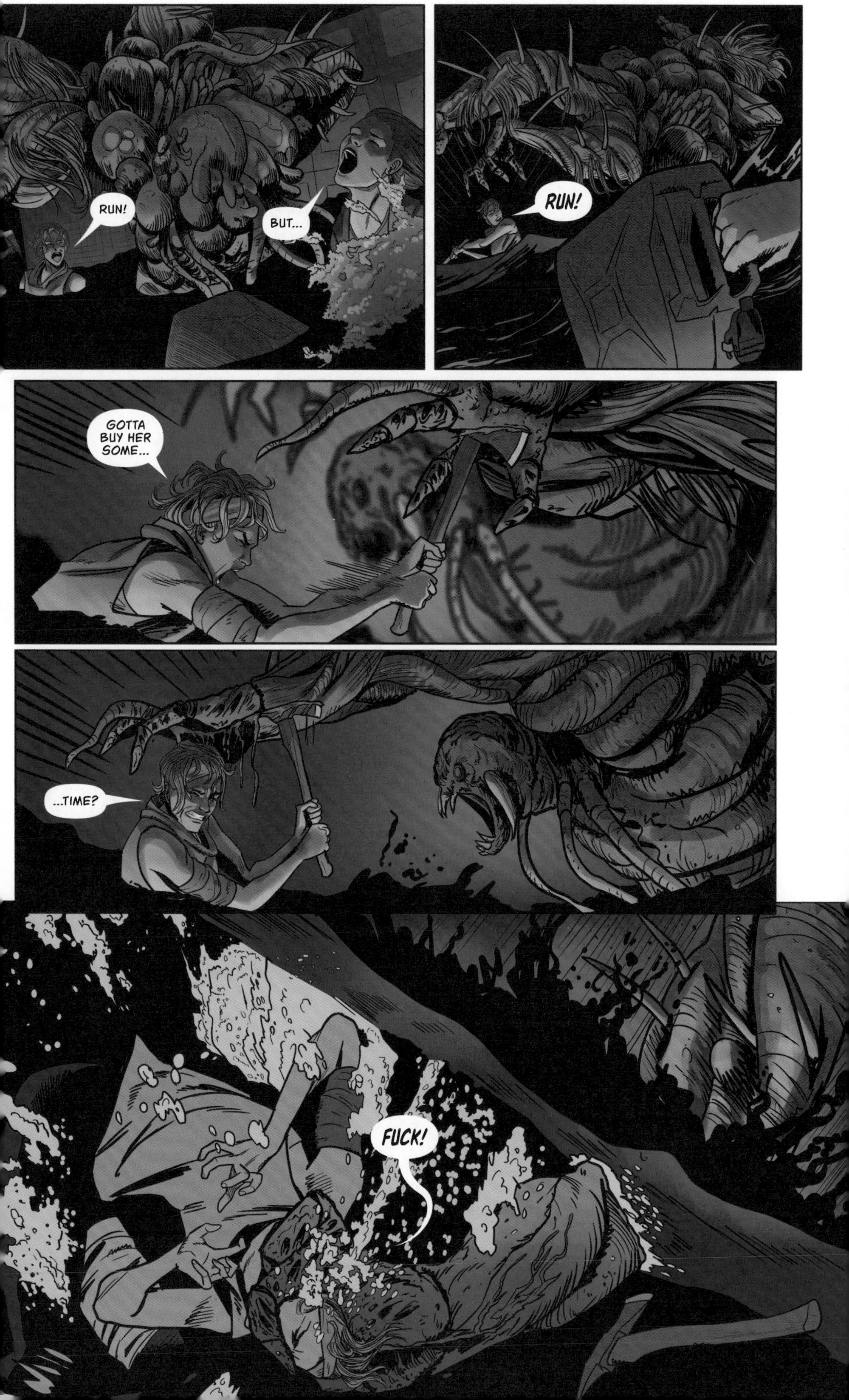
RUN!
BUT...
RUN!
GOTTA BUY HER SOME...
...TIME?
FUCK!

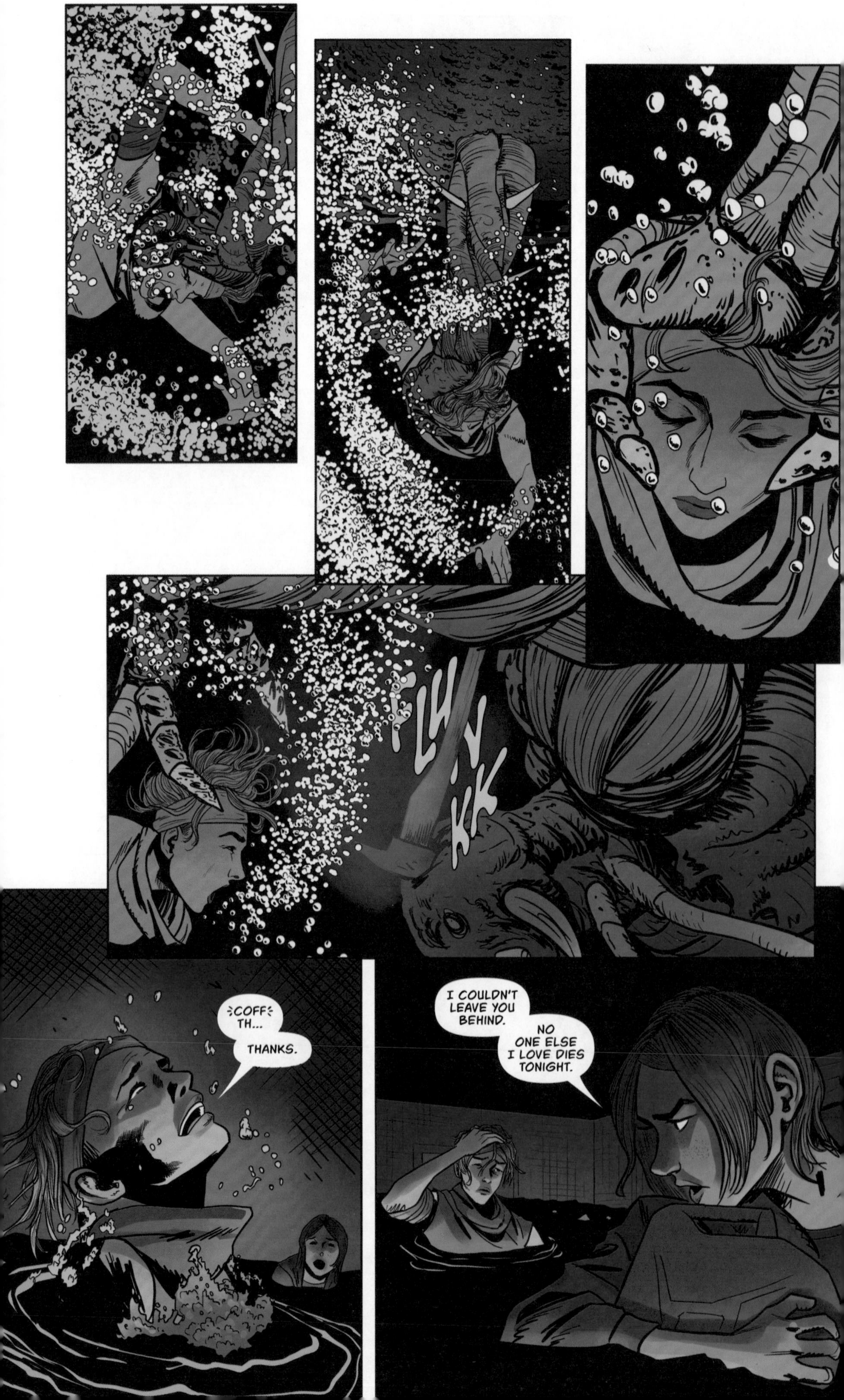
FLUNKK
COFF
TH...
THANKS.
I COULDN'T LEAVE YOU BEHIND.
NO ONE ELSE I LOVE DIES TONIGHT.

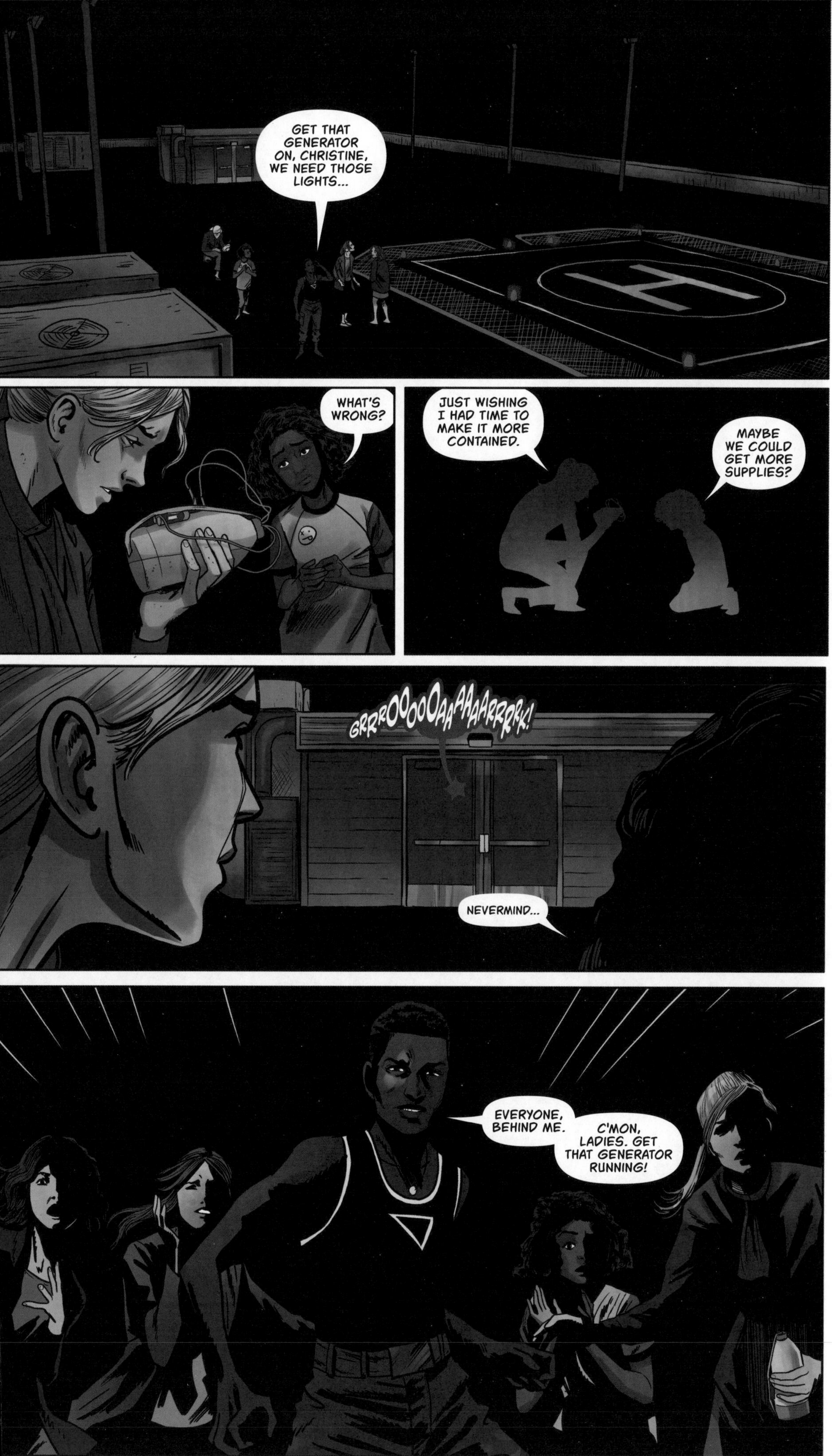
GET THAT GENERATOR ON, CHRISTINE, WE NEED THOSE LIGHTS...
WHAT'S WRONG?
JUST WISHING I HAD TIME TO MAKE IT MORE CONTAINED.
MAYBE WE COULD GET MORE SUPPLIES?
GRRROOOOOOAAAAAARRRRK!
NEVERMIND...
EVERYONE, BEHIND ME.
C'MON, LADIES. GET THAT GENERATOR RUNNING!

I'LL SEE IF THERE'S ANYTHING ELSE TO PUT IN FRONT OF THIS DOOR!
I DON'T THINK YOU'LL WANT TO BE ANYWHERE NEAR THE WATER WHEN I TURN THIS THING ON.
ALRIGHT, HIT IT!
HRRRRAAAAAUUUUK!
KREAK
SKPLSH
FRY, YOU BASTARDS!

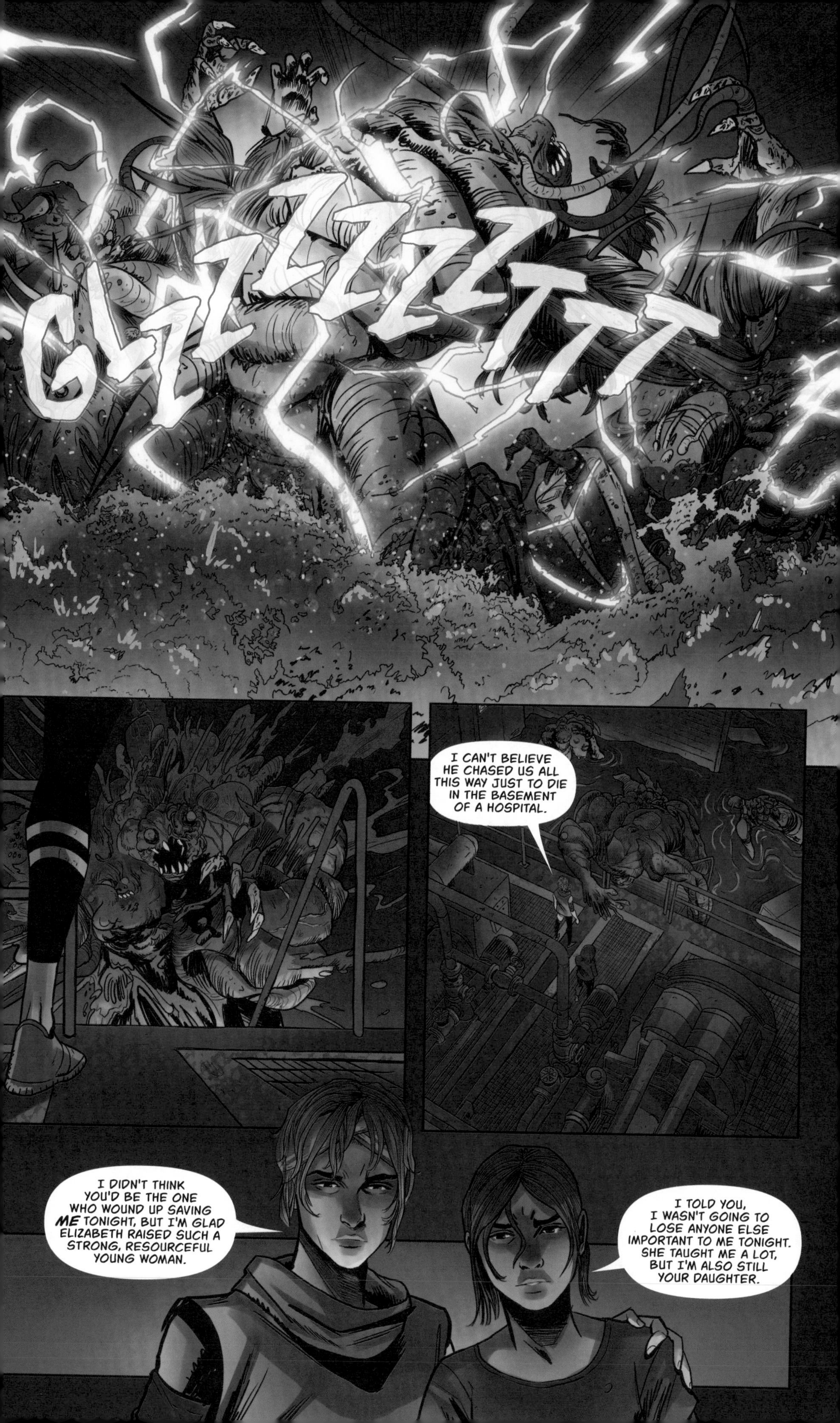
GLZZZZZTTT
I CAN'T BELIEVE HE CHASED US ALL THIS WAY JUST TO DIE IN THE BASEMENT OF A HOSPITAL.
I DIDN'T THINK YOU'D BE THE ONE WHO WOUND UP SAVING ME TONIGHT, BUT I'M GLAD ELIZABETH RAISED SUCH A STRONG, RESOURCEFUL YOUNG WOMAN.
I TOLD YOU, I WASN'T GOING TO LOSE ANYONE ELSE IMPORTANT TO ME TONIGHT. SHE TAUGHT ME A LOT, BUT I'M ALSO STILL YOUR DAUGHTER.

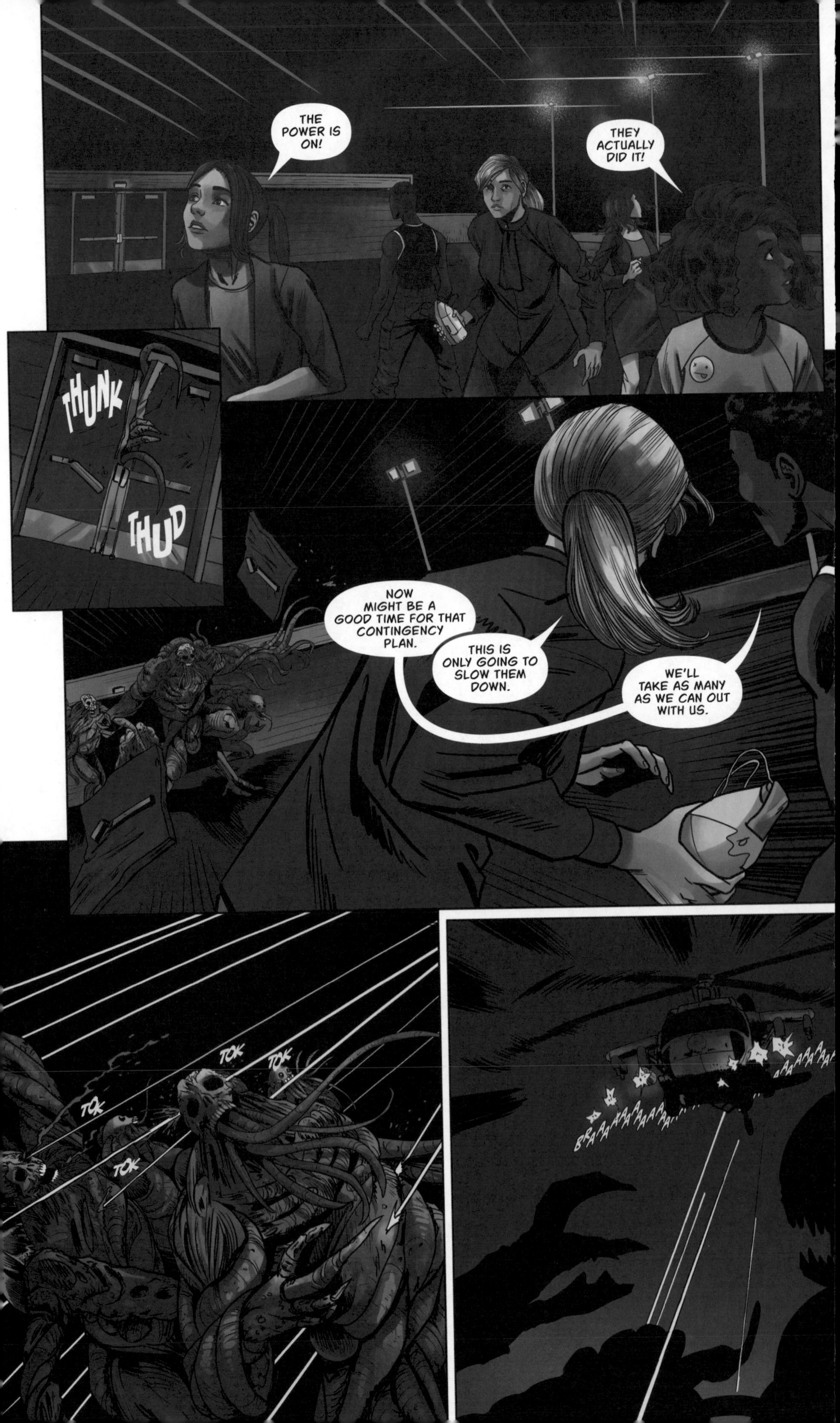
THE POWER IS ON!
THEY ACTUALLY DID IT!
THUNK
THUD
NOW MIGHT BE A GOOD TIME FOR THAT CONTINGENCY PLAN.
THIS IS ONLY GOING TO SLOW THEM DOWN.
WE'LL TAKE AS MANY AS WE CAN OUT WITH US.
TOK
TOK
TOK
TOK
BRAAAAAAAAAAAA...

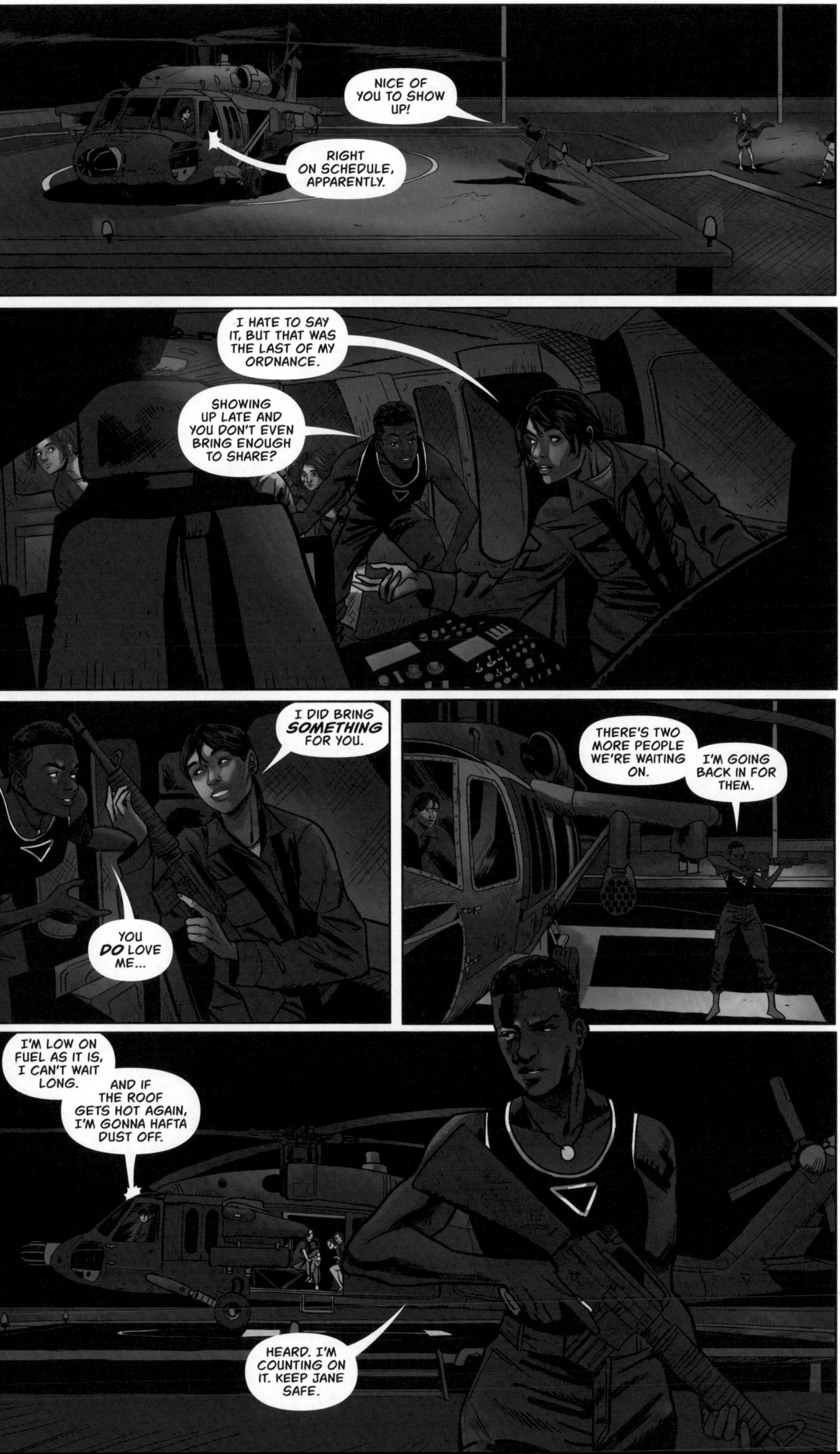
NICE OF YOU TO SHOW UP!
RIGHT ON SCHEDULE, APPARENTLY.
I HATE TO SAY IT, BUT THAT WAS THE LAST OF MY ORDNANCE.
SHOWING UP LATE AND YOU DON'T EVEN BRING ENOUGH TO SHARE?
I DID BRING **SOMETHING** FOR YOU.
YOU **DO** LOVE ME...
THERE'S TWO MORE PEOPLE WE'RE WAITING ON.
I'M GOING BACK IN FOR THEM.
I'M LOW ON FUEL AS IT IS, I CAN'T WAIT LONG.
AND IF THE ROOF GETS HOT AGAIN, I'M GONNA HAFTA DUST OFF.
HEARD. I'M COUNTING ON IT. KEEP JANE SAFE.

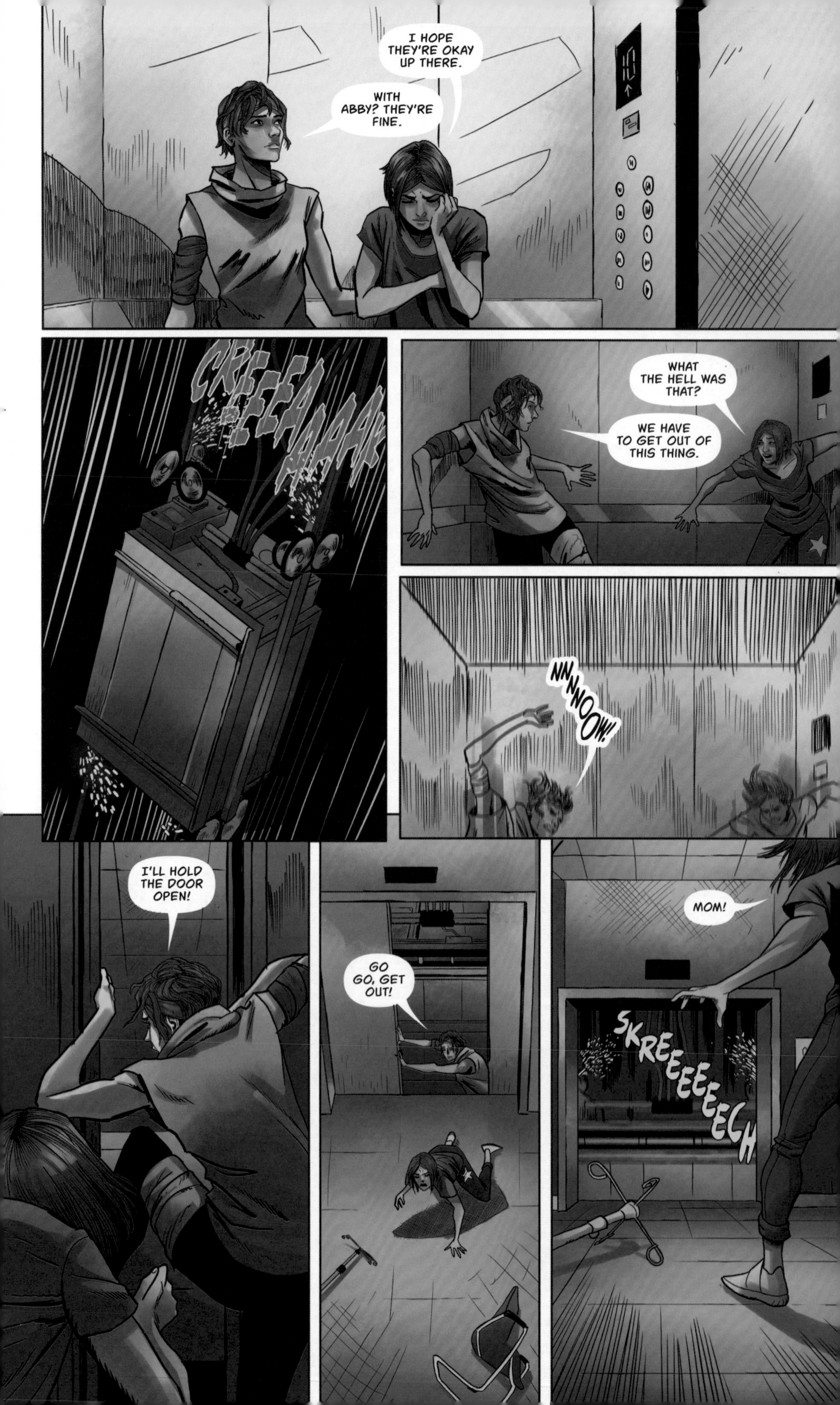
I HOPE THEY'RE OKAY UP THERE.
WITH ABBY? THEY'RE FINE.
CREEEAAAAK
WHAT THE HELL WAS THAT?
WE HAVE TO GET OUT OF THIS THING.
NNNOOW!
I'LL HOLD THE DOOR OPEN!
GO GO, GET OUT!
MOM!
SKREEEEEEECH

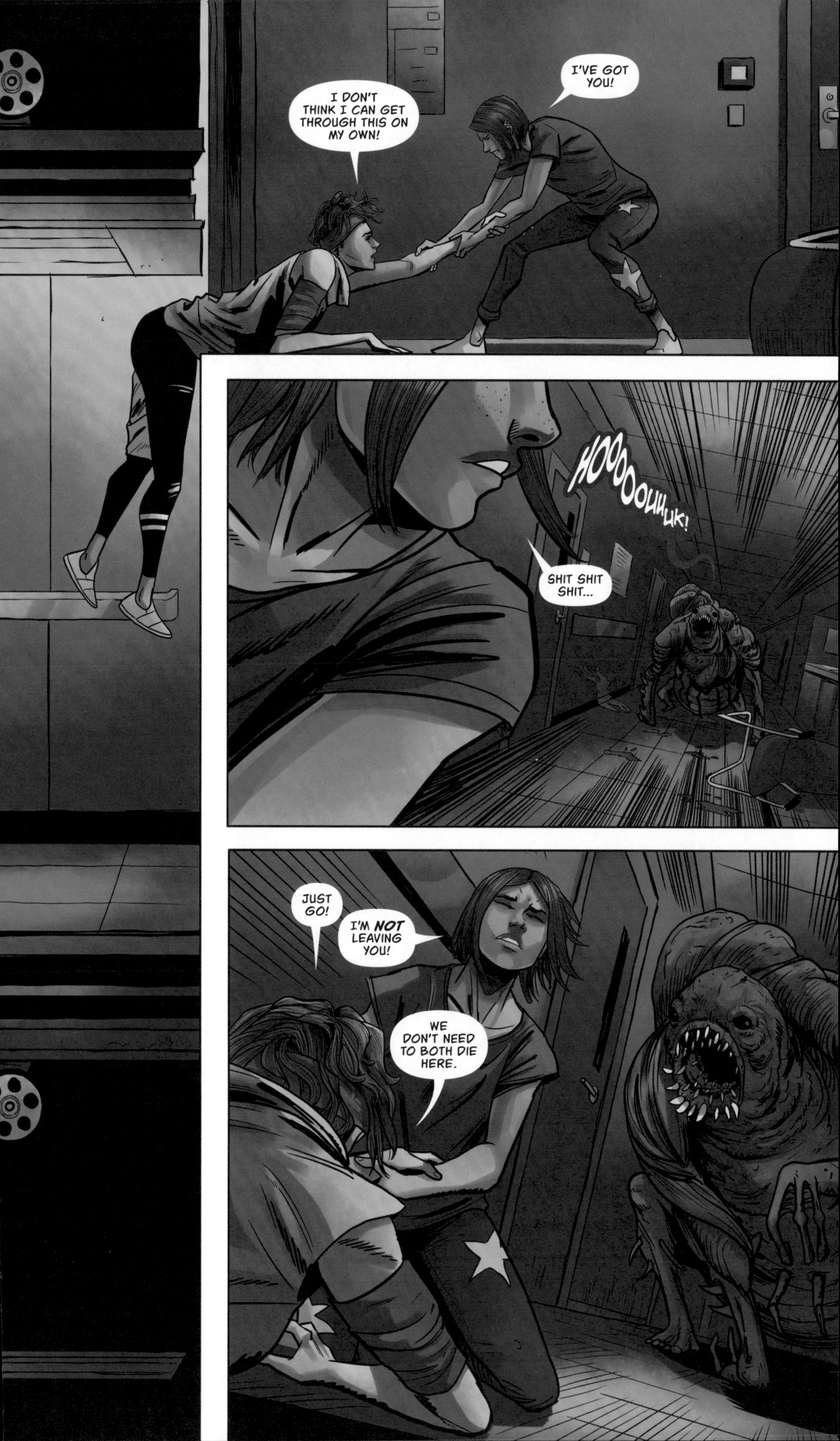
I DON'T THINK I CAN GET THROUGH THIS ON MY OWN!
I'VE GOT YOU!
HOOOOOuuuuk!
SHIT SHIT SHIT...
JUST GO!
I'M **NOT** LEAVING YOU!
WE DON'T NEED TO BOTH DIE HERE.

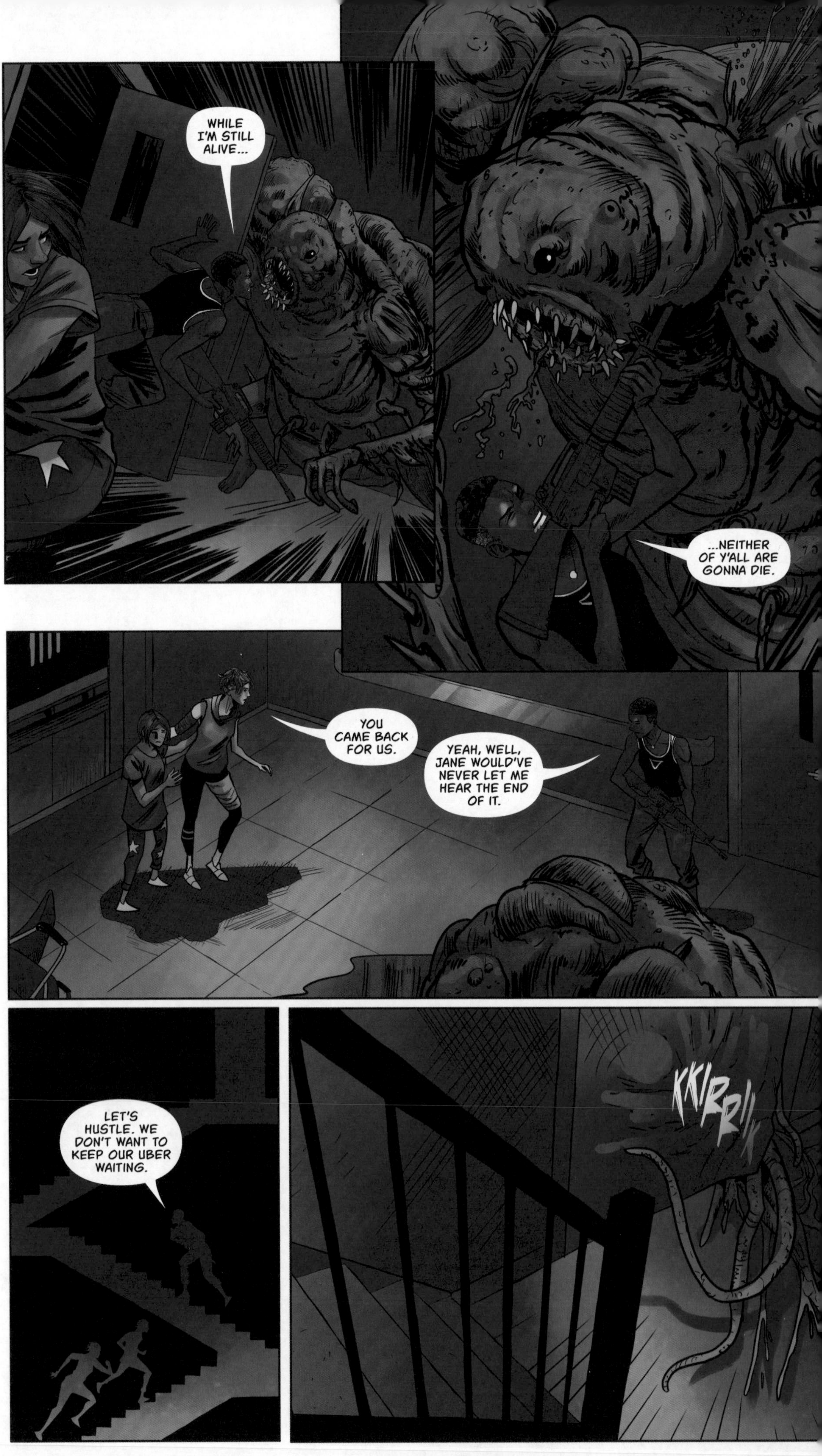
WHILE I'M STILL ALIVE...
...NEITHER OF Y'ALL ARE GONNA DIE.
YOU CAME BACK FOR US.
YEAH, WELL, JANE WOULD'VE NEVER LET ME HEAR THE END OF IT.
LET'S HUSTLE. WE DON'T WANT TO KEEP OUR UBER WAITING.
KKIRRIIK

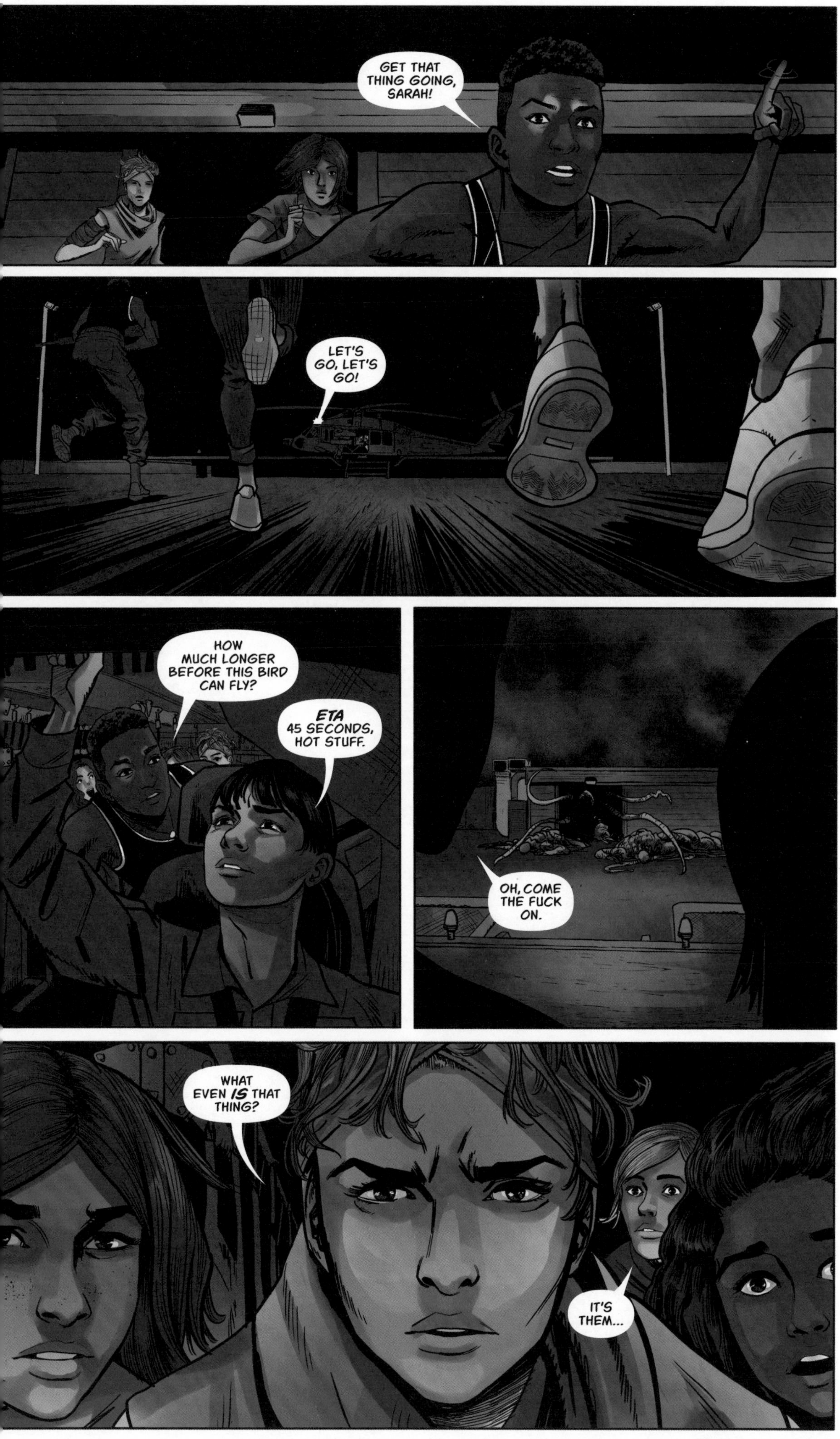
GET THAT THING GOING, SARAH!
LET'S GO, LET'S GO!
HOW MUCH LONGER BEFORE THIS BIRD CAN FLY?
ETA 45 SECONDS, HOT STUFF.
OH, COME THE FUCK ON.
WHAT EVEN IS THAT THING?
IT'S THEM...

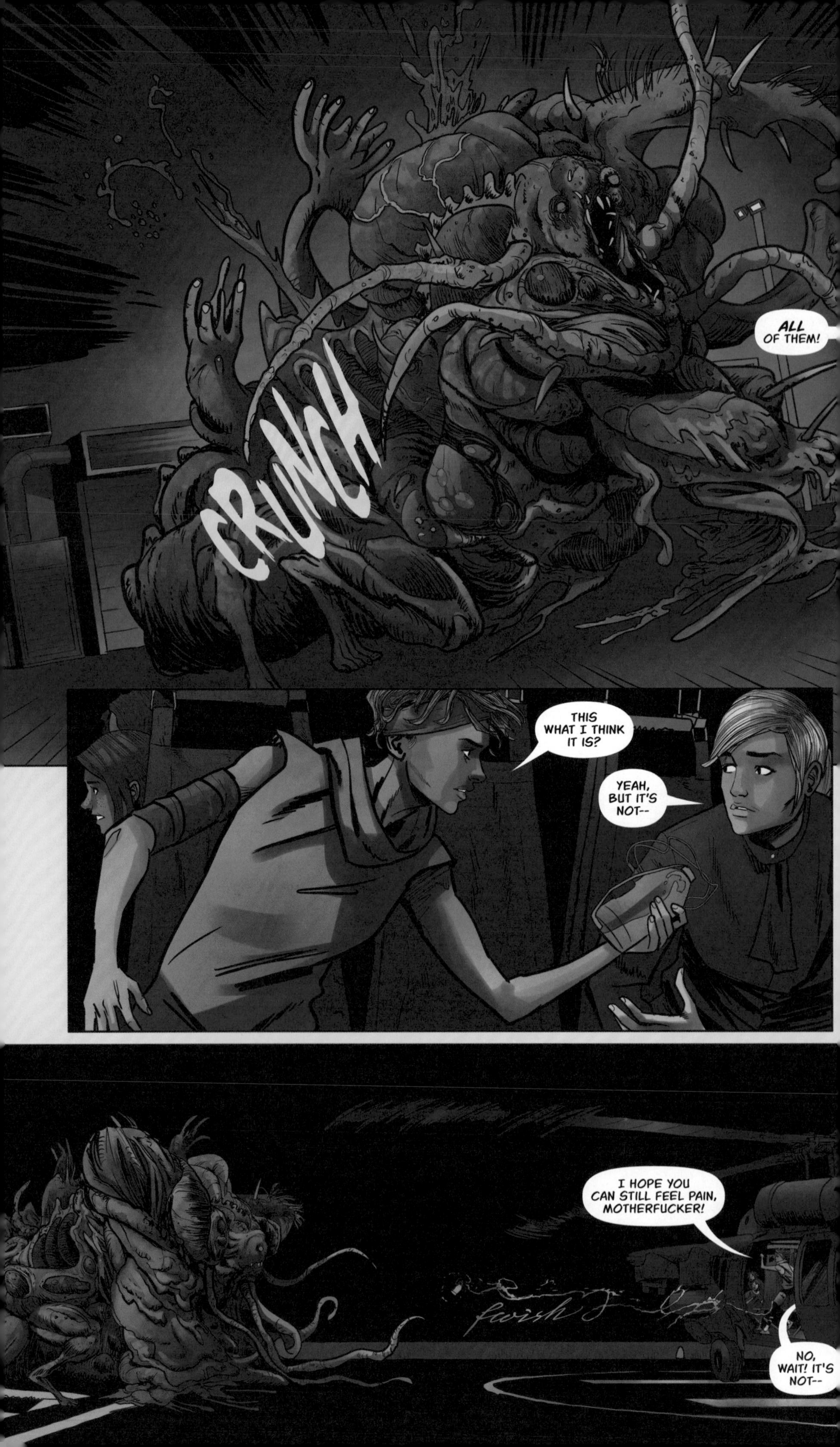
CRUNCH
ALL OF THEM!
THIS WHAT I THINK IT IS?
YEAH, BUT IT'S NOT--
I HOPE YOU CAN STILL FEEL PAIN, MOTHERFUCKER!
fwish
NO, WAIT! IT'S NOT--

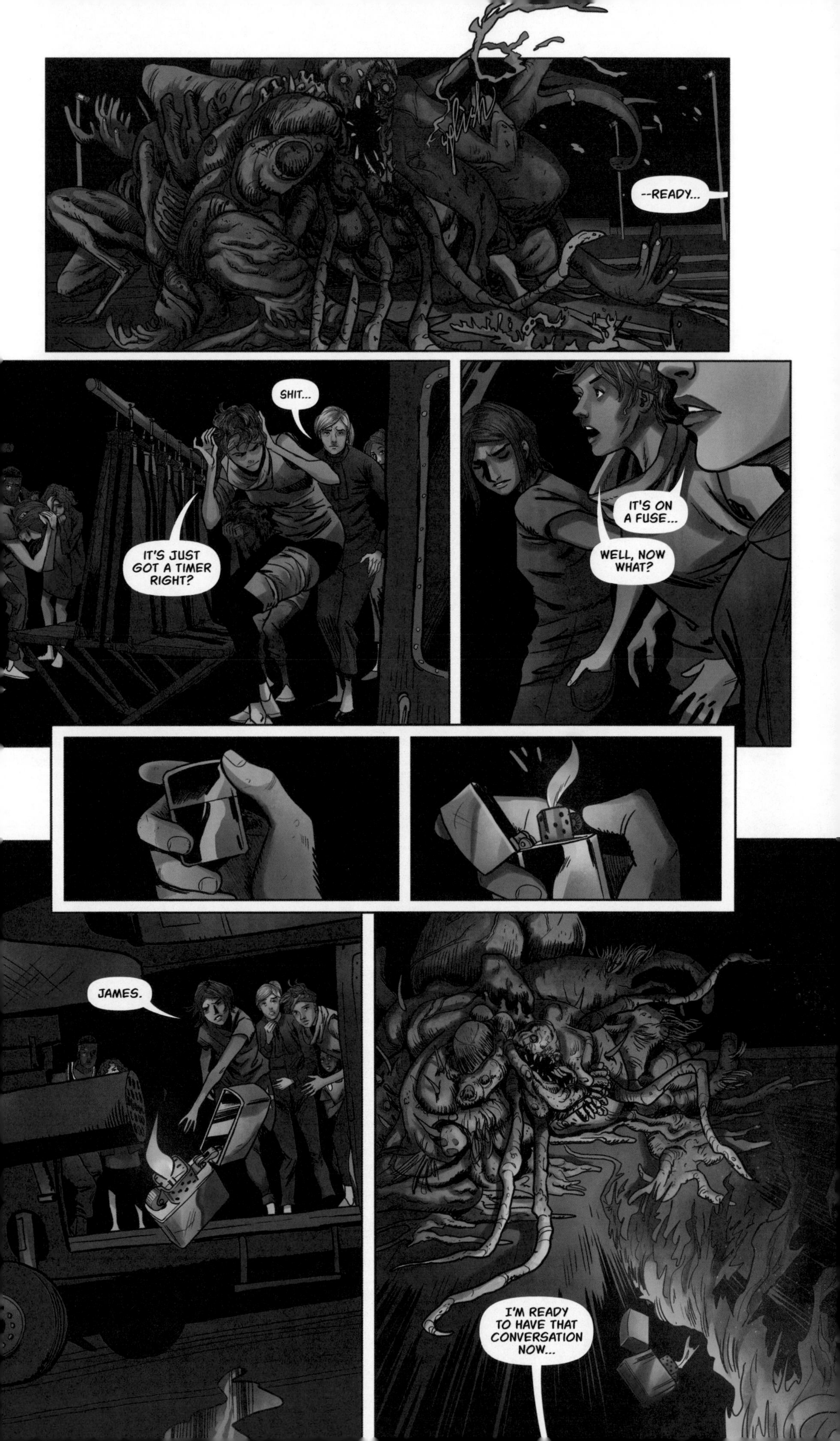
splish
--READY...
SHIT...
IT'S JUST GOT A TIMER RIGHT?
IT'S ON A FUSE...
WELL, NOW WHAT?
JAMES.
I'M READY TO HAVE THAT CONVERSATION NOW...

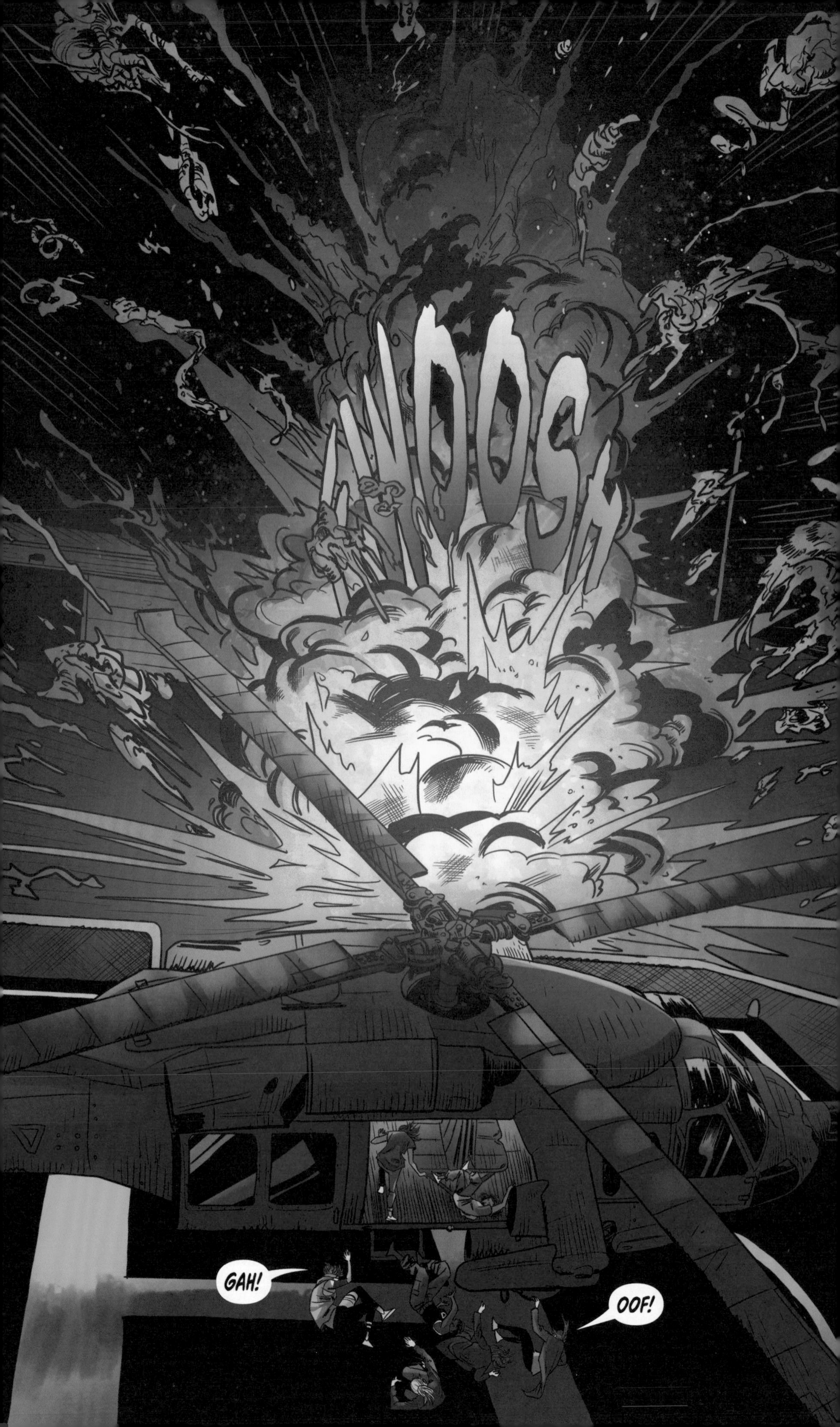
WHOOSH
GAH!
OOF!

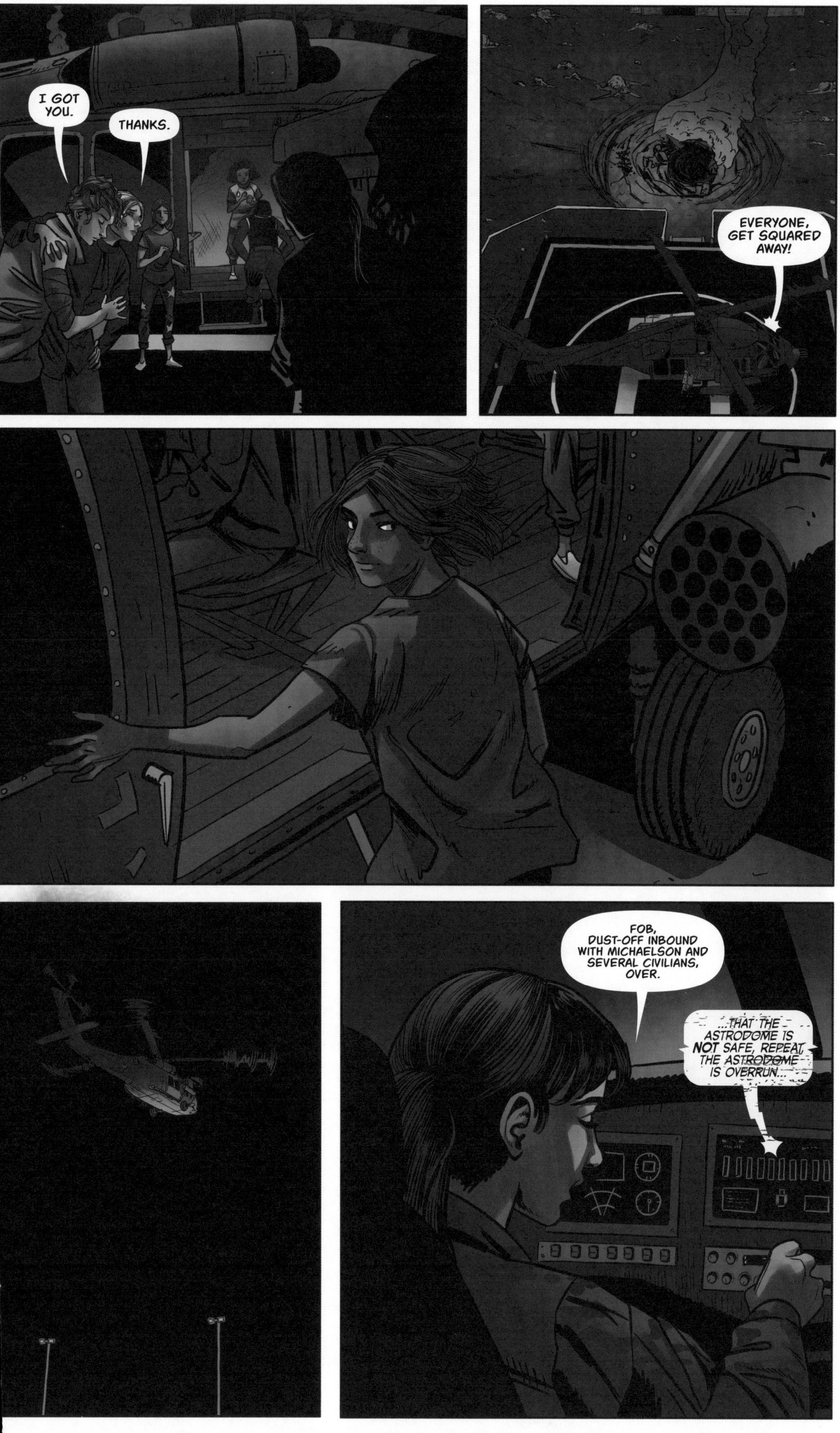
I GOT YOU.
THANKS.
EVERYONE, GET SQUARED AWAY!
FOB, DUST-OFF INBOUND WITH MICHAELSON AND SEVERAL CIVILIANS, OVER.
...THAT THE ASTRODOME IS NOT SAFE, REPEAT, THE ASTRODOME IS OVERRUN...

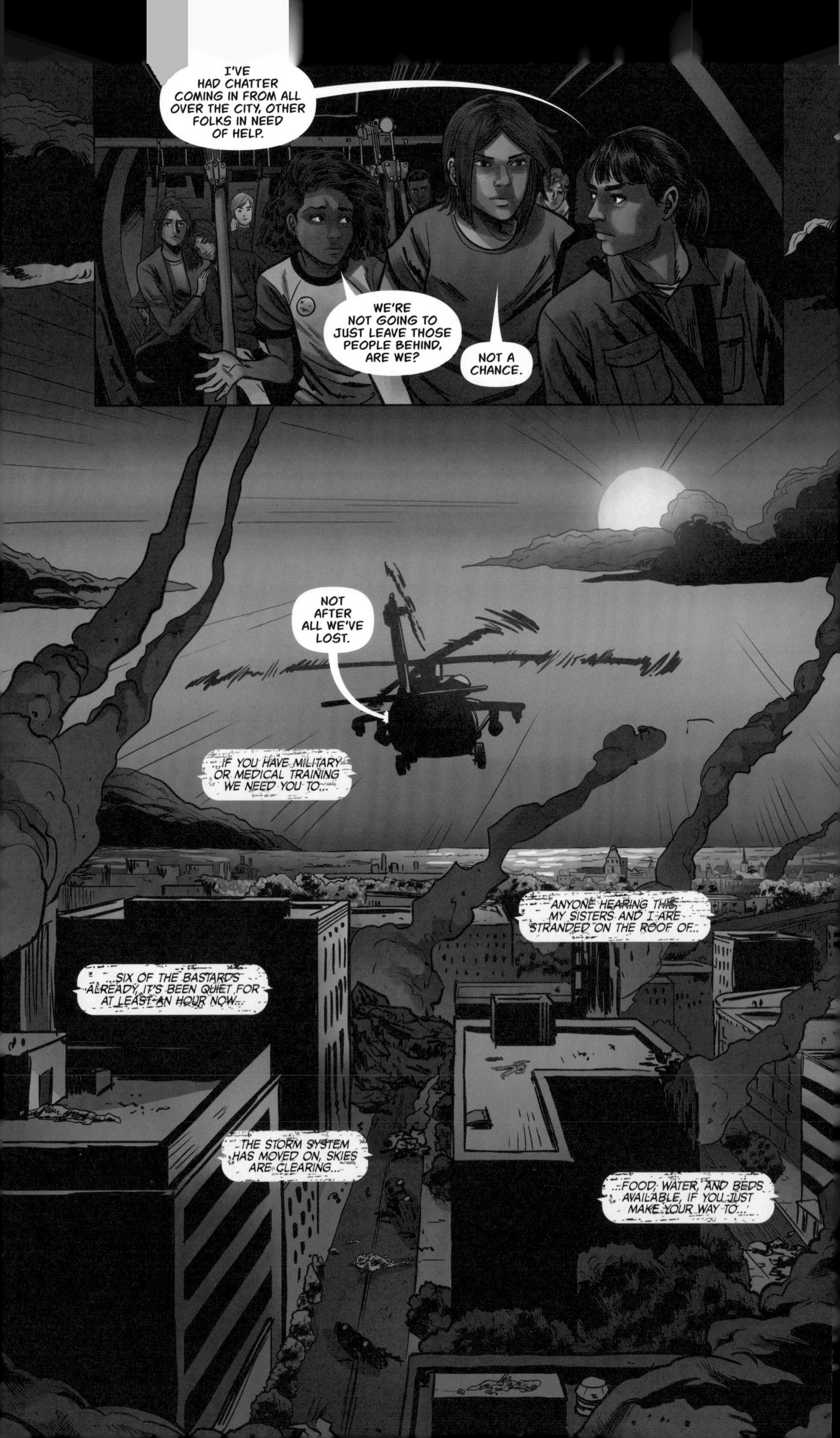
I'VE HAD CHATTER COMING IN FROM ALL OVER THE CITY, OTHER FOLKS IN NEED OF HELP.
WE'RE NOT GOING TO JUST LEAVE THOSE PEOPLE BEHIND, ARE WE?
NOT A CHANCE.
NOT AFTER ALL WE'VE LOST.
...IF YOU HAVE MILITARY OR MEDICAL TRAINING WE NEED YOU TO...
ANYONE HEARING THIS, MY SISTERS AND I ARE STRANDED ON THE ROOF OF...
...SIX OF THE BASTARDS ALREADY, IT'S BEEN QUIET FOR AT LEAST AN HOUR NOW...
...THE STORM SYSTEM HAS MOVED ON, SKIES ARE CLEARING...
...FOOD, WATER, AND BEDS AVAILABLE, IF YOU JUST MAKE YOUR WAY TO...

ORIGINAL COVER ART BY
MARIA NGUYEN

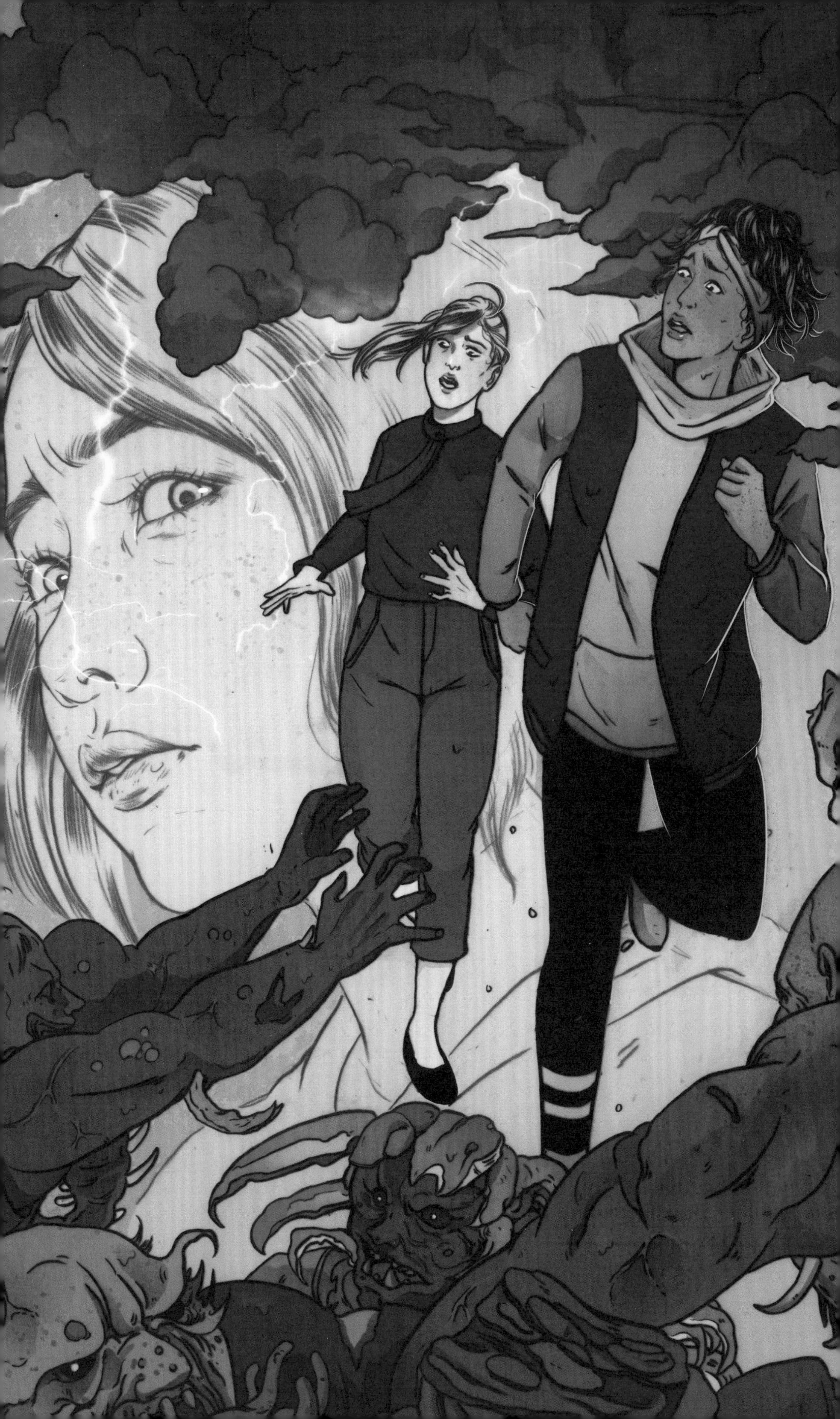

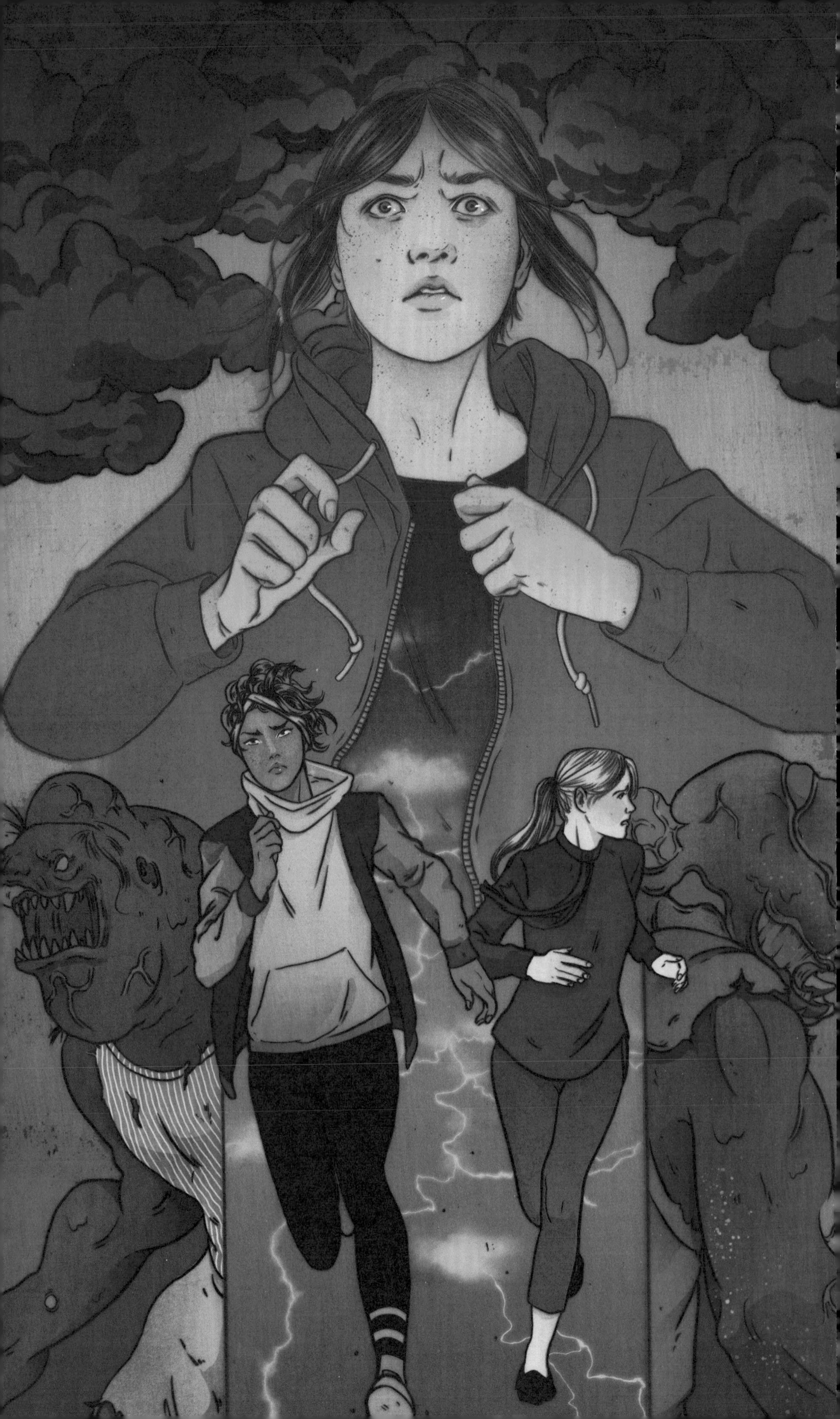

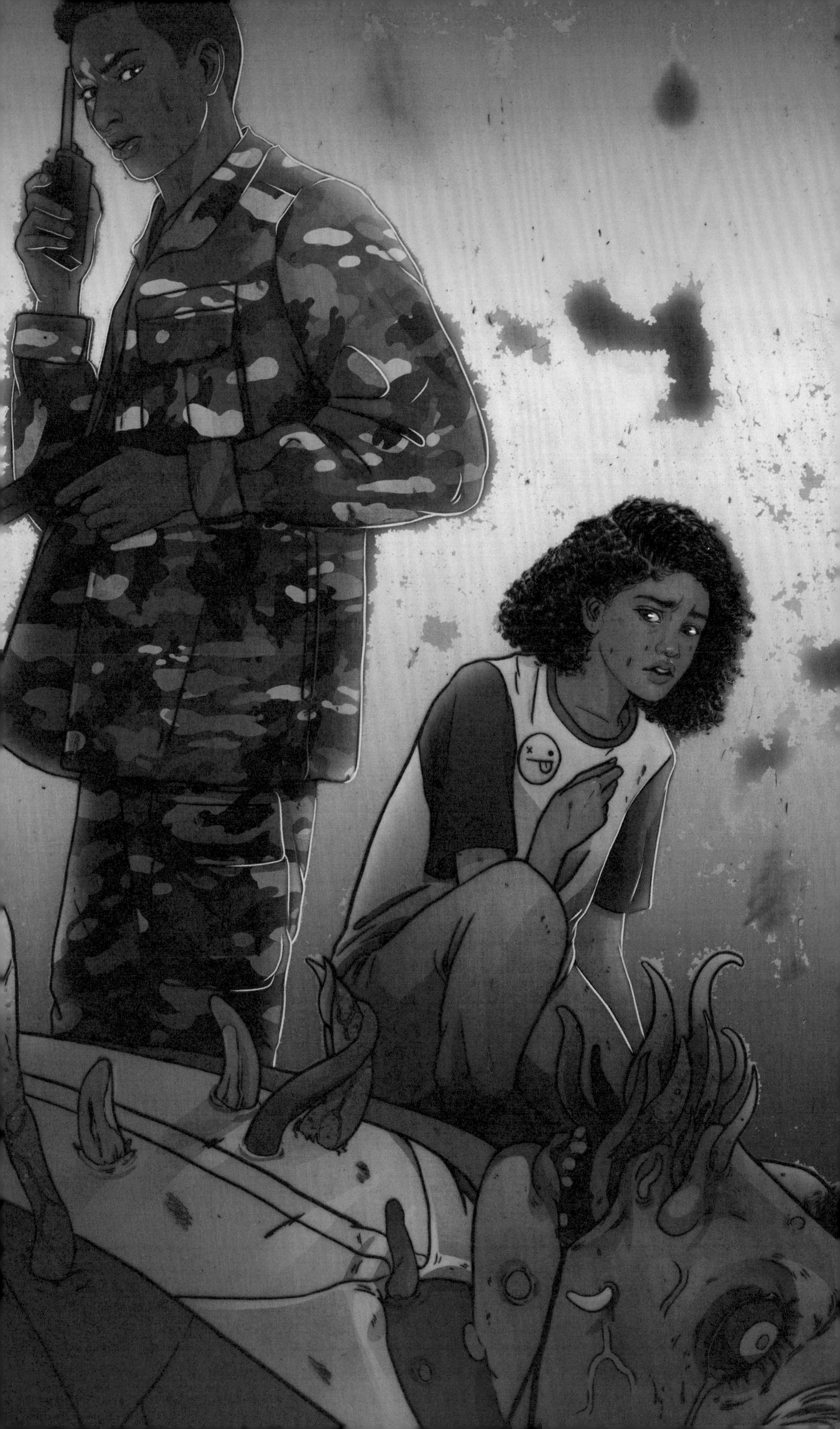

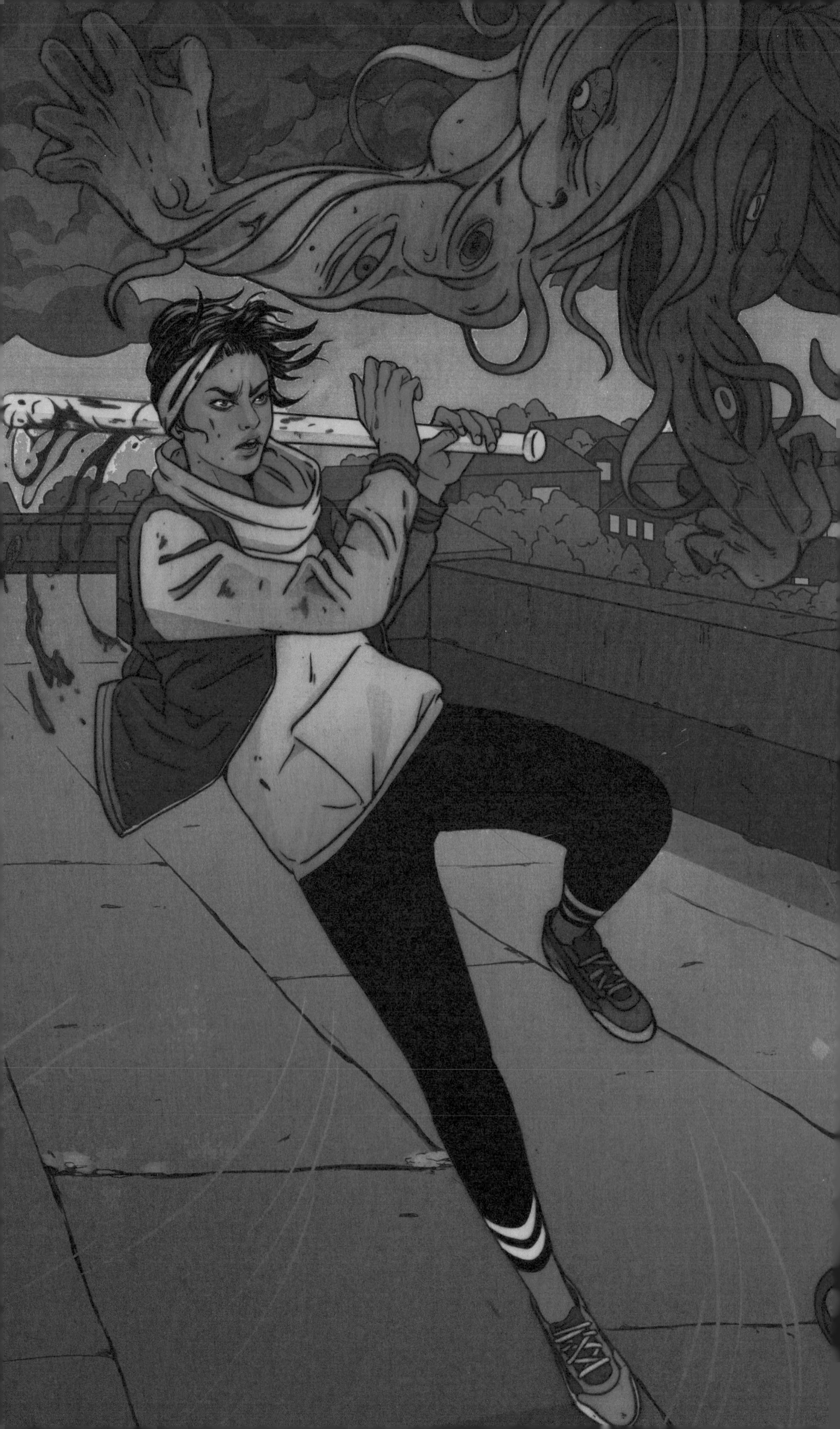

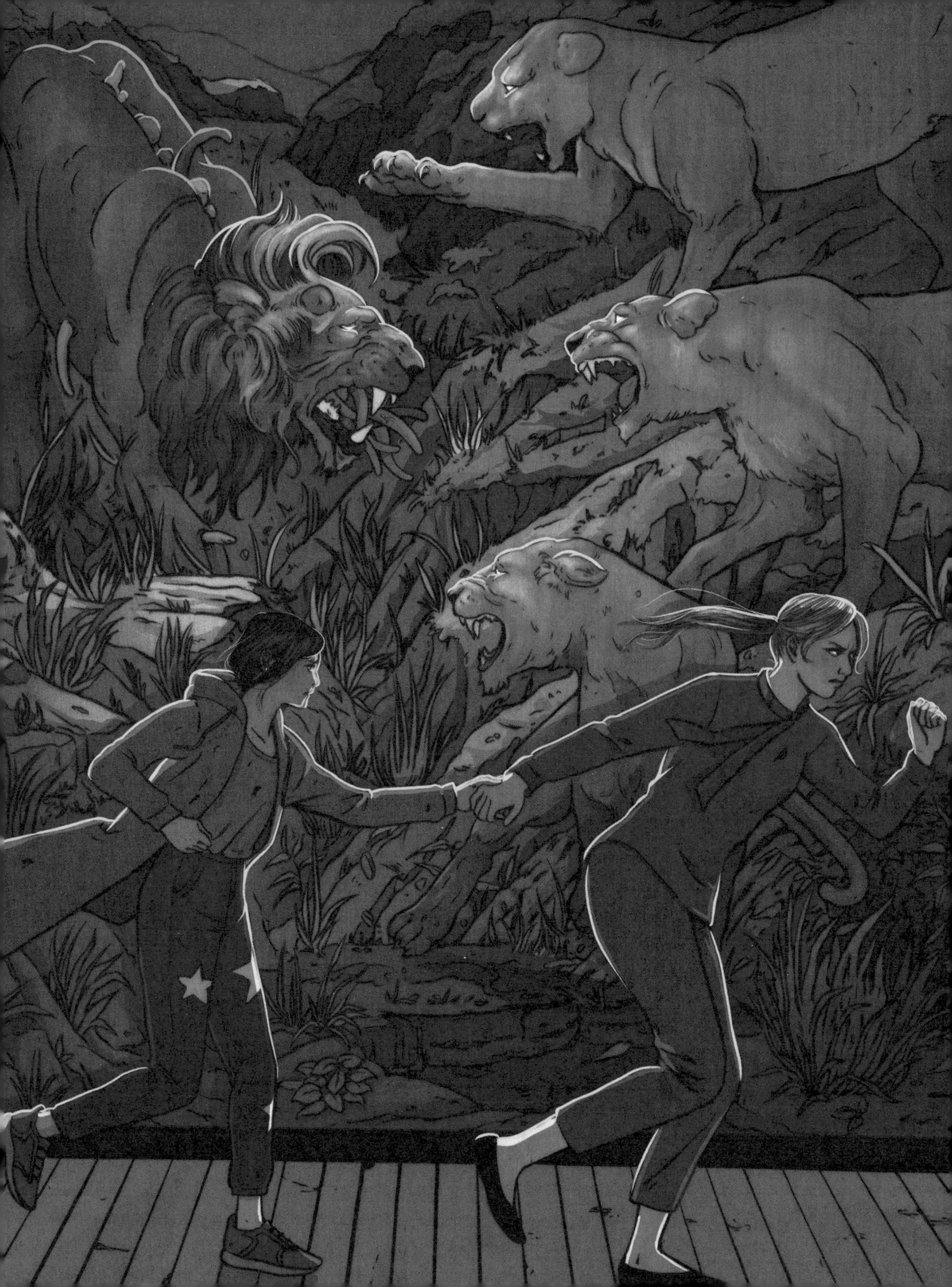

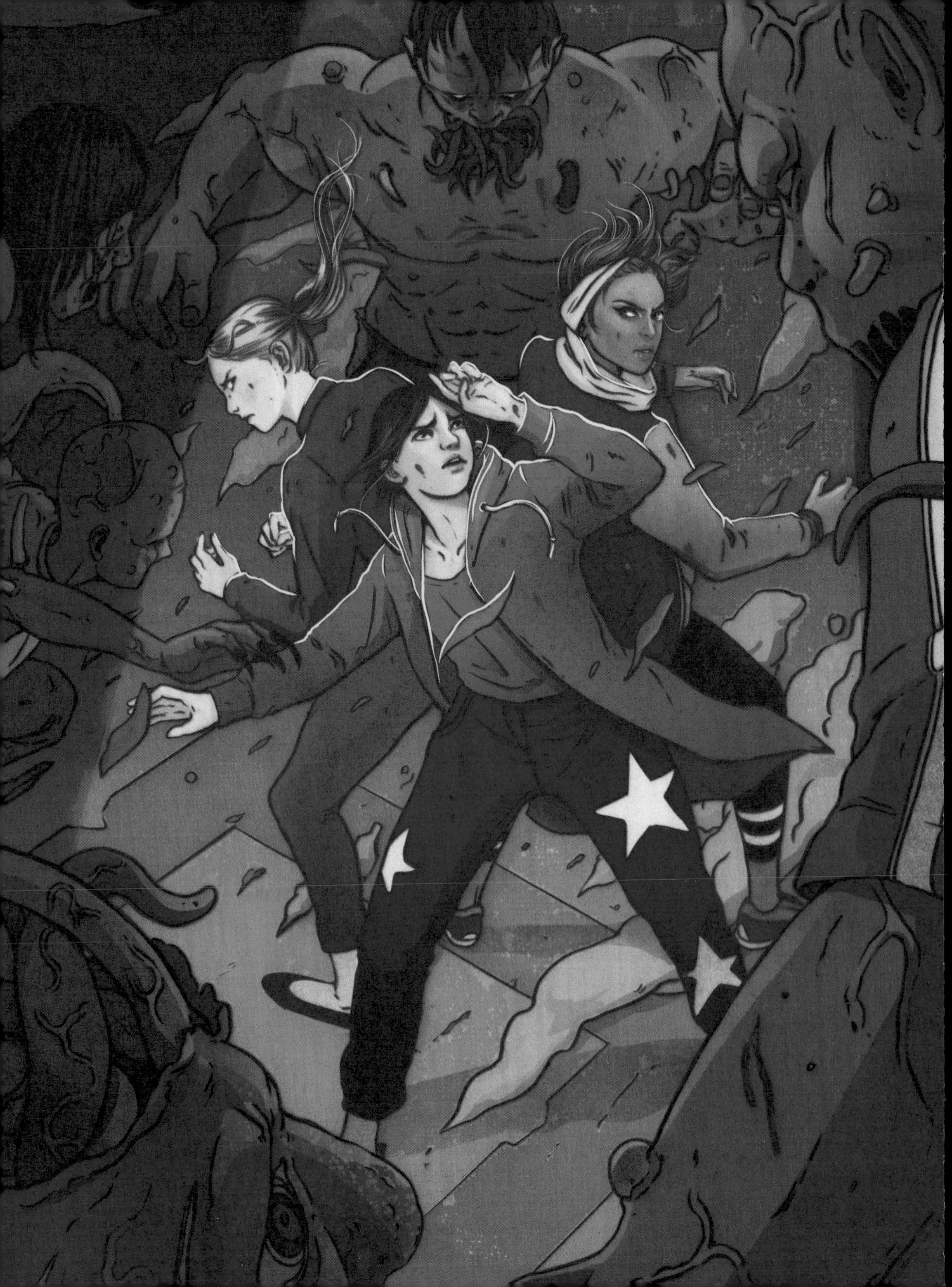

CREATORS

SALVATORE A. SIMEONE | WRITER

Salvatore Simeone was born in Queens, NY. Growing up on Long Island he developed a love for video games, comic books, Dungeons & Dragons, and local hardcore music. While working as a chef in NYC he spent many a late night watching old horror and sci-fiction films scrounged from bins at Kim's Video Underground. Although he's always enjoyed dabbling in various mediums of art, EVE OF EXTINCTION is his first foray into professional writing.

STEVEN SIMEONE | WRITER

Steven Simeone was born in New York but grew up on the internet. A steady regimen of science fiction, fantasy, and horror way before he understood what any of it was has left him well-equipped with a constant need to check under beds and over his shoulder. He is a graduate of the University of Houston's Creative Writing Program, where he was co-editor of their undergraduate literary journal GLASS MOUNTAIN during the year it won the National Program Directors' Prize for content. His previous work is buried somewhere in the annals of the University of Houston library in his senior honors thesis and centers around themes of fraudulence and non-belonging.

NIK VIRELLA | ARTIST

Nik Virella is a native New Yorker and School of Visual Arts alumnus. Her previous work includes THE MORTAL INSTRUMENTS: CITY OF BONES graphic novel, IDW's G.I. JOE, and Marvel titles such as RETURN OF THE LIVING DEADPOOL, 1872, HYPERION, ALL-NEW WOLVERINE, STAR WARS and BLACK WIDOW. In addition, she's had her work featured in Marvel QuickDraw, VOGUE Italia and ENTERTAINMENT WEEKLY.

ISAAC GOODHART | ARTIST

Isaac Goodhart is a 2010 graduate of the School of Visual Arts with a BFA in cartooning. He got his start in comics in 2014 as one of the winners of the Top Cow Talent Hunt. After drawing ARTIFACTS #38, he moved on to illustrating Matt Hawkins' POSTAL for twenty-six consecutive issues. He is currently contributing to DC Comics with UNDER THE MOON: A CATWOMAN TALE and VICTOR AND NORA: A LOVE STORY.

RUTH REDMOND | COLOR ARTIST

Ruth Redmond is an Irish comic book colorist living in Canada. Her previous work includes DEADPOOL, AMAZING SPIDER-MAN: RENEW YOUR VOWS, THE WORST X-MAN EVER, IMAGINE AGENTS and more.

ARIANA MAHER | LETTERER

Ariana Maher is a comic book letterer who works with both independent imprints such as Little Foolery and publishers such as Image Comics, Dynamite Entertainment, and Skybound. Recent projects include EVE OF EXTINCTION, JAMES BOND 007, RINGSIDE, SFEER THEORY, FLAVOR, and Outpost Zero.

SEBASTIAN GIRNER | EDITOR

Sebastian Girner is a German-born, American-raised comic editor and writer. His editing includes such series as DEADLY CLASS, SOUTHERN BASTARDS and THE PUNISHER. He lives and works in Brooklyn with his wife.

TKO STUDIOS

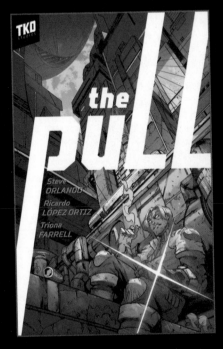

THE PULL

by Steve Orlando, Ricardo López Ortiz
& Triona Farrell

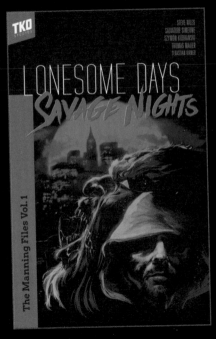

LONESOME DAYS,
SAVAGE NIGHTS

by Steve Niles, Salvatore Simeone
& Szymon Kudranski

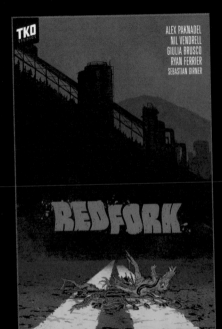

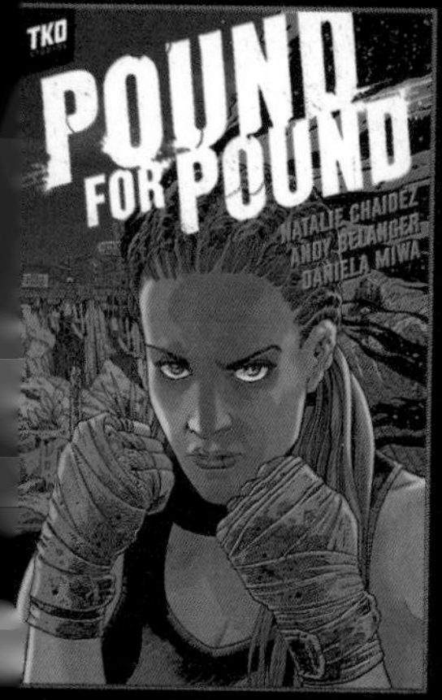
TKO
POUND FOR POUND
NATALIE CHAIDEZ
ANDY BELANGER
DANIELA MIWA

POUND FOR POUND

by Natalie Chaidez, Andy Belanger & Daniela Miwa

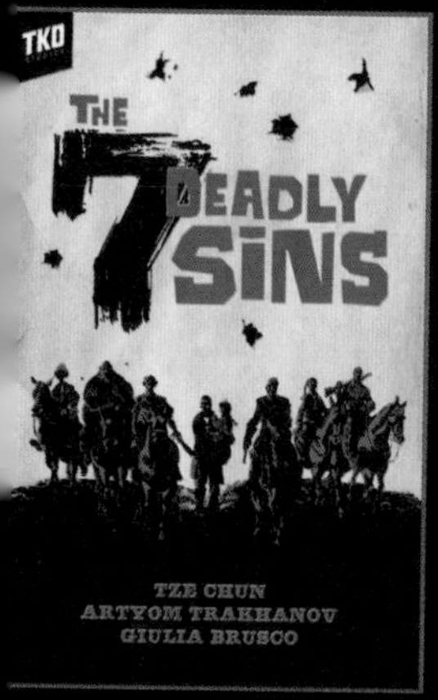
TKO
THE 7 DEADLY SINS
TZE CHUN
ARTYOM TRAKHANOV
GIULIA BRUSCO

THE 7 DEADLY SINS

by Tze Chun, Artyom Trakhanov & Giulia Brusco

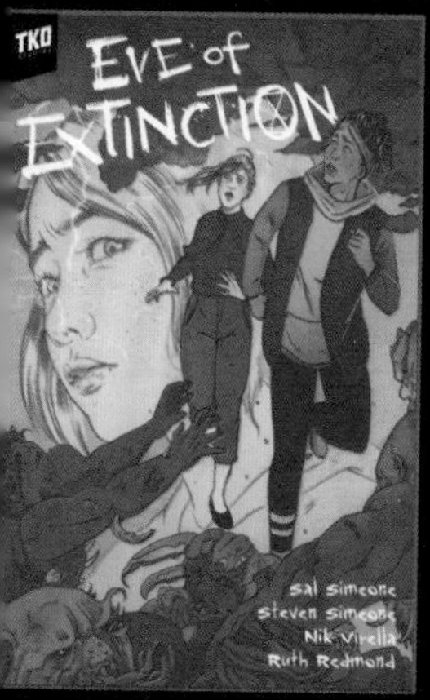
TKO
EVE of EXTINCTION
Sal Simeone
Steven Simeone
Nik Virella
Ruth Redmond

EVE OF EXTINCTION

by Sal Simeone, Steve Simone, Nik Virella & Ruth Redmond

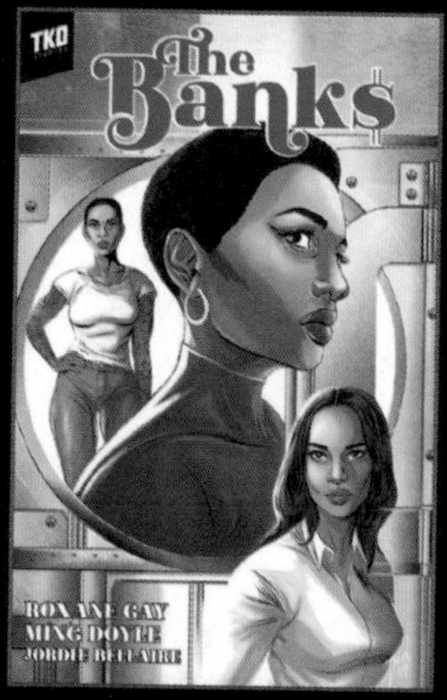
TKO
The Banks
ROXANE GAY
MING DOYLE
JORDIE BELLAIRE

THE BANKS

by Roxane Gay, Ming Doyle & Jordie Bellaire

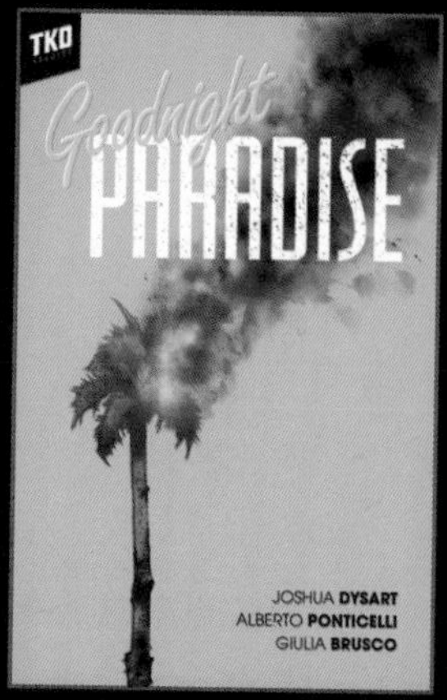
TKO
Goodnight PARADISE
JOSHUA DYSART
ALBERTO PONTICELLI
GIULIA BRUSCO

GOODNIGHT PARADISE

by Joshua Dysart, Alberto Ponticelli & Giulia Brusco

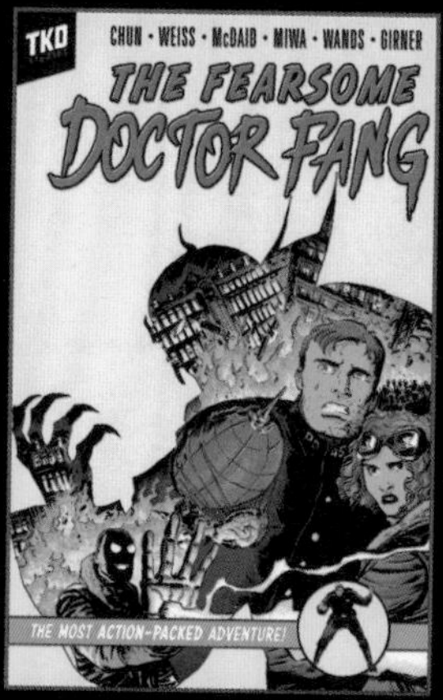
TKO
CHUN • WEISS • McDAID • MIWA • WANDS • GIRNER
THE FEARSOME DOCTOR FANG
THE MOST ACTION-PACKED ADVENTURE!

THE FEARSOME DR. FANG

by Tze Chun, Mike Weiss, Dan McDaid & Daniela Miwa

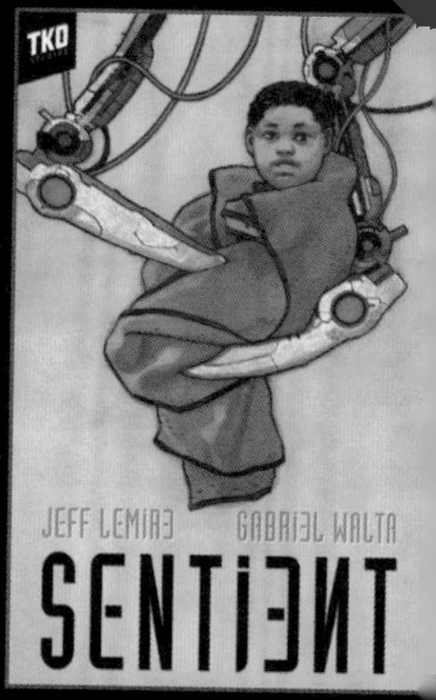
TKO
JEFF LEMIRE
GABRIEL WALTA
SENTIENT

SENTIENT

by Jeff Lemire & Gabriel Walta

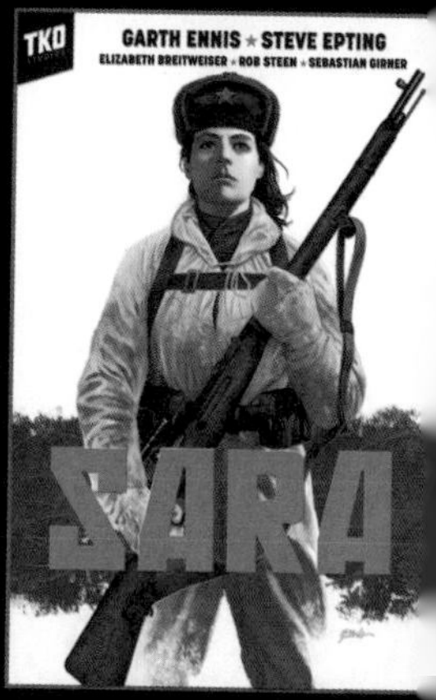
TKO
GARTH ENNIS ★ STEVE EPTING
ELIZABETH BREITWEISER • ROB STEEN • SEBASTIAN GIRNER
SARA

SARA

by Gath Ennis, Steve Epting & Elizabeth Breitweiser

AVAILABLE NO
TKOPRESENTS